T0347539

STUDIES IN HIGHER EDUCATION
DISSERTATION SERIES

Edited by
Philip G. Altbach
Monan Professor of Higher Education
Lynch School of Education, Boston College

A ROUTLEDGEFALMER SERIES

STUDIES IN HIGHER EDUCATION
PHILIP G. ALTBACH, *General Editor*

POWER AND POLITICS IN UNIVERSITY GOVERNANCE

GOVERNANCE

Organization and Change at the
Universidad Nacional Autónoma
de México

Imanol Ordorika

RoutledgeFalmer
New York & London

Published in 2003 by
RoutledgeFalmer
29 West 35th Street
New York, NY 10001
www.routledge-ny.com

Published in Great Britain by
RoutledgeFalmer
11 New Fetter Lane
London EC4P 4EE
www.routledge.co.uk

10 9 8 7 6 5 4 3 2 1

Library of Congress Cataloging-in-Publication Data

Ordorika, Imanol.
  Power and politics in university governance : organization and change at the Universidad Nacional Autónoma de Mexico / by Imanol Ordorika.
    p. cm. — (RoutledgeFalmer dissertation series in higher education)
  Includes bibliographical references.
  ISBN 0-415-93515-6
  1. Universidad Nacional Autónoma de México. 2. Higher education and state—Mexico—Case studies. I. Title. II. Studies in higher education, dissertation series.
LE7.M599 .O73 2002
378.72'53—dc21   2002069896

A Imanoltxu y Amaya, porque arrasan
todo con su alegría y su intensidad.
A Mireya, porque eres el centro desde el
que lanzamos todas nuestras campañas y
al que corremos a refugiarnos en las
desventuras.
A los estudiantes en lucha que fueron el
impulso que dio sentido a mi vida política
y académica y que en México son un
punto de referencia para quienes
luchamos por transformar a nuestro país
y a la Universidad. A los estudiantes de
entonces y a los de ahora.

Contents

Preface

This book is based on my doctoral dissertation *Power, politics, and change in higher education: the case of the National Autonomous University of Mexico*. It is a product of my long involvement with student and faculty struggles at the *Universidad Nacional Autónoma de México* (UNAM). It entails an effort to understand the nature of political processes in higher education. This understanding is in itself important in the contemporary context of increased conflict in colleges and universities at the worldwide level. It is also relevant at a local level in order to inform future efforts for the transformation of our National University and in this way participate in the democratization of Mexico.

This work is an attempt to make sense of my own life as a political activist and a researcher. I have been marked forever by my early memories of the student movement of 1968, by the years of despair and hopelessness of many defeats, and by the marvelous experience of the *Consejo Estudiantil Universitario* from 1986 to 1990. Images of its student gatherings, its huge demonstrations, the strike, the University Congress, and the public debates with University authorities will remain in my memory as some of the most exciting and fulfilling experiences in my life. I hope that I will never lose the generosity, spirit, commitment, passion, and collective will that student struggles gave many of us during the memorable journeys of the *Consejo Estudiantil*.

This research on the power and politics of higher education is based on an intense theoretical reflection about political processes occurring in colleges and universities. The study of the *Universidad Nacional Autónoma de México* is founded on these theoretical considerations. An important part of this research is the product of interviews with key political actors within this institution. I want to thank them, Jesús Aguirre Cárdenas, Francisco Barnés, Daniel Cazés, Luis de la Peña, Jorge Del Valle, Luis Javier Garrido, Henrique González Casanova, Gilberto Guevara Niebla, Carlos Imaz Gispert, Javier Jiménez Espriú, Jorge Madrazo Cuéllar, Salvador Martínez Della Rocca, Jaime Martuscelli, Eliezer Morales Aragón, Humberto Muñoz García, Inti Muñoz, Manuel Peimbert Sierra, Evaristo Pérez Arreola, Fernando Pérez Correa, Guillermo Soberón Acevedo, Luis Villoro, Miguel José Yacamán, and Sergio Zermeño for their willingness to participate in these interviews and their support for this research. I also want to thank Celia Ramírez, director of the *Archivo Histórico* de la UNAM, as well as Alicia Alarcón, and other members of the executive office of the University Council for allowing me to use archival material in this research.

The initial ideas for this work originated in multiple discussions with student and faculty colleagues in political gatherings and academic settings at UNAM. I recall many sessions with fellow student and faculty leaders among whom my brother Antonio Santos, as well as my comrades Óscar Moreno, Inti Muñoz, and Adolfo Gilly should be noted. I thank them for their solidarity and friendship in good and bad times.

The first notions of university elites and the study of power relations in higher education emerged from never–ending discussions with Humberto Muñoz, my advisor at UNAM, and my friend and colleague in spite of political differences.

At Stanford I came in contact with Martin Carnoy, Hank Levin, Patti Gumport, and John Meyer among other faculty members. As my advisor Martin provided intellectual guidance and a thorough understanding of political issues in Mexico. Martin and Hank not only offered the theoretical foundation for my own work, but also helped me develop a critical stance towards mainstream theories and polished my views on power and politics in education. Patti Gumport opened the field of higher education for me. She introduced me to literature, research methods, and colleagues that have become fundamental in my academic and professional development within this field. John Meyer read my work at its early stages and offered a thorough and supportive critique as well as invaluable suggestions. Lorenzo Meyer provided the historical structure for my dissertation and rooted my work in the Mexican reality. Lorenzo's enthusiastic support and good humor became a soothing remedy during the toughest part of the writing process.

My student colleagues were the source of the most interesting intellectual challenges and the best times at Stanford. With my brothers Brian Pusser and Ihron Rensburg, I shared academic and political passions. Sandy Stein, Chris Mazzeo, and I enjoyed together the early years of this academic journey. Luis Benveniste, Diana Rhoten, and Michel Welmond helped me bring this project to a closure in our humorous but effective writing group that will not be forgotten.

Ken Kempner and Gary Rhoades read important sections of this manuscript and provided good insights that have improved my work. They have become intellectual comrades in diverse academic projects.

My Mexican colleagues and *compañeros* Hugo Casanova, Alma Maldonado, Alejandra Recillas, and Roberto Rodríguez were the objects of my constant requests for help and information. My teachers and friends at the UNAM have always been a source of support and encouragement for me in many situations. I thank Alipio Calles, Ana María Cetto, Montserrat Gispert, Raúl Gómez, Marili, Pepe, and Vivianne Marquina, Annie Pardo, Manuel Peimbert, Luis de la Peña, and Rosalía Ridaura at the *Facultad de Ciencias*; Arturo Bonilla, Fernando Carmona, José Luis Ceceña, Elvira Concheiro, and the late Sergio de la Peña at *Investigaciones Económicas*; as well as Alejandro Álvarez, Alfredo López Austin, and Jorge Martínez Stack. I also thank the UNAM and the *Instituto de Investigaciones Económicas* for supporting my doctoral studies at Stanford.

Phil Altbach encouraged me to review my dissertation and publish this book. In addition to constant support, Phil provided academic insights and editorial guidance. I feel deeply indebted to him.

Finally, I want to thank my wife Mireya. She worked on my dissertation and this book as if it were hers and provided thoughtful insights into the understanding of our University. Mireya also coped with my anger and frustration, pushed me to continue working, and enjoyed the conclusion of this process. This work would have been impossible without you.

Mexico City
Spring of 2002

List of Main Acronyms Used in Text

CCH	Colegio de Ciencias y Humanidades
CEU	Consejo Estudiantil Universitario
CNH	Consejo Nacional de Huelga
CONACYT	Consejo Nacional de Ciencia y Tecnología
ENP	Escuela Nacional Preparatoria
ENEP	Escuela Nacional de Estudios Profesionales
IPN	Instituto Politécnico Nacional
PAN	Partido Acción Nacional
PNR	Partido Nacional Revolucionario
PRI	Partido Revolucionario Institucional
PRM	Partido Revolucionario Mexicano
SEP	Secretaría de Educación Pública
SPAUNAM	Sindicato del Personal Académico de la Universidad Nacional Autónoma de México
STEUNAM	Sindicato de Trabajadores y Empleados de la Universidad Nacional Autónoma de México
STUNAM	Sindicato de Trabajadores de la Universidad Nacional Autónoma de México
UAM	Universidad Autónoma Metropolitana
UNAM	Universidad Nacional Autónoma de México

CHAPTER 1

Introduction

A mí siempre me ha parecido intolerable la mezquindad con la cual un escritor pretende esconderse detrás de sus palabras, como si nada de él se filtrase en sus oraciones o en sus verbos, aletargándonos con una dosis de supuesta objetividad. Seguramente no soy el primero en notar esta dolosa trampa, pero al menos quiero dejar constancia de mi desacuerdo con este escandaloso intento por parte de un autor de borrar las huellas de su crimen.

Jorge Volpi. *En busca de Klingsor*

Universities can be considered among the most political institutions in society. The evolution of these establishments since the foundation of the first universities is a history of political conflicts (Brunner 1990; Luna Díaz 1985; Perkin 1984). These confrontations within higher education institutions become increasingly relevant given the centrality of education in a globalized world (Carnoy 1998; González Casanova 2001) and in light of the growing number of political confrontations within universities at the worldwide level. There are many examples of new political struggles and conflicts within these institutions. Most notable among these are the disputes over graduate student unionization in the United States and Britain (Rhoades and Rhoads 2000), the conflict over affirmative action policies at the University of California and other universities in this country (Pusser 1999), and the ten month student strike over tuition at the *Universidad Nacional Autónoma de México* (UNAM) (Rosas 2001).

Only a small number of works in the field of higher education has addressed the political nature of colleges and universities (Kogan 1984). In spite of the emergence of new conflicts, what I call a phenomenon of university re-politicization, decreasing interest in the politics of higher education since the early 1970s (Hardy 1990) has not changed significantly.

The harshness and complexity of political confrontations like the one at the UNAM (Rosas 2001), permanent tensions between government and

1

public higher education institutions over financing (Slaughter and Leslie 1997), as well as conflicts and new political dynamics within governance bodies (Pusser and Ordorika 2001) are some of the issues that require new studies that are grounded on political perspectives.

The study of politics, power, and conflict in higher education is the object of this work. This effort to understand political processes within higher education runs in two directions. On one hand, it addresses the absence of political theories of higher education with the development of a conceptual framework founded on theories of the State, sociological perspectives of education, studies about conflict in higher education and the nature of the academic profession, and theories of power and politics. In itself, the development of alternative models that enable us to capture the political essence of higher education is important in the context of contemporary higher education.

Secondly, this book provides a thorough understanding of the *Universidad Nacional Autónoma de México* by addressing the political nature of this university. The theoretical model constitutes the foundation for a study of power relations, political processes, and conflicts at the UNAM. Being the largest and most important single institution of higher education in the country, a political study of the UNAM is important in itself. The case, however, is also enlightening for the study of higher education institutions in general because of the massive nature of this university, its centrality in Mexican higher education, and the opportunity to gather data on the nature of these conflicts and tensions.

UNIVERSITIES AND CONFLICT IN A HISTORICAL PERSPECTIVE

The term *universitates*, originally referred to communities, technical associations, or publicly accepted corporations in Europe during the Twelfth century (Rashdall 1936). Educational corporations emerged from the confluence of teaching and the dynamics of guilds (Le Goff 1980). Students approached renowned professionals, called doctors, in order to learn a trade. These relationships were "very similar to those established by the contracts between the apprentices and the masters of the guilds" (Le Goff 1993; Luna Díaz 1987b). Teaching slowly evolved into a special activity and a way of life. Scholars attempted to create their own special corporate arrangement *vis-à-vis* the Church, secular authorities, and the rest of society (Le Goff 1980).

Due to these privileges and broad jurisdiction, educational corporations became very powerful. However, they were not completely autonomous from Church or State and there were cases of external intervention. The first universities in Bologna and Paris were different because of their distinct historical contexts. Bologna emerged from the impulse of students in the late Twelfth Century. The University of Bologna thrived from the confrontation between the Pope and the Emperor and acquired extensive privileges and jurisdiction (Luna Díaz 1987b). Nevertheless, it was also shaped by conflicts with both the Church and the State. Consequently, the Church gained the right to supervise the hiring of teachers and establish indirect controls over the university. Students, however, essentially ran the university by providing professorships (Valadés 1974), establishing schedules, and deciding on the length of lectures (Wences Reza 1984). The *universitas scholarium* was a corporation, based on traditional privileges and professional values (Luna Díaz 1987b).

In Paris, the university was strongly related to the Church. It was created from the cathedral schools of Notredame also in the late Twelfth Century. Professors ran the university (Le Goff 1993; Wences Reza 1984). The Church, however, maintained control over the provision of degrees in this *universitas magistrorum* (Luna Díaz 1987b). In spite of their differences, both institutions shared a profound corporate nature. The acquisition of such a large degree of autonomy, and the broad extent of their privileges and jurisdictions, can only be explained in the absence of a unique centralized source of power in medieval twelfth–century societies (Luna Díaz 1987a).

In these universities' attempt to perform their functions with a relative degree of freedom, both institutions were involved in diverse disputes with the Church and the Crown (Luna Díaz 1985; Perkin 1984). The Catholic Church, the States, and local authorities competed in their endeavor to exercise external control over these universities (Le Goff 1993; Luna Díaz 1987b). These tensions between the preservation of freedom and external attempts to control were accompanied by political conflicts about the organization and internal distribution of power (Brunner 1990). Faculty and student migrations were often the consequence of these internal and external conflicts.

The lay and student–centered university model in Bologna influenced the creation of new universities. Migrations from Bologna were the origin of the universities of Vicenza (1204) and Padua (1220) in Italy (Perkin 1984). Salamanca, Alcalá, Barcelona and Lisbon, among others, were established later in Spain and Portugal (Brunner 1990). The Italian model eventually succumbed to external controls by the Pope and the commune, but it gave birth to a strong tradition of student participation (Perkin 1997).

The faculty–centered and church–controlled model of Paris was also linked to the creation of new universities. Oxford (1167) was the product of migrations from Paris. Cambridge (1209) was the product of migrations from Oxford. In the end, the model of the University of Paris was to give birth to the dominant university tradition in which scholars control students and the learning process (Perkin 1984).

The university as an institution grew all over Europe. In the Sixteenth Century, it was transferred by the colonial powers to the New World (Sánchez 1944). Universities were involved in processes of intense political and social change, gaining preeminence with the Reformation and declining during the Enlightenment. Tensions between university traditions and State needs permeated higher education institutions during the Enlightenment and the Industrial Revolution. Eventually, control over higher education shifted from the Church to the State (Perkin 1984; Perkin 1997). National governments attempted university reforms (Germany) or created parallel institutions (France) (Ben-David 1992).

Universities in the New World were also subject to conflicts involving religious and government authorities during the Sixteen, Seventeen, and Eighteen Centuries (Brunner 1989; González-Polo y Acosta 1983; Lanning and Valle 1946). Disputes over higher education in Latin America continued in the early years of independence. Among the most relevant conflicts between the University and the State in the early Twentieth Century is the struggle over autonomy that took place in Córdoba, Argentina, in 1918 (Portantiero 1978).

After a period of notable expansion in the post–WWII era, political conflicts in higher education became evident again during the 1960s with the emergence of student movements all over the world (Ehrenreich and Ehrenreich 1969; Lipset and Altbach 1969). The images of student revolts in France; Mexico; and Germany; or Berkeley, Columbia, and Kent State in the United States; encouraged scholars to address the political nature of higher education for more than a decade (Mets and Peterson 1987).

Still, after eight centuries of existence, the essence of the university has been preserved, to such an extent, that we can continue to identify it as a unique institution (Perkin 1984). The history of higher education evidences, however, that universities have changed much, along these eight hundred years. Meanings and objectives have been transformed in order to adapt to the requirements and conditions of diverse societies and different times.

Many of the most relevant changes in higher education have occurred as a consequence of political conflicts. Following Brunner (1990) it is possible to say that throughout the history of the university, these political conflicts have emerged along two dimensions. One dimension involves the relations of the university with established external powers (the Church, the State, or economic powers). The second dimension involves power relations within these institutions' governance and organization, as well as faculty and student participation.

THE STUDY OF POLITICS AND CONFLICT IN HIGHER EDUCATION TODAY

New tensions and conflicts have affected higher education in the post–welfare State era. In the last three decades, increasing demands at the internal and external levels have impacted universities worldwide (Cameron and Tschirhart 1992; Cole, Barber, and Graubard 1994; Kerr 1995; Slaughter 1990). Sources of funding for higher education have shift-

ed from the public to the private realm. Public state and federal appropriations have been significantly reduced, and higher education institutions
have become less isolated from market forces (Massy 1992; Massy 1996).
Some of the most important effects of these demands upon universities
include large increases in student enrollment, growth in faculty, diversification of tasks, and bureaucratic expansion.

The information age and economic globalization have also increased
many of these pressures on higher education. Colleges and universities
nowadays are affected by demands upon governments to reduce public
spending in education and the search for alternative sources of funding for
public higher education systems. At the same time, knowledge requirements
of international competition force governments to expand knowledge production and skilled–labor training in order to attract foreign capital.
Knowledge production and training require the expansion of postsecondary
education. Competition establishes the need to meet international standards. The quality of higher education systems is assessed through testing
programs in order to meet these standards (Carnoy 1998).

The process of globalization has unprecedented effects upon nation
states (Castells 1996). The redefinition of the State in its role as organizer
of the economy, as well as the constructor and bearer of national identity,
has a strong impact on higher education institutions. The University loses
its linkage to the nation state as a "producer, protector, and inculcator of
an idea of national culture" (Readings 1996 p. 3). With this, the university has lost one of its most important sources of legitimacy.

These demands for rapid changes in the role and nature of higher education institutions are the source of tensions and conflicts within colleges
and universities and between them and other State institutions. Universities
appear as conservative and reluctant to change at the pace required by
external demands. At the internal level, faculty and students react against
administration's attempts to produce reforms that contravene traditional
perceptions about the role of the institution, as well as established rights
and practices.

This work attempts to contribute to the study of the relation between
political processes and change in higher education. It constitutes an effort
to explain why increasing demands have not produced rapid responses
from the university. It tries to understand why this lack of response has
generated internal and external tensions and conflictive dynamics. In
addressing these issues I draw from a revealing case study and a theoretical construct in order to generalize some patterns that will enable our
understanding of other cases and institutions.

This study examines the process of change at the National Autonomous
University of Mexico (UNAM) in the presence of new internal and societal
exigencies, from a historical perspective. Three issues of major relevance
are addressed. The first issue is the construction of a conceptual model that

will focus on change as a consequence of politics and conflict in higher education. An outcome of this is the exposition of the political nature of UNAM and higher education organizations in general. The second issue is an effort to reassess the limits of University autonomy and the relation between UNAM and the Federal Government in Mexico. The third issue is to examine the process of change at UNAM and to examine its limits and basic characteristics.

AN ALTERNATIVE CONCEPTUAL FRAME

The mismatch between increasing demands and institutional reactions is a matter of concern in many studies of higher education (Finn and Manno 1996; Massy 1996). University resistance to change has also been a major subject of inquiry (Guevara Niebla and Alba Alcaraz 1981; Kerr 1995; Massy 1992; Muñoz García 1989; Peterson 1985). Some literature tries to address the concern over the lack of fundamental change in higher education organizations by establishing that universities are conservative institutions (Altbach 1974).

It is often argued that faculty possess strong resistance to change, or that the objectives of university reform are excessively ambitious (Cerych 1984). Clark (1983) writes that higher education can only evolve gradually, that "incremental adjustment is the pervasive and characteristic form of change" in higher education systems (p. 235). Other authors propose that universities in Latin America have assumed a conservative stance when attempting internal changes. This attitude seems to be in open contradiction with a traditional anti *status quo* external image that frequently permeates this type of institution (Levy 1986).

Among the most important contemporary theories about change in higher education is Clark's (1972) idea of increasing complexity based on Durkheim's model of societal differentiation. Adaptation to market demands is increasingly assumed by mainstream scholars to be the fundamental cause of change (Massy and Zemsky 1996; Zemsky and Massy 1990). A few alternative studies have suggested that transformations in post–secondary organizations can be attributed to internal politics (Baldridge 1971) or resource dependency (Pfeffer and Salancik 1978; Slaughter and Leslie 1997).

A case is made here for an alternative explanatory model. This alternative conceptual frame[1] builds a bridge between the university and its societal context using theories of the State. It looks at educational change (institutional and organizational) as a consequence of conflict, and at the political manifestations of these struggles (Carnoy and Levin 1985). This conceptual frame will enable a better understanding of the processes of change by integrating the objects of conflict, the levels in which it takes place, and the actors involved in power struggles in their specific historical context.

THE NATURE OF POLITICS AND AUTONOMY AT UNAM

University authorities have held that UNAM gradually adapts to evolving environmental demands. However, many critics, from different perspectives, agree that despite increasing exigencies and profound changes in its historical context, the National University of Mexico has not undergone a fundamental transformation. The ways in which knowledge is created, delivered and distributed have not changed much in the last fifty years. Relations involving the essential actors of university life, and those between the University and the governing apparatus of the Mexican State, have remained the same since the early 1970s (Guevara Niebla and Alba Alcaraz 1981; Martínez Della Rocca and Ordorika Sacristán 1993; Muñoz García 1989).

It has often been argued that internal organizational, academic, or political processes essentially determine change, or the lack of it, in Mexico's National Autonomous University. The argument is based on the assumption that UNAM has considerable latitude from the Mexican government in determining its own policies and transformation projects.

This matter is extremely complex. Congress legally established the relations between the Mexican government and UNAM in 1910, 1929, 1933, and 1945. The development of these legislation episodes will be analyzed in the next chapters of this work. For the time being it may suffice to establish that since 1929, the Mexican government granted institutional autonomy to the National University. With historical variations, the government granted UNAM an autonomous statute; the legal rights to administer its resources, make academic decisions, and appoint university authorities.

The extent to which this autonomy really exists in the presence of a highly centralized and authoritarian political regime is a matter of contention. Opinions about governmental influence over the university in Mexico range from absolute autonomy to absolute control. Almost everybody holds a view about the real limits of university autonomy. Many of these are based on personal experiences within the university. However, few of them are grounded in any type of research. Few studies have thoroughly researched the relation between the National University and the government.

One of the notable exceptions is Daniel Levy's work *University and Government in Mexico: Autonomy in an Authoritarian System*. In 1980, Daniel Levy published this extensive study on the relation between universities and government in Mexico. Levy provided a working definition for autonomy as the location of authority "*somewhere* within the university," (p. 4) or "as university control over [the] components [of institutional self–government]" (1980 p. 7). This characterization is compatible with Berdahl's classical definition where autonomy is "the power of a university or college ... to govern itself without outside controls" (Berdahl, Graham, and Piper 1971 p. 8).[2]

Levy assessed the extent of autonomy in three broad areas or components of institutional self–government: appointive, academic, and financial (Levy 1980 p. 7). Appointive autonomy includes the hiring, promotion, and dismissal of professors; as well as the selection and dismissal of deans, rectors, and administrative personnel. Academic autonomy includes the definition of access and career choice policies, curriculum and course selection, establishment of degree requirements, and academic freedom. Financial autonomy includes the definition of funding levels and criteria, preparation and allocation of the university budget, and accountability.

Levy provided an operational frame for the study of *who decides*, on each of these policy realms. The foundation for this assessment is the characterization of the Mexican political system as an authoritarian regime and of the University as a conservative institution reluctant to adapt to government policies. The study focused essentially on who makes policy decisions in each of these realms.

After analyzing each of these policy areas, Levy concluded that there is substantial autonomy in the three dimensions. According to Levy, academic autonomy is almost absolute and there is almost no noticeable government interference in the definition of access policies, curriculum, and academic programs. He argued that the government's monopoly over university funds does not imply the exercise of control through the flow of resources. He established that autonomy in the hiring and promotion of faculty is essentially an internal matter. Levy recognized the problematic nature of procedures for the appointment of university authorities. He concluded however, that although limited and probably the subject of external intervention, these procedures are more university based than most of the United States and Latin American universities are. In summary, Levy stated that "public university autonomy in Mexico, though certainly far from complete, is relatively strong—stronger than government control and considerably stronger than university autonomy in most other Latin American nations" (Levy 1980 p. 19).

This work contests the first part of Levy's argument. It shows that the degree of autonomy of UNAM has changed according to different historical circumstances. Also that effective autonomy is weaker than what Levy argued. This might seem a simple matter of appreciation about the degrees of autonomy. It is more than that.

This work shares Levy's definition of autonomy as the power to make decisions within the University. It also agrees with his distinction of autonomy levels, in different realms of university policymaking. I have arranged these levels into: (a) political autonomy, including appointment of authorities and conflict resolution; (b) academic and campus autonomy; including access, academic freedom, and free speech; and (c) financial autonomy, including tuition and salary policies among other issues.

The main differences in assessing the nature and limits of autonomy at the National University are the consequence of different theoretical perspectives and consequently of evaluating the historical evidence. First, he establishes a complete distinction between the University and the government. Even though he claims that the "autonomous university is a power *within* a power" (p. 4), he later conveys the idea of two distinct entities which are mutually dependant. The State is external to the institutions and operates on them through diverse mechanisms (*i.e.* financial control). Perhaps the most revealing statement is that "democracy, participation and intra-university power distributions are important issues, but should not be confused with autonomy" (p. 4). I agree that autonomy and internal democracy should be distinguished as to distinct relations. However, there is a direct connection between these two. In the next chapters, I will show that the nature of the political relations between social actors within the University has a strong influence on the nature and extent of University autonomy.

Second, Levy's study of University—government relations is based on a static evaluation of formal decision–making realms and structures as determined by laws and statutes. While Levy recognized the limitations of such a study, he did not go beyond a superficial exploration of real decision–making performance by university authorities and collective bodies.

The basic assumptions of this work go in a different direction. It looks at internal conflict in its articulation with broader struggles in a historical perspective in order to assess relations between UNAM and the government. This study highlights the connections between actors in conflict at the level of the State and its higher education institutions. It also looks at power beyond the instrumental study of decision–making, by focusing on agenda control (Levy makes a brief reference to the issue of non–decision-making), and the cultural dimension of political confrontation.

Based on this alternative perspective, the conclusion of this study contrasts with Levy's findings. I agree that the *Universidad Nacional Autónoma de México* is not fully captured by the government and that it enjoys substantial formal autonomy as established in the 1944 Organic Law. However, I will show that, in reality, university autonomy has been limited by constant State intervention in the appointment and removal of Rectors. I will provide evidence of interference to hamper reform projects and democratization attempts. I will show that the government has forced admissions and tuition policies upon the University. I will provide evidence of how the heavy reliance of University authorities on government support in the face of conflict and the political expectations of a bloated bureaucracy have created linkages that subordinate University decisions to government projects and practices.

I argue that the levels of confrontation of opposing reform projects determine the limits of University autonomy. Overt or covert conflict operates as a counter balance to the most powerful political actors within the university (bureaucrats and university elites). In the absence of conflict, these dominant groups act within the parameters of the dominant political discourse and educational projects at the broader State level. This is not to say that relations between these dominant groups operating at different levels of the State are exempt of tensions. The autonomy of the university is shaped and constrained by societal and internal conflicts and by the articulation and tensions within the dominant groups.

THE PROCESS OF CHANGE AT UNAM

Perspectives on change in higher education are strongly determined by mainstream formulations about autonomy and the University. In the case of UNAM, it is often argued simplistically that university resistance to reform is the product of student reluctance to lose acquired privileges, like low tuition as well as slack academic standards and requirements (Levy 1980; Ornelas 1995; Ornelas and Post 1992). Most of the literature dealing with issues of governance and change in Mexican higher education comes from what I have labeled elsewhere as organizational and societal functional perspectives (Ordorika 1999a). Organizational views explain the lack of change at UNAM because of its size, internal inefficiencies (Carpizo 1986), and authoritarian structures of governance (Jiménez Mier y Terán 1987). Kent (1990) looks at a process of conservative modernization and bureaucratization, as well as the development of academic markets and their impact on academic cultures as the main explanation of university stagnation.

While many approaches recognize the existence of political conflict within the university, most of the explanations view students (and sometimes faculty) as interest groups that have stopped reform processes (Levy 1980; Levy 1986). Some authors develop this idea further and recognize the existence of conflicting reform projects in Mexican higher education (Ornelas 1995; Ornelas and Post 1992). Their explanation is based on the assumption that university bureaucracy is the driving force for a modernizing reform that is opposed by a populist project, supported by sectors of faculty and students.

This research shows that the process of university reform in Mexico is quite different from what the current literature reveals. I will show that the most significant changes that have occurred at the National University have been driven by political conflict. Some transformations are a direct outcome of the confrontation between the University and the State. Other instances of change are the product of attempts to preserve the political arrangement of these institutions in the face of internal challenges. The outcomes of these preservation attempts in turn shape and constrain the process of change in the University. This study provides evidence on the increased political dependency of the University elite on the State, and the expansion of its bureaucratic constituency as consequences of the union-ization struggles in the 1970. I argue that the presence of these powerful political interests, as well as that the political dependency and the bureau-cratization of the University, have shaped and heavily determined the rationale and dynamics of change.

METHODOLOGY AND DATA SOURCES

The characteristics of the political process at UNAM and the high intensi-ty of the confrontation that takes place within this institution have shaped and determined many aspects of this research. My role as a researcher has been heavily influenced by my position as an active political actor within UNAM. The selection of the topic and the theoretical approach to this study are shaped by my own experience at the University. This condition presents advantages and disadvantages in the collection and interpretation of data.

My situation as a political actor in University conflicts during the 1980s, gave me access to sources of information that would have been out of the reach of other researchers. These sources include interviews with current and former University and government officials, as well as student and union leaders. On the other hand, this same condition limited my access to other sources such as interviews with former Rector Sarukhán[3] or access to the archives of the University Council and the Governing Board at UNAM.[4] In themselves, these refusals were revealing of the political char-acteristics of the institution in which official university information has become part of the political dispute. Some of these obstacles were over-come using additional primary (media accounts and interviews) and sec-ondary sources (other authors that had been granted access to primary sources).

In the collection and interpretation of the data I benefited from my extensive knowledge of UNAM and its history. My previous experience at UNAM constituted an intense period of participant observation. This expe-rience provided guidelines for data collection and research design. On the other hand, it required a careful process of triangulation to reduce biased interpretations. Triangulation was based in the use of multiple sources and contrasting voices, the collection of databases, and the codification of the data before proceeding to the interpretation.

In this context, I considered that this research should take the form of a historical case study. It is historical in that it addresses a temporal span of university life by focusing on the process of political confrontation and uni-versity change. It is a case study because the analysis of the single case of UNAM attempts to describe the political process and generate theory.

Periodization. This work looks at the history of the National University from its creation in 1910 to the unionization conflicts in the 1970s and early 1980s. The periodization for this historical study is based on relevant historical events in the relationship between the university and the Mexican State. Notably, this periodization corresponds to distinct historical periods at the broader societal level.

The first period of this study goes from the foundation of the University in 1910, to the creation of the Board of Former Rectors and discussion of the new Organic Law for the University (in 1944). This period roughly corresponds to the revolutionary wars (from 1910 to 1917) and the *emergent* phase of the authoritarian regime (from 1916 to 1944).

The second period goes from the establishment of the first Governing Board (in 1945) to the student movement of 1968. This period corresponds to the phase of *consolidation* of authoritarianism (1944 to 1968).

The third and final period goes from the aftermath of the 1968 student movement, in 1969, to the unionization struggles in the 1970s. This period corresponds to the *crisis* or declining phase of the authoritarian political system.

Guidelines of historical research. The history of the National University in the next chapters follows these guidelines:

1. conflict within the University and at the broader State level and the relation between these levels of confrontation,

2. transformations in the relationship between the Mexican government and the National University,

3. changes in dominant perceptions about the University and its role in the Mexican society,

4. evolution of governing structures and changes in university laws, rules, and regulations,

5. configuration of competing social formations, coalitions, and alliances.

I have used different data sources for each period of this historical study.[5] For the study of the three periods I have utilized several historical descriptions and analyses; personal memoirs and testimonies; chronologies and biographies; and University yearbooks. I also looked into the history of University unions as well as media and key actors' depictions of different student movements. Finally, for the three historical periods I have reviewed public statements by government and University officials.

In each of these periods, I drew from specific sources. For the first period, from 1910 to 1944, I studied the 1910, 1929, and 1933 Organic Laws; and their accompanying position papers; as well as the 1934, 1936, and 1938 University statutes. I also reviewed University Council minutes from 1924 to 1944.

For the second period from 1944 to 1968, I reviewed accounts of the discussions within the *Directorio Universitario* (University Directorate) and studied the debates of the *Consejo Universitario Constituyente* (Constitutive University Council) in 1944 that finally gave birth to the Organic Law of 1945. I studied this law and its position paper. I reviewed the 1945 University statute and changes that were introduced until 1968. I also drew from the minutes of the University Council from 1945 to 1968.

Since 1960, I have relied increasingly on different data from the printed media. These include paid political advertisements, press releases, statements, press accounts, feature articles, op–ed pieces, and editorials. In addition to data from the media, I drew information from a database on University political biographies that I collected for most members of the governing board at UNAM, and for the upper echelons of the University bureaucracy. Throughout the text this database will be labeled University Biographies.

For the third period, from 1969 to 1980, the availability of historical accounts is greatly reduced. I relied on first–hand collected data from media sources; official documents and statements by diverse organizations and actors involved in the political conflicts; political biographies of Governing Board members and University officials; and interviews with key political actors.

There is no single method in historical inquiry (González y González 1988). The theoretical construct presented in Chapter 2 illuminates a set of issues to which I attempt to give meaning in their historical context. These issues offered direction and focus for this historical research. An "interim image of the past" (González y González 1988) provided a course of action for the periodization and the collection of data. On this basis, I proceed to the analysis and interpretation of this data into a combination of narrative and structural history. The validity of this process is established through triangulation (Denzin 1989) in an attempt to correct for problems of authenticity, exactness, sincerity, and interpretation (González y González 1988).

In this study of the political history of UNAM, I focus on the political dispute along three dimensions: *instrumental, agenda control,* and *dominant culture.*

A study of university elites. The analysis at the *instrumental* level is a study of elites. For the purpose of this dissertation, I followed C. Wright Mills (1956) and Domhoff's (1983) reputational and positional methodologies for the study of power elites. Data for the reputational analysis was drawn from the interviews I conducted with key political actors in the University. They were asked to provide a list of the individuals that they considered more influential in University decision–making.

For the positional study, I selected governing bodies and administrative positions that would be included in this research. This selection includes members of the governing board (from 1945 to 1997), patrons (from 1945 to 1990), Rectors (from 1960 to 1990), and other University officials (1972 to 1990).[6]

I collected political biographies for most of them. In the biographies, I was able to obtain information about disciplinary or professional background, administrative postings in the University and the federal government, and political affiliation among others.

Finally, I brought together the data from the positional and reputational sources. I looked at overlaps between these two lists and analyzed the information according to disciplines and professions, political affiliations, and public postings. I followed political trajectories and looked at different types of relations between members of the governing board (*i.e.* friendship, kinship, schooling, professional collaboration, university appointment, and work provision).

Agendas. In this study, I have focused essentially on issues and non–issues in University decision–making and not in the processes through which elites establish agenda control. I examined policy statements, reform projects, and public statements by University officials from 1960 to 1980. I searched for the most relevant issues that became part of the decision–making agenda of the University Council or the University administration.

I also examined proposals, themes, and topics that were put forward by alternative actors (staff and faculty unions, collegial bodies, and student organizations) and their inclusion or exclusion from decision–making agendas. I draw data essentially from official statements; union publications; recommendations, petitions and demands towards governing bodies; media accounts of political discourses; and faculty and student assemblies.

Data is analyzed in search of patterns of inclusion and exclusion from University decision–making agendas. I searched for continuities and disruptions that would shed light into the nature of the political process at UNAM.

Dominant political culture. In the presentation of the theoretical frame, I argue that dominant culture is always part of an active creation and recreation process. I also established that the recreation of a dominant culture involves actors in conflict within institutional settings. Dominant actors establish their hegemony through the selection of traditions in order to consolidate a dominant identity.

Open conflict is a privileged site for data collection on competing perceptions about the university. It is in the process of institutionalization of new relations of forces that the elements of a dominant political culture are established. I looked at the data in its historical context and focused on moments of salient conflict.

Data was gathered from position papers and public statements that surrounded the approval of the Organic Law in 1945. I collected a new set of data from seven Rectors' inauguration speeches; and from a variety of public statements by Rector Soberón during the conflicts with staff and faculty unions in the 1970s. Additional data stems from the interviews I conducted.

Through this historical study, I focus on the selection traditions by dominant social formations and the configuration of these traditions into a dominant political discourse. In addition to this, cultural perceptions of the university will be classified according to topics. Competing perceptions will be identified and organized for each of these topics. This will highlight identifiable patterns, as well as processes of evolution and change of dominant political discourse.

§

Since the very beginning of this research I have been much more than a participant observer. My long experience as an activist and my own position as a researcher have committed me to radical reform in Mexico's National Autonomous University. Inevitably, my own biases tint this research through the selection of the topic, the theory, and the methodology.

It is argued here that the crisis of higher education in Mexico is essentially a consequence of the lack of academic leadership and legitimacy of governing bureaucracies. It also shows that the vested interests of the dominant elite and the university bureaucracy are so powerful that they have been successful in resisting internal and external pressures in favor of university reform. These interests have determined the rationale and dynamics of change.

The political nature of university reform and the issue of legitimacy of the transformation process are emphasized throughout this work. It attempts to expose the myths about the neutrality and the apolitical nature of the University as mechanisms to exclude faculty and students from the process of reform.

The overall purpose of this research has been to identify the main factors that have prevented the transformation of colleges and universities in Mexico by drawing from the experience of UNAM. I have emphasized the political nature of the obstacles for the reform of the National University and probably of the whole public higher education system in Mexico.

The conviction that the only path towards University reform is the democratic participation of faculty and students has guided this and other works. Let us hope that a broader audience can share it and that this work contributes to the transformation of Mexico's National Autonomous University.

NOTES

[1] By conceptual frame, I mean a theoretical base understood as a set of "conceptual schemes that order and inform the process of inquiry into social life"

(Giddens 1984). Also following Giddens I argue that in setting down this conceptual frame I can use ideas from very diverse sources.

> To some this may appear as an unacceptable eclecticism, but I have never been able to see the force of this type of objection.... If ideas are important and illuminating, what matters much more than their origin is to be able to sharpen them so as to demonstrate their usefulness, even if within a framework which might be quite different from that which helped engender them (p. xxii).

[2] In a normative attempt to establish an adequate relation between autonomy and state coordination, Berdahl also suggested a distinction between substantive and procedural autonomy. Substantive autonomy refers the "goals, policies, and programs that an institution has chosen to pursue" and procedural to the "techniques selected to achieve the chose goals" (Berdahl, Graham, and Piper 1971 p. 10).

[3] During his stay as a visiting scholar at Stanford University I requested an interview with former Rector Dr. José Sarukhán. Dr. Sarukhán replied that we could meet but he would not grant me an interview because of "personal as well as institutional principles" (email from Sarukhán, September 8, 1997).

[4] There is no official policy regarding the nature of many official documents at UNAM. While the University Council sessions are open to the public, in many occasions access to the minutes of this body have been denied to University researchers. The office of the University Council also holds the Governing Board minutes. My request to access the minutes for the University Council session of January 1945, when the first Governing Board was elected, was denied.

[5] For a detailed description of data sources see Appendix 1.

[6] These include administrative secretaries, treasurers, University attorney generals, secretaries of the interior, humanities and social sciences coordinators, sciences coordinators, and planning secretaries from 1972 to 1990.

A Model for the Study of Politics, Governance, and Change in Higher Education

> Believing, with Max Weber, that man is an animal suspended in webs of significance he himself has spun, I take culture to be those webs . . .
>
> Clifford Geertz. *The Interpretation of Cultures*

In order to assess the explanatory power and limitations of diverse approaches to governance and administration in higher education I have elsewhere organized this body of literature along two dimensions (Ordorika 1999a pp. 172–173). The epistemological dimension distinguishes between subjective versus objective approaches (Burrell and Morgan 1979; Milam 1991). The second dimension varies between organizational and social-historical approaches (Brunner 1988). These dimensions establish the boundaries of four analytical perspectives: organizational-functional, organizational-interpretive, societal-functional, and societal-interpretive (Ordorika 1999a; Ordorika 1999b).

In looking at the literature it is very evident that the major body of work approaches governance from a functionalist perspective by either focusing exclusively on structures or looking at decision–making processes as deterministic causal relations between social actors. Organizational–functional approaches to governance in higher education provide important elements that help us perceive some relevant aspects of university organizations. They have contributed to inform a basic understanding of the structures and processes of higher education institutions. These approaches have focused on organizational goals, technologies, and work. According to these perspectives universities change through rational responses to internal inefficiencies, organizational growth and increased complexity (Clark 1983). Fewer studies suggest that internal politics and interest articulation within the university drive change within higher education institutions (Baldridge 1971). In most cases, however, organizational–functional theories assume internal homogeneity and fail to acknowledge the impact of external requirements upon universities as well as the contested nature of internal and external demands. However, in many occasions universities' organizational development responds to dynamics that contradict the internal rationality of bureaucratic or collegial arrangements. Organizational boundaries are difficult to establish and goals are vaguely defined (Cohen and March 1974). The historical evolution of the organization and governance structure of UNAM cannot be understood strictly as a product of rational responses to increased complexity or institutional growth and in isolation from its historical context.

Societal–functional approaches to university governance, contrast with organizational perspectives. Societal–functional theories have focused their attention on the relation between postsecondary institutions and their environments. According to these views, university organizations and governance structures are determined by external factors. They look at the environment in terms of the internal strategies to adapt or to minimize the influence of surroundings upon organizations. Some perspectives within this frame explain change within higher education as organizational responses to market dynamics (Massy 1992). Resource dependency theories argue that universities change in order to increase their chances to survive within an environment where resources are scarce (Pfeffer and Salancik 1978; Slaughter and Leslie 1997). There is no doubt that markets and resources are extremely relevant in the transformation of higher education. These theories, however, are limited in their ability to explain why universities like UNAM have remained unresponsive to labor and economic market demands maintaining an archaic organization of academic disciplines and professional schools as well as remaining virtually tuition free. Resource dependency also fails to explain situations in which universities make conscious choices that limit their access to financial resources. Such is the case of the National University in Mexico during the early–1930s when this institution rejected State demands even at the cost of losing government appropriations.

If we evaluate external and internal approaches in terms of their results on the field, it is possible to find that the strengths of one perspective are the weaknesses of the other. It becomes clear that none of them is able to advance a full understanding of change in higher education without including elements from the other approach (Brunner 1988).

Interpretive approaches have shed light on processes more than structures. They have brought our attention to issues of culture and meaning. They have also increased our awareness and understanding about the relation between research and the subject matter. In this way, they have constituted a theoretical alternative for the study of higher education governance. These cultural perspectives have also focused alternatively on the organizational and societal levels. Following Berger and Luckman's (1966) views on the social construction of reality, a number of researchers have focused on symbolic as well as substantive interactions, enacting myths and belief systems that are essential for organizational legitimacy (Meyer and Rowan 1978; Weick 1976). Institutional theorists explain change in higher education in response to social and cultural demands for conformance to prevailing sets of shared beliefs (Clark 1983; Meyer and Rowan 1978).

Institutional perspectives have successfully brought the cultural dimension into the study of higher education. Like other perspectives, these approaches do not deal with the fact that cultural perceptions in the organization and its environment are contested. There is no recognition that institutional myths and cultural perceptions shape and are in turn shaped by political contests at the organizational and societal levels. In the historical evolution of the National University in Mexico, it is possible to see how the University reacted to cultural expectations within the organization, at the broader State level, and even in relation to global paradigms of higher education. However, these reactions—resistance and adaptation—have been a constant object of confrontation and political struggle.

In the light of these limitations, it is possible to argue that some of the theoretical challenges—in dealing with governance and change in higher education—lie in the possibility to bridge some of the gaps between these four analytical frames. On the one hand, it is necessary to focus on the connections between societal and organizational processes. On the other hand, it is important to look at the linkages between structure and culture. The foundation of this theoretical construct is the contested nature of higher education organizations themselves.

LIMITATIONS OF EXISTING MODELS AND ANALYTICAL PERSPECTIVES

In trying to move in this direction, it is possible to identify that a large proportion of current research on higher education shares a number of significant limitations. One of the most important limitations is that most studies of higher education do not include an understanding about the State and the place of higher education institutions in society. Historically, the State has been seen either as a source of funding or as an intrusive force interfering with the development of professional and scientific expertise (Slaughter 1988). American scholarship on education, in general, and particularly in higher education, has not addressed the understanding of the State and its relation with education organizations (Carnoy and Levin 1985; Rhoades 1993).

Underlying this lack of concern is an implicit view about the State. This view is fueled by a powerful myth of the apolitical nature of education (Wirt and Kirst 1972). Based on an extensive review of current literature on higher education, Gary Rhoades (1993) has shown that this implicit view about the State and the apolitical nature of post–secondary education is also promoted by the views of university scholars about themselves and their institutions. It is assumed that higher education institutions are politically neutral and autonomous organizations rooted on professional competence and rational behavior (as opposed to the politically driven irrational State) (Rhoades 1993).

Usually the State is viewed as opposed to Academe. Higher education is considered autonomous and independent of bureaucratic and political practices. The State is seen as external and adversary. In most cases, the State is perceived as equal to formal political bodies, inefficient and intrusive. Most of these views are not grounded on any explicit State theory. Rhoades, however, argues that these assumptions are rooted in a structuralist and pluralist view of the State that permeates the work of higher education scholars.

Only a small amount of literature openly acknowledges the presence of power and politics in higher education governance. Many of the stated and underlying views of power in these perspectives are also founded on pluralistic models. These views, based on the Weberian notion of power, argue that power exists only in the presence of conflict. When there is no conflict, the notion of power is deflated and substituted for a Weberian concept of authority.

Most of the views we have reviewed make some sort of distinction between governance, management, and leadership. This distinction implicitly confines the locus of power to the restricted notion of governance as decision–making. This distinction is based on the assumption that the university is essentially a technical institution. Following Wolin (1991), I argue that the political nature of the university is obscured by the argument of the neutrality of techniques in their intent to disengage technical analysis from political judgment.

The absence of an understanding about the State and the position of post–secondary organizations within society, and the deficient comprehension of theories of change, can explain the limited success in the attempt to grasp the complex relation between "internal" and "external" processes. The distinction between internal and external levels in higher education is extremely problematic (Gumport 1993). An understanding of the broader issues of political economy[1] and power relations within the higher education organizations and between these and external sources is necessary to comprehend power and change in higher education.

THEORETICAL FOUNDATIONS OF A HEGEMONIC MODEL

Perhaps one of the most important limitations in the field of higher education research is the absence or misuse of theories developed within other social science disciplines. In the development of the conceptual frame for this research, I draw from several sources that enable me to combine diverse levels of explanation.

I agree with Rhoades that most higher education scholars have an underlying or implicit pluralist view of the State (Rhoades 1993). It is assumed that the State is the representative of the "common good," of the national interests. A few other works have addressed the study of higher education from different perspectives that view the State, not as representative of the common interest, but as the representation, in some way or another, of the interests of the economic ruling class.

The Capitalist State: Hegemony and Contest

These perspectives are not homogeneous. They are founded in theories that range from classical Marxist ideas about the "instrumental" State[2] (Lenin 1965; Marx 1972; Miliband 1969); to views on hegemony[3] (Gramsci 1971) and ideological apparatusses[4] (Althusser 1971; Poulantzas 1973); to the State as a site of struggle[5] (Poulantzas 1978) or an autonomous organizer of capitalist production (Offe 1975). These perspectives vary essentially along two dimensions. The first dimension is the degree of autonomy or "capturedness" of the State by the capitalist class. The second is the weight of the economic structure versus the superstructure in the process of domination.

Clyde W. Barrow (1993) argues that non of these competing theories of the State have been proven by historical or empirical evidence. Theories are selected on the basis of their power to address some particularly relevant features to the eyes of the researcher. In this case, I will use the concept of hegemony and the idea of the State as a site of conflict as expressed by Gramsci and Poulantzas. In my view, these theories are particularly suitable to address the problems of governance and change in higher education from a political perspective by:

1. providing an understanding of the capitalist State as a dynamic institution, the product of historically evolving relations between competing classes in society,

2. looking at this contest at the level of economic relations and emphasizing the importance of the development of dominant ideologies,

3. providing a theory of social change as a product of the confrontation between dominant and subaltern sectors of society, and

4. situating higher education in a broader context as a State institution.

Education: A Contested Terrain

Alternative perspectives about education in a capitalist society developed in correspondence with these different views on the State. Although these perspectives on education vary enormously, it is possible to group them in three broad trends. Instrumentalist and structuralist views of the State provide the foundation for different notions on education as a mechanism for the reproduction of the capitalist society[6] (Bernstein 1971; Bourdieu and Passeron 1977; Bowles and Gintis 1976; Carnoy 1974). Perspectives about the State as a relatively autonomous organizer of capital accumulation in balance with the pursuit of legitimacy (Offe 1975) are the basis for notions of education as a source of "compensatory legitimation" (Weiler 1983).

The concept of hegemony and the idea of the State as a site of struggle are the foundations of two different views of education as a site of conflict. In the first case, the confrontation within education is the consequence of resistance to the reproductive role of education. Resistance is based on the development of conscience through action in education. This action essentially takes place through the transformation of hidden curricula (Apple 1982; Freire 1970; Giroux 1981). This perspective emphasizes the conflict over ideology.

The second perspective argues that conflict within education is the product of competing demands, for capital accumulation on one hand, and equalization on the other. The tension between these two opposing dynamics shapes the nature of the education system. Contests shaping education take place within education and in society at large. This perspective emphasizes conflict over the purpose, operation, and resources of education (Carnoy and Levin 1985).

Building upon these perspectives of education as a site of conflict, I developed a conceptual frame on power and politics in higher education governance. Gramsci employed the concept of ideology broadly and dialectically, rooting it in actual conflict between classes in a variety of "state apparatuses." The State was simultaneously an actor in its own right, a multi-faceted resource, and State institutions an arena of class struggle over public policy and, much more important, over hegemony. On occasion, the working class could effectively control parts of the State apparatus.[7] Poulantzas further developed the idea of the State as a site of struggle between the classes. The State is the historical product of economic class relations in the form of struggle (Carnoy 1984 p. 126).

Based on these perspectives I argue that higher education is an institution of the State. It is therefore a site of struggle and contestation. Its reproductive nature is challenged. As a consequence of social movements and struggles, it is also a site of equalization and democratization of social relations in society (Carnoy and Levin 1985). Taken together, these theories enhance our understanding of the process of change in higher education and provide the foundations for a political theory of governance by:

1. establishing the importance of looking at political contest in education as a confrontation over ideology and resource allocation,

2. looking at decision–making structures and processes in education as historical products of the relations between dominant and subaltern groups in education and the broader State,

3. explaining the dynamics of educational reform as consequences of competing demands for the reproduction of ideology and skills on one hand and struggles for equalization and acquisition of conscience on the other, and

4. establishing the linkages between internal and external political contests in shaping educational reform.

But how does this conflict over ideology and resource allocation, between dominant and subordinate groups within the university really take place? In what ways, if any, is the dispute in higher education distinct from other educational institutions?

Poulantzas' theory of the State as a site of conflict and Carnoy and Levin's analysis of education have shed light on the ways in which underlying tensions, essentially linked to the dynamics of the workplace (reproduction of the labor force versus equalization) explain educational reform. I have said that these perspectives provide powerful tools to understand the nature of competing projects for educational reform. In my view, however, contest theories of education have two interrelated shortcomings for a full comprehension of governance within higher education organizations. The first of these is the fact that contested State perspectives have been developed for the democratic State. That is, it is assumed that democracy is a "principal form of subordinate–class contestation in the class State" (Carnoy 1984 p. 126). The second shortcoming is the absence of a theory about the political process of contestation itself. The conditions of participation within a democratic State suggest the idea that political processes follow the patterns of interest group politics and the struggle for power as described by pluralist political theories. These shortcomings become evident when dealing with higher education institutions in authoritarian political systems —as is the case of this study.

In addition to these limitations, it is also very important to expand the theory in order to establish what makes higher education distinct from other institutions of the State. That is, it is necessary to understand what makes higher education particular even with regard to education in general.

In the next sub–sections I will focus on the particular features of conflict within higher education institutions and provide the theoretical foundations on the nature of the political system as well as the dimensions of political conflict.

Conflict Over Higher Education

According to Sheila Slaughter (1990), the conflict between demands for capital accumulation and demands for equalization is expressed within higher education around "major policy issues." These issues are access, social uses of knowledge (career preparation as well as research and service), and allocation of resources. I will call these the *objects* of conflict in higher education organizations.

The objects of conflict. Access is shaped by attempts to regulate the reproduction of skilled labor and social demands for higher education as a mechanism for upward social mobility. The regulation of access is based on a

> meritocratic ideology [where] those with the greatest intellectual capacity enter into a strenuous competition with their fellows, in which the winner is named the fittest, or the most meritorious, and, claiming a credential rather than the means of production, invariably goes on to a long and prosperous life (Slaughter 1990 p. 30).

Beyond the fact that this merit–based argument is all about social Darwinism, it is important to understand that in the certification process that will allow access to higher education, the dominant culture rewards

> skills and attitudes possessed in abundance by the middle class —cultural literacy, numeracy, perseverance, self–confidence, appropriate assertiveness, and social agreeable manners– and not found as frequently among immigrants, the working class, or the working poor (p. 31).

There is a great deal of debate about the social uses of knowledge in career preparation, research, or service. In the first case, this debate has to do with the hierarchy and orientation of academic disciplines and professions, as well as with expansion or contraction of student access to academic programs that yield the highest returns. In the case of research, debate affects science policies and the prioritization of some disciplines, usually more related to production, over others more related to public needs.

Finally, resource allocation deals with the sources of funding (public or private) and the transfer of costs (from the State to individuals), as well as with expenditure patterns within higher education.

Tensions from within higher education. Societal tensions are played out in higher education over different directions of reform dealing with access, uses of knowledge, and resource allocation. Higher education organizations also possess inherent contradictions having to do with the nature of academic disciplines and professions, as well as the characteristics of work within the organization.

The conflict over the uses of knowledge drives much of the tension between academic disciplines and professions. The internal logic of the disciplines themselves accounts for conflict within the disciplines and between the disciplines. These confrontations are also played out over access, recognition within the knowledge status structure, and over resources.

The conflict over the nature of work is a product of the distinction of two types of activities within higher education organizations. Some of these activities can be characterized as bureaucratic, the others as academic or professional (Blau 1973). The characterization is problematic.

> Universities and colleges have some bureaucratic characteristics, such as formal division of labor, an administrative hierarchy, and a clerical apparatus. But they do not have other bureaucratic attributes; for example, there is no direct supervision of the work of the majority of employees, the faculty, and there are no detailed operating rules governing the performance of academic responsibilities (Blau 1973 p. 11).

On the other hand the characterization of academics and their activities as professional is also problematic. In terms of classic theory, academics differ from professionals in that they do not serve clients (Hughes 1981) and in the absence of a common basic body of knowledge that defines the profession. These two caveats can be minimized if we establish that their clienteles are non–traditional (students in the case of teaching, users of knowledge in the case of research), and we assume that we have multiple professions each of them with its own common body of basic knowledge (Blau 1973).

There are however, a number of very important similarities between academic and professional work. The most important of these is that academic work is autonomous and self–regulated (it can only be evaluated by peer specialists), as well as the fact that professional associations establish required standards. According to Blau,

> [s]uch authority of professionals, including now academics, which rests on institutionally recognized expert knowledge, conflicts with administrative authority, which is based on official positions in a bureaucratic hierarchy. Hence administrative and faculty expectations tend to come into conflict (Blau 1973 p. 13).

But the nature of academic work is evolving rapidly. Managerial requirements are producing changes in the autonomous and self–regulated components of faculty work (Rhoades 1998). At a theoretical level a study of this development is beyond the scope of this work. It should be understood however, that this is one of the most important causes of internal conflict in contemporary higher education.

The sectors. Societal and organizational contradictions involve actors from four different sectors in the University. These sectors are students, faculty, staff, and administrators. In the previous paragraphs I addressed the nature of the contradictions between faculty and administration (or bureaucracy). Here I will look at the organizational characteristics of students.

According to some scholars, academic organizations are "people–processing" institutions. Individuals—in this case students—with specific needs come into the organization from the environment, the organization acts upon them, and they are returned to society. This is a very important condition. This situation becomes problematic when we consider that students, as stakeholders, are part of the organization itself. They participate in decision–making within the organization and, in spite of their transient condition, they are part of internal confrontations, and they contribute to shape the institution. While student struggles are an expression of the contest between different directions for reform, they are also partly involved in inherent contradictions between teaching and research, and professional versus bureaucratic activities.

There is only a small amount of literature on the characteristics of staff and their role in higher education institutions. What exists has addressed the evolving nature of what used to be clerical or manual labor, to include a certain type of academic professional, a shift from academic to technical work (Rhoades 1998). But if staff has not gained a space in academic analysis, they have certainly appeared as a relevant factor in university conflicts since the beginning of the 1970s. It is that presence that I will address in this work.

The Nature of the Political System

The attempt to extend Carnoy and Levin's theory of education as a site of contest beyond "the democratic State" shall be addressed by incorporating the analysis of political systems into the study of the contesting social movements. The analysis of the most relevant features of the political system in each case will shed light on the particular forms that this political struggle assumes and on the nature and evolution of competing demands for education reform. Historically, capitalist States have assumed different political systems. The most traditional forms have been classified as democratic, authoritarian, and totalitarian (Smith 1979). Some authors include populist as a distinct variety of political system.

By including dimensions associated with the nature of each political system in the construction of this theoretical frame, it is possible to extend the theory to any type of political system (democratic, authoritarian, or totalitarian). These dimensions focus on four crucial aspects of the competition that shapes higher education governance and drives educational policy. These are:

1. the extent or limits of democratic political competition,

2. the nature of the dominant ideology,

3. the degrees of political mobilization or citizen participation, and

4. the nature of leadership (the role of political parties and other State institutions, *i.e.* the army).

In this section, I have addressed the issue of incorporating the political system dimensions into a conflict theory of education at a general level. For the purpose of this case study, I analyze the specific conditions of political contest within an authoritarian State with particular political features. This analysis of political conflict in the National Autonomous University of México is grounded on a characterization of the State as a product of the Mexican revolution, and the evolution of the authoritarian political system. This discussion is presented at the beginning of Chapter 3.

Dimensions of the Political Struggle for Power

The development of a political theory of conflict within education will be addressed by looking at the struggle for power, understood as the potential to determine outcomes (Hardy 1990), on three dimensions (Lukes 1974). The first dimension is that of the actors, structure, and process of decision–making (Dahl 1966; Weber, Mills, and Gerth 1946). The second is about the control over the political agenda (Bachrach and Baratz 1970). The third dimension is the process of shaping and incorporating perceptions, cognitions, and preferences (Lukes 1974) into a dominant ideology[8] (Gramsci 1971).

The actors of decision–making: bureaucracies and elites. Elite studies were originally developed by classical theorists Gaetano Mosca (1939), Vilfredo Pareto (1935), and Robert Michels (1958) as a response to Marxist depictions of society as divided in classes (Parry 1969; Smith 1979). Classical elite theorists recognized unequal distribution of power as inevitable. The minority that possessed the largest share of power was defined as the governing or political elite (Pareto 1935). For Pareto and Mosca, the character, abilities, and expertise of political leaders determined the power structure of society (Parry 1969).

For traditional Marxists on the other hand, political leaders were representatives of the dominant economic class. The class–structure of society determined the political system. Theorists like James Burnham and C. Wright Mills attempted the first syntheses between elitism and Marxism. They looked at elite power as a consequence of the control over the means of production (Burnham 1942), or as a consequence of the occupation of positions in key institutions in society (Mills 1956). Ralph Miliband (1969) and William Domhoff (1967; 1970) provided new formulations for the role of elites by establishing an analytic distinction between class and State. The ruling–class rules through colonization of key positions in the State apparatus. The nature of the capitalist State was historically contingent upon the relation between ruling class and State apparatus. The unity of the elites was essentially accomplished through ideology.

Structuralists criticized Miliband and Domhoff's instrumental views. Based on a profound dichotomy between structural determinism and historical agency, Poulantzas (1973) argued that according to these perspectives the capitalist nature of the State was determined by individual agency at the elite level and not by structural relations in capitalist society. In his early work he suggested alternatively that structures produced by the confrontation between classes at the level of production determined the capitalist nature and the shape of the State. I already mentioned that Poulantzas' later work suggested that the State itself was a site of struggle with absolute autonomy in relation to the classes (Poulantzas 1978). While the State is still shaped by structural relations between the classes (now inside the State itself), it is the operation of bureaucracies or political elites that defines policy.

In the study of higher education governance it is important to look at the different political dimensions that affect policy–making. It has already been established in previous sections that this model is based on the idea that the confrontation between dominant and subaltern social groups shapes the political structures and processes of State institutions. Struggles at the level of institutions and the broader State also establish the broad lines of university reform. Within these, however, the bureaucracy and the university elite define the particular forms of policy and establish the continuity of the dominant projects for higher education. The study of this bureaucracy and university elite, and their connections with those of other State institutions, is a fundamental component of any understanding of governance as a political process within higher education.

The issues of higher education reform. When talking about power, it is important to establish a difference between the sources and the exercise of power. While elite theorists from different perspectives focused on the sources of power, their pluralist critics looked at the exercise of power (Lukes 1974). Pluralists have equated power with participation in decision–making processes (Bachrach and Baratz 1970). In this perspective the study of power is centered on outcomes. Pluralist methodology is based on participants' successes or defeats in getting their initiatives adopted, or vetoing the initiatives of others over *key* issues. Successes and defeats are computed, and participants with higher rates of success are considered the most powerful or influential (Dahl 1966). Power is only present when decisions are made over key issues, that is, when decisions involve actual, observable conflict (Lukes 1974).

Bachrach and Baratz (1970) criticized pluralist perspectives on power and decision–making. They argued that power had two faces: decisions and non–decisions. Non–decision is the mechanism through which issues and demands for change can be eliminated even before they are voiced (Lukes 1974). Beyond the importance of initiating, deciding, or vetoing, "power may be, and often is, exercised by confining the scope of decision–making to relatively 'safe' issues" (p. 6). Non-decision–making is the primary method for maintaining "mobilization of bias" that is

> a set of predominant values, beliefs, rituals, and institutional procedures ('rules of the game') that operate systematically and consistently to the benefit of certain persons and groups at the expense of others. Those who benefit are placed in a preferred position to defend and promote their vested interests. More often than not, the "status–quo defenders" are a minority or elite group within the population in question (Bachrach and Baratz 1970 p. 43).

There are several forms of non-decision–making. *Force* is the direct and extreme form of preventing demands for change from reaching the political process. *Coercion* is the threat of negative (potential deprivation) or positive (cooptation) sanctions to inhibit challenging demands. *Invocation of existing biases* is the use of norms, precedents, rules, or procedures, to do away with threatening issues. *Reshaping or strengthening of the mobilization bias* is also an indirect form of non decision–making (Bachrach and Baratz 1970).

Bachrach and Baratz's two–dimensional view of power provides a very important tool for the understanding of political conflict. In this research we will use their model for the study of agenda control, of issues and potential issues, of decisions and non–decisions.

It is important however, to understand the limitations of this perspective. Following Lukes (1974) I identify that: First, non decision–making is assumed to be an individualistic process. It does not acknowledge that individual actions are constrained by mobilization bias and that this is an expression of collective forces and social arrangements. Second, it is assumed that there is power only in the presence of conflict. This is problematic because it does not account for the use of power in preventing conflict through the process of shaping the very demands of potentially challenging actors. Finally, it is assumed that the absence of grievances implies that consensus has been reached. Once again, this perspective does not account for the use of power to prevent grievances by shaping perceptions, cognition, and preferences. In spite of these limitations the two-dimensional model is extremely useful for the study of issues and potential issues in the decision–making agenda. The shortcomings will be addressed by looking at a third dimension in the study of power.

Cultural hegemony. As I established earlier, this theoretical model is based on the idea that the State and State institutions are a site of struggle and that this struggle takes place at the level of the economic structure but also, and in very relevant manner, at the level of cultural hegemony. Raymond Williams (1977) emphasizes "the full possibilities of the concept of culture as a constitutive social process, creating specific and different 'ways of life'" (p. 17), and the utility of cultural history as a methodology for cultural analysis.

In this sense, he ascribes himself fully to the Gramscian tradition from which he extracts analytical concepts and practices to be applied to cultural approaches of reality. For Williams,

> [h]egemony is always an active process, but this does not mean that it is simply a complex of dominant features and elements. On the contrary, it is always a more or less adequate organization and interconnection of otherwise separated and even disparate meanings, values, and practices, which specifically incorporates in a significant culture and an effective social order.

> This process of incorporation is of major cultural importance. To understand it, but also to understand the material on which it must work, we need to distinguish three aspects of any cultural process, which we can call traditions, institutions and formations" (p. 115).

In the study of the process of creation and recreation of a dominant identity, I will draw from Raymond Williams' approach to cultural hegemony. For Williams, tradition is an active, shaping force and constitutes in practice "the most evident expression of the dominant and hegemonic pressures and limits." Tradition is radically selective. In a certain culture, certain meanings and practices are selected and others are neglected or excluded. A hegemonic process successfully presents this selection as "tradition." It actively provides a "deliberately selective and connective process which offers a historical and cultural ratification of a contemporary order" (p. 116).

The establishment of a selective tradition depends on identifiable institutions. Nevertheless it is an underestimation of this process to suppose that it depends on institutions alone. It is also a question of social formations; "those effective movements and tendencies, in intellectual and artistic life, which have significant and sometimes decisive influence on the active development of culture and which have a variable and often oblique relation to formal institutions" (p. 117).

The importance of institutions in the process of socialization of a selected set of meanings and values is unquestionable. Yet it cannot be assumed that the sum of institutions constitutes an organic hegemony precisely because hegemony is not only socialization. It is a much more complex process full of contradictions and unresolved conflicts. Hegemony cannot be established with mere training or coercion. It implies effective self–identification with the hegemonic forms. Social formations are therefore fundamental for the comprehension of hegemony. They are the space for re–creation and questioning of tradition; the direct link between culture and society; and the "active social and cultural substance" (p. 120).

These three levels of political struggle are deeply interrelated. The analytic distinction between levels allows for the possibility of a systematic study of the political process within State institutions, as in the case of higher education. On the other hand, acknowledging the relationship between the three levels allows us to understand the political nature of processes that had been traditionally considered as non–political. In cases where there is absence of open political conflict, and lack of identifiable grievances in the process of collegial consensus building or the exclusion of potential issues in the political agenda (Lukes 1974), this model still enhances the political nature of governance and decision–making.

THE HEGEMONIC MODEL OF POLITICS AND GOVERNANCE IN HIGHER EDUCATION

In the previous sections I have provided the theoretical foundations of a hegemonic model for the study of politics and governance in higher education. In presenting these foundations and establishing the connections between the different levels of theory I also put on view the main features of this analytical conceptual frame. In this section I will try to summarize the model in its abstract form. The model is divided in five levels.

The first level, or State–theoretical level, is grounded on the assumption that the class State is a site of conflict between dominant and subaltern sectors of society. Demands for increased capital accumulation and demands for social justice, equality, and democracy drive conflict. This conflict takes the form of a struggle for hegemony, a confrontation over ideology and resource allocation, and it takes place at the level of the State and State institutions.

A second theoretical level looks at higher education as a State institution. Therefore colleges and universities are also a site of conflict. External competition for capital accumulation versus equalization takes a particular form within higher education. Demands for the reproduction of dominant ideology and a skilled labor force; as well as the production of knowledge geared towards the enhancement of productivity and capitalist accumulation (Slaughter 1990) are opposed to exigencies for increased access, enhancement of the social mobility function of education, and increased democratic participation. Conflict assumes the form of competing projects for educational reform. These alternative projects deal with the social function of higher–education institutions, access, academic orientations, and resource allocation policies.

The third theoretical level provides the instantiation of the political contest within the particular forms of the political system at the level of the university and the broader State. The political system is shaped by four basic elements. These are the limits of democratic political competition; the nature of the dominant political ideology; the degrees of political mobilization or citizen participation; and the nature of political leadership.

The previous three theoretical frames provide the guidelines for a historical study of politics, power, and change in higher education and enable us to understand the historical evolution of decision–making structures and processes as well as norms, rules and regulations. The fourth theoretical level provides the dimensions for the study of the political process within higher education. The first is the instrumental dimension. It deals with the study of the central actors (political elites and bureaucrats) of decision–making. The second is the policy dimension. It deals with the control over agendas and the historical development of issues and non–issues in university policy–making. The third is the hegemonic dimension. It deals with the creation and recreation of dominant cultures and identities through the political process. The three dimensions are interconnected. In the process of political confrontation with subaltern social movements and alternative political options, elites and institutional arrangements shape and are in turn shaped by ideological constructs. Decision and non–decision-making (agenda control) is constrained and determined by actors and dominant cultural perceptions.

Finally there is a fifth theoretical level that directly guides the process of data collection and analysis in the inquiry about the previous dimensions of political contest and within the context of the first three theoretical levels. The instrumental dimension of political contest will be addressed through the study of political elites. It will follow C. Wright Mills and Domhoff's theory of elites and both reputational and positional methods. The policy dimension will be studied through a historical study of the development of real and potential issues for policy–making. This study is based on theories of agenda control. The hegemonic dimension will study the creation and recreation of dominant cultures and identities by identifying the process of selection of traditions by dominant social formations.

The following table provides a summarized account of theoretical foundations for the hegemonic model for the study of governance and politics in higher education:

State theory	Theory of education	Political system	Theory of political conflict	Elites, agenda control, and selection of traditions
The State and State institutions are the site of conflict between dominant and subaltern sectors of society Conflict is driven by tension between demand for increased capital accumulation and demands for social justice, equality and democracy	Higher education is a State institution it is also a site of conflict Conflict in education is driven by demands for the reproduction of ideology, labor skills, and productivity oriented knowledge production on one hand, and demands for access, equality and democratic participation on the other	The political system is the particular expression of the forms in which competition takes place within the State The nature of the political system (democratic, authoritarian, populist, or totalitarian) shapes the interaction between dominant groups at the broader State and education level as well as the nature of conflict with social movements.		
Conflict takes the form of an hegemonic struggle over resources and ideology	Conflict takes the form of a struggle over the ideological content and the allocation of resources between competing projects of university reform	The forms of conflict are determined by the extent or limits of democratic political competition; the nature of the dominant ideology; the degrees of political mobilization or citizen participation; and the nature of leadership (the role of political parties and other State institutions, i.e. the army).	The political contest takes place at three interrelated dimensions: The instrumental dimension dealing with actors The policy dimension, dealing with control over agendas, and	Instrumental: Study of political elites and bureaucracies within the university Policy: Historical continuity of issues and non–issues
			The hegemonic dimension, dealing with dominant culture and identities	Hegemony: Creation and recreation of dominant culture and identities through selection of traditions

CONCLUSION

The study of higher education requires new theoretical developments focusing on political processes in university governance and change. Researchers should be capable of grounding their observations and analyses on theories that emerge from such social sciences as economics, sociology, political science, history and psychology.

This systematic organization of different theoretical layers presented here, stemming from political sociology, provides the foundations for a set of studies about political processes, tensions, and conflicts in higher education. This theoretical perspective integrates distinct levels of analysis and processes, from the broadest and more general level of the State to the more particular spaces of higher education organizations. The integration of these processes and levels in this model is grounded on theories of the State and the political system; conflict theories of education and higher education as a site of struggle; and theories of power in its instrumental, agenda control, and ideological construct dimensions. All of these theories focus on the analysis of conflict and politics. The integration of these levels of analysis and diverse theories constitutes a powerful tool for a wholistic understanding of the complex arrangement of actors, norms, agendas, and cultural views in which domination within higher education institutions is founded.

Ideological or cultural domination is largely based in a lack of capacity to understand the totality of power relations within institutions. The theoretical approach in this chapter has been developed with the purpose of presenting a full perspective on the complexity of these power relations and the conflicts that develop within colleges and universities.

The repossession of theories of power and conflict from the social sciences and their use in the context of higher education goes against the grain of dominant contemporary analytic models. The attempt here is precisely to build theoretical tools that will enable a re-politicization of the study of higher education *vis-à-vis* technocratic and economicist trends (Readings 1996; Slaughter 1991; Wolin 1991).

NOTES

[1] In *The Grundrisse*, Marx explains his methodology for the study of a social formation. It is based in the systematic study of "concrete" and "real" facts, and the economic and social relations established between them. The "chaotic conception of a whole" can be avoided by moving analytically towards simple concepts. This movement goes "from the imagined concrete towards ever thinner abstractions until I had arrived at the simplest determinations" (Marx 1972 p. 237). From here, the process has to be retraced until the original concept is reconstructed "not as a chaotic conception of the whole, but as a rich totality of many determinations and relations" (Ibidem). For Marx, "the concrete is concrete because it is the concentration of many determinations, hence unity of the diverse. It appears in the process of thinking, therefore as a process of concentration, as a result, not as a point of departure, even though it is the point of departure in reality and hence also the point of departure for observation and conception" (Ibidem). Assuming this path, the abstract determinations lead towards a reproduction of the concrete by the way of thought.

Based on these premises, political economy has come to mean the analysis of the structures and the relations of production within a determined social formation. It is associated with the study of economic categories, in a particular mode of production, in their relation to one another. The suggested order of analysis goes from "the general, abstract determinants which obtain in more or less all forms of society;" to the categories which make up the inner structure on which the fundamental classes rest and their interrelation; to the concentration of society in the form of the State, and from here to the analysis of these relations at the international level (Marx 1972 p. 244).

2 Marx and Engels originally developed this idea. Based on the separation of society in economic structure (forces of production and relations of production) and superstructure (Marx 1972) their idea of the State is that of an instrument of the ruling class. There are two main ideas about this instrumental State: (a) it is the "monopoly of legitimate violence," and (b) the State is part of the superstructure and it is determined by the economic structure.

For Marx and Engels, ideology is reproduced through the process of production (Marx and Engels 1967). The State is part of the ideological superstructure and plays no role in reproducing ideology. Its function, as political committee of the ruling class, is to defend the interests of this class through repression. Lenin agreed with Marx and Engels's instrumental view and stressed the idea of the necessary overthrowing of the State as the only revolutionary strategy for the working class in opposition to other views within the Second International (Lenin 1965; Miliband 1969). Later versions of instrumental views have focused on the complexity of the State and the existence of State apparatuses and have argued that Marx's work also suggested a "reformist" strategy in which socialists could make use of the capitalist State before overthrowing it (Miliband 1977).

3 Gramsci developed an alternative Marxist view of the State. Even though his work is based on Marx and Engels, he emphasized "...the role of the superstructure in perpetuating classes and preventing the development of social consciousness" (Carnoy 1984 p. 66). Gramsci's conception of the State as dictatorship + hegemony, and his idea of hegemony as established through the mediation of ideology, provide a new and powerful view of this category. For Gramsci ideology is the terrain "on which men move, acquire consciousness of their own position, struggle," it is "a practice producing subjects" (Gramsci 1971).

Gramsci considers that: "a world-view is manifest in all action and that it expresses itself in a very elaborate form and at a high level of abstraction —as is the case with philosophy— or else it is expressed in much simpler forms as the expression of 'common sense'... These world-views are never individual facts but the expression of the 'communal life of a social bloc', which is why Gramsci calls them organic 'ideologies'" (Mouffe 1979).

4 The Gramscian perspective opened the way for two further developments in class–based State theory. The first one is the structuralist view (Althusser and early Poulantzas). According to Althusser, there are three kinds of structures in society: the economic (in traditional Marxist terms the structure), the political, and the ideological (in traditional Marxism both of these would constitute the superstructure). The ideological structure is autonomous but functional to the economic structure in the last instance. The State is part of both the political and the ideological structures. In Althusser's view the State is the combination of ideological apparatuses and repressive apparatuses (Althusser 1971). Ideological State Apparatuses (ISA's) are structures in which the dominant ideology is embedded. The dominant ideologies, and therefore the relations of production, are reproduced through "subject interpellation" by these ISA's. The educational system is part of the ISA's.

5 A different development following Gramsci's view is that of the State as an arena of class struggle. This approach was essentially developed by Pietro Ingrao and in Poulantzas's later work (Carnoy 1984). This "class struggle" analysis of the

State argues that the capitalist State itself is an arena of class conflict, and that whereas social-class relations shape the State, it is also contested and is therefore the product of class struggle within the State. Politics is not simply the organization of class power through the State by dominant capitalist-class groups, and the use of that power to manipulate and repress subordinate groups. It is also the site of organized conflict by mass social movements to influence State policies, gain control of State apparatuses, and gain control of political apparatuses outside the State. Politics, in this view, also takes place in the economic structures themselves: these are struggles for greater control of the work process and for power over surplus (Carnoy 1984 p. 7).

[6] The structuralist approach to the State is the strongest foundation of most early reproductivist theories in education. Since there is no ideological contestation within the ISA's, the educational system is viewed essentially as a site in which the dominant ideology and the existing relations of production are reproduced.

[7] This interpretation of Gramsci's view is not consensual. I base it essentially in Gramsci's identification of the concept of "passive revolution" and that of "war of position" in the *Prison Notebooks* (Gramsci 1971 pp. 104–106). It can also be extrapolated from diverse parts of the text. One example is the following:

> The massive structures of the modern democracies, both as State organizations, and as complexes of associations in civil society, constitute for the art of politics as it were the 'trenches' and permanent fortifications of the front in the war of position: they render merely 'partial' the element of the movement which before used to be 'the whole' of the war, etc. (Gramsci 1971 p. 243).

Several authors like Mouffe (1979) and Portantiero (1981) suggest a similar interpretation of Gramsci's work. Carnoy's review of Buci-Glucksmann is particularly useful:

> ...in that very consciousness that could consent to the relations of capitalist society lay the foundations of a strategy for gaining the active consent of the masses through their self-organization, starting from civil society, and in all the hegemonic apparatuses—from the factory to the school and the family" (Carnoy 1984 p. 69).

Other authors diverge. Carnoy argues that Gramsci "began to open the way for serious discussion of the Capitalist State as a site of class struggle" (Carnoy 1984 p. 153) but nevertheless maintained a Leninist view about the siege (war of position) and later overthrowing of the capitalist State (war of maneuvers or frontal attack). Probably a discussion about the terms of the "siege" could generate a common understanding of this issue.

[8] Gramsci distinguishes between rule and domination. A group rules or leads when it is able to exercise power in a hegemonic way. To do this the group has to establish previously an "intellectual and moral leadership" (one of the principal conditions of winning such power). Even if the group holds power firmly, it must continue to lead as well (Gramsci 1971).

The State, the Political System, and the University
The University and the Emergence of Authoritarianism

> ...the whole movement, therefore, seems to turn in a vicious circle, out of which we can only get by supposing a primitive accumulation preceding capitalistic accumulation; an accumulation not the result of the capitalist mode of production but its starting–point.
>
> The primitive accumulation plays in political economy about the same part as original sin in theology.
>
> Karl Marx. Capital

This chapter sets the historical foundations for the political analysis of the *Universidad Nacional*. The first section provides an overview of the Mexican State and the essential characteristics of the authoritarian political system in three phases: emergence (1917–1944), consolidation (1944–1968), and decline (since 1968). The following sections of this chapter trace the relation between the National University and the Mexican State since the end of the armed phase of the revolution and until 1945. Except for a short phase from 1922 to 1924, the University as a whole remained distant, refusing to become involved in populist education projects, when not openly confronted with the State apparatus. Several authors have argued that during this period the University became the space in which urban middle class intellectuals acquired a distinct identity *vis-à-vis* the Revolutionary State and established relations of cooperation or resistance against its populist projects (Garciadiego Dantan 1996; Guevara Niebla 1980). In addition to this, in the following sections, I show that during this period, intellectual groups within the National University developed strong traditions and ideological configurations in the midst of intense confrontations with the government in 1929 and 1933. I also show that by 1945 changes at the level of the State and within the University allowed for a redefinition of the relations between these two institutions.

In this chapter I also analyze the process through which the *Universidad Nacional Autónoma de México* was reorganized and a new governance structure was set in place in 1945. I show that the establishment of this political arrangement sanctioned a new relationship between the University and the Mexican State, and institutionalized the balance between competing political forces within the University. Populists and radical conservatives were defeated in 1933 and 1944 respectively, allowing for the establishment of this new dominant alliance between University and State. I argue that the new formation became institutionalized in a new political system that constrained the legitimate space for political action within a well–defined discourse of de–politicization and academic meritocracy. Finally, I show how university liberal groups connected to the State were able to strengthen their political influence on UNAM through a process of *primitive accumulation of power.*[1]

This development has been broadly described in many historical accounts. Typically, it has been characterized as a technical reform of University structures, contributing to the myth of de-politicization of the modern University. With the exception of President Ávila Camacho, Alfonso Caso, or the Board of Former Rectors, no actors or interests are usually named. González Oropeza's (1980) historiography constitutes the only attempt to provide information about the actors, the discourse, and the mechanisms that gave birth to the current political system at UNAM.

Based on this different interpretation of historical data on the resulting governance structure at UNAM, I challenge this characterization. I show that what others view as the "de–politicization" of the University in this period was, in fact, the incorporation of UNAM into a particular political structure. This incorporation took place through a political process that tied the University closely to the State apparatus. A close analysis of this historical development sheds light on the process, discourse, and structures through which the dominant coalition and the articulation with State interests were institutionalized[2] into the new political system at UNAM. This will be particularly relevant to understanding the political developments and processes of change analyzed in the following chapters.

THE MEXICAN STATE AND THE AUTHORITARIAN POLITICAL SYSTEM

I have argued that a full understanding of the evolution of university politics and its processes of change is not possible without studying the ever–changing relationship between this institution and the State. Consequently, this section develops a concrete analysis of the Mexican State as it emerged from the Mexican Revolution and a characterization of the corresponding political system. This section is fundamental in order to understand the relationship between the National University and the State apparatus as well as essential characteristics of the political arrangement within the University.

The evolution of the National University in Mexico from 1910 to the present is deeply embedded in the development of the modern Mexican State. Originally, this State was the product of almost ten years of a revolutionary process of enormous proportions and complexity. It was precisely the complex interrelation of the defeated peasant armies of Villa and Zapata combined with former regional political elites of the Porfiriato, represented by Carranza, and the emerging middle–class farmers from Sonora that formally gave birth to the Mexican State in the 1917 Constitution.

The Revolution and the Mexican State

The 1917 Constitution was put together based on two distinct programs. On the one hand, the proposal of a liberal State, with strong executive presence, limited parliamentary attributions, and direct presidential elections, put forward by Carranza (Córdova 1973). On the other, were elements of the radical program promoting national sovereignty over national resources, State provided non–religious education, peasant communities' access to land, and protection of labor rights, put forward by Múgica and the Obregonistas (Hamilton 1982).

According to the Constitution, the emerging State was to be the representative of the revolutionary classes. In the discourse of the Revolutionary State, these classes were ambiguously defined. They supposedly included the peasantry, the workers, and the urban poor, but on occasion even the military and the members of the government were considered part of this sector. The State was entrusted with the role of creating the conditions for capital accumulation and promoting economic growth and development. The interventionist nature of the Mexican State was enhanced by the incorporation of the masses, the subaltern classes, through corporatist organizations and the official party. At the same time, it was limited by two factors. First, it was constrained by the restricted availability of resources and the limitations of the economic base. Second, it was historically constrained by the presence of foreign capital, heavy debts to the United States and European nations, and the need for foreign exchange and capital. These elements, characteristic of underdeveloped or dependent countries, have allowed foreign capital and world powers, most significantly the United States, to play a defining role in the historical development of the Mexican State (Meyer 1981a).

The Political system: Mexican authoritarianism

The characteristics of the State mentioned above constitute the foundations for the existing authoritarian political system in Mexico. Juan Linz (1975) described the basic features of authoritarian political systems.

> Authoritarian regimes are political systems with limited, not responsible, political pluralism; without elaborate and guiding ideology (but with dis-

tinctive mentalities); without extensive nor intensive political mobilization (except at some points in their development); and in which a leader (or occasionally a small group) exercises power within formally ill–defined limits but actually quite predictable ones (p. 255).

The Mexican political system fits within Linz's broad theoretical guide-lines. It is important to analyze the particularities of the Mexican authoritarian regime as it has historically evolved through three distinct phases. I will denote these phases as the *emergence, consolidation,* and *crisis* of Mexican authoritarianism. They will be especially useful in establishing historical periods for the study of governance, conflict, and change at UNAM.

The limits of political participation. The most relevant feature of authoritarianism is restricted political competition. This was also the most salient characteristic of the Mexican political system from 1917 to 2002. While formally a democratic regime, elections in Mexico have been completely dominated by the government parties since 1916. During the *emergence* phase, from 1916 to 1938, electoral competition ranged from a multiparty system with limited electoral content to a unique national coalition of revolutionaries (the *Partido Nacional Revolucionario* in 1929). According to Lorenzo Meyer (1981a), during the early years of the revolution

> political victory did not depend on ballot results but on the recognition of this [election] by the central authorities. The political fortune of the members of the revolutionary elite —chiefs of military operations, governors, legislators, labor and peasant leaders, local caciques,3 etc. —depended very little on the electoral result and much on relations with coalition leader in the center" (p. 1195).

Centralized control over the electoral competition *consolidated* with the creation of the *Partido de la Revolución Mexicana* in 1938. During this period, "the contest for power [was] effectively restricted to supporters of the regime, the circle that has become known as the 'revolutionary family'" and genuine political competition only existed within those limits (Smith 1979 p. 50).

The *consolidation* phase lasted until 1968. In that year, the student movement challenged the foundations of the authoritarian regime. The movement itself and the violent response by the government initiated a long *crisis* of the political system. The phase of *crisis* has evolved in the midst of vast social and political conflicts up to this day.

Political mobilization and citizen participation. Mexican authoritarianism has developed a set of distinctive features over time. In spite of its bureaucratic and authoritarian nature, the Mexican State is not totally exclusive of subaltern sectors. The Mexican political system reflects the limited inclusive nature of the State. In exchange for people's acceptance of an authoritarian bureaucracy, the State, to a limited extent, has provided protection and delivered goods for peasants and workers.

At the political level, inclusion does not take place through traditional citizen participation or political mobilization as it does in a democratic political system. In Mexico, it develops essentially through two political processes. The first of these is the corporatist relation of social organizations with the State party. The inclusion of marginal sectors in the political system *began to emerge* at the end of the armed struggle. This corporatist political arrangement finally *consolidated* with the development of the *Partido de la Revolucion Mexicana* (PRM) in 1938. Precursor movements for independent unions (like those of teachers and railroad workers) took place in the late–fifties. However, the long decline of the corporatist relations only started after the 1968 *crisis* with the emergence of independent union movements in universities, electrical and automotive workers, as well as other sectors of society.

The second process of political inclusion is cooptation. By cooptation, I mean the process of assimilation of new or opposing elements into the leadership of an organization as a mechanism to avoid conflict and obtain legitimacy and stability. During the *emergent* phase of authoritarianism, cooptation was used to overcome political fragmentation in the early years after the Revolution (Anderson and Cockroft 1972). The party would not tolerate any external centers of power. "If cooptation failed, strong–arm methods were used" (p. 233). The cooptation–repression pattern became a salient feature of the *consolidated* authoritarian political system. It was the system's growing inability to co–opt and its increasing use of repression, during the 1960s, that led to the student movement and its tragic conclusion in 1968. With it, came the beginning of the crisis of the authoritarian regime.

The nature of leadership and the role of State institutions. It can be seen that Mexican authoritarianism is distinct from that of other nations when we examine the nature of presidential leadership, the State party, and other institutions. It differs from Linz's original formulation in several ways. The strong executive model presented by Carranza in 1917 (Córdova 1973) developed into a perfected political system in which the president has ruled over legislative and judicial powers as well as states and local powers (Carpizo 1978). The president is also the head of the State party with absolute power to designate his successor, the official party presidential candidate (Meyer 1981a).

The State party is a primary political institution (Garrido 1982). "It is visible and valuable, both as a means for claiming legitimacy and, especially, as an instrument of cooptation and control" (Smith 1979 p. 57). Diverse authors agree that in spite of its political clout, the power of the

State party to influence government policy decreased considerably (Meyer 1981a; Smith 1979) during the *consolidation* period.

Absolute control by the president over other branches of government, over the State party, and over limited political competition has given name to the Mexican version of authoritarianism: *el presidencialismo*. *Presidencialismo* has become a political culture of personal authoritarianism, subordination of collegial structures to executive authorities, and substitution of institutional duties for personal loyalties that has permeated every other institution of the State (Ordorika 1988). Beyond the faculties awarded by the Constitution and ordinary laws, presidential powers are rooted in the authoritarian nature of the Mexican political system. *Presidencialismo* is based on three fundamental meta–constitutional faculties: a) the undisputed leadership of the State party, b) the unwritten right to designate its own successor, and c) control over the designation and removal of state governors (Carpizo 1978).

In addition to the lack of political competition, these faculties give the president control over the judicial and legislative branches of government. They provide him with strong influence over individual political careers and consequently over the competition within the State party. Given the corporatist incorporation of social organizations to the official party, the president's influence is extended to peasants and workers unions, labor federations, and even some professional organizations (Garrido 1982).

In the peak of authoritarianism (from 1944 to 1968) this situation provided the president with enormous control over political competition with the State party. Given that the president constituted the point of articulation between State institutions, *presidencialismo* gave the struggles within the State apparatus a high degree of isolation and lack of connection. In this way, the political system has largely determined the nature of contestation processes within the Mexican State.

The "ideology" of the Mexican revolution. Diverse authors have extensively analyzed ideology of the Mexican revolution. Some argue that it is not an ideology in a strict sense but a set of doctrines (Anderson and Cockroft 1972; Smith 1979). Córdova (1973) described that while there is

> [a] dominant ideology, that absolutely responds to the interests of the dominant class, it is not systematically and permanently expressed by representatives of that class, but it is preferably left, to be produced and manifested by the political groups that directly control State power, through pragmatic solutions that are linked to State politics (p. 37).

In spite of pragmatic party and government interpretations, there are some relevant features of the dominant ideology of the Mexican State (Córdova 1973).

1. The State is conceived as playing a central role in the accumulation of goods and the organization of society. It is not until very recent times that this idea has been challenged.

2. Private property has been considered the basic tenant of social organization.

3. Democratic ideas and organizations as well as citizen liberties are valued as essential components of the political regime. They have been sacrificed, however, in the name of future development and social equality.

4. Social order and societal institutions are not the product of citizen participation. They are imposed by the State, in many cases, against society itself.

5. Social order is established through conciliation of classes and interests, mediated and arbitrated by the State.

6. Popular masses are essential for development policies. They are included through social reforms and mobilized in order to control and discipline other social groups.

7. Opposition is slandered with the image of "reactionary threats" to social reforms "conquered" by the Revolution.

8. Nationalism is the unifying ideology and the condensation of the common good.

9. In spite of nationalist posturing, foreign intervention is surreptitiously accepted in return for acceptance of State intervention on internal economic affairs.

Political discourse is handled with unlimited pragmatism. The ideological foundations of the Revolution are interpreted, used, and discarded according to the requirements of different political situations.

Overall, it is important to note that the Mexican authoritarian political system has been founded on a very broad and heterogeneous social base. This is the product of social reforms, political inclusion through cooptation or corporatism, and ideological conformity. In turn, the broadness of its social base has provided the Mexican State and its authoritarian political system with a large degree of internal legitimacy. It was not until 1968 that this legitimacy started to erode.

ANTECEDENTS OF THE *UNIVERSIDAD NACIONAL*: DEVELOPMENT OF A
POLITICAL CULTURE

Since its foundation in the early colonial days, the National University in
Mexico has had a long history of political conflict. There are many historical accounts of the University during the colonial and early independent historical periods (Carreño 1961; González González 1987;
González-Polo y Acosta 1983; Lanning and Valle 1946; Luna Díaz 1985;
Luna Díaz 1987c). Few of them have emphasized the political features of
the University during those days. These narratives however, provide
interesting data for the study of political processes in Mexican higher
education. Some of the strongest political traditions of the University
originated during the era of the *Real y Pontificia Universidad de México*,
ending in 1867.

University Traditions in the Colonial Era

The *Real y Pontificia Universidad de México* was founded by royal
decree in 1551, and officially inaugurated in 1553. It was organized in
the scholastic tradition of the *Universidad de Salamanca* in Spain
(Jiménez Rueda 1955). This institution inherited two basic features of the
University of Salamanca: autonomy, as well as democratic election of university officials and professors.[4] The founding royal decree established
that the University would receive annual appropriations from the *Real
Hacienda* (Royal Treasury) (Attolini 1951).[5]

While the *Real y Pontificia Universidad de México* enjoyed formal
academic, administrative, and appointive autonomy, there were many
instances of external interference by government authorities and the
Church. Occasional viceroy interventions in the internal affairs of the
University were the sources of several conflicts in the history of the *Real
y Pontificia Universidad de México* (Carreño 1961; González González
1987). Additionally, the academic content of lectures and readings was
heavily controlled and policed by the Church. Autonomous
decision-making was also limited by the institution's financial accountability to the Crown (Menegus Bornemann 1987).

In spite of these limitations, modern Mexican higher education inherited four strong traditions from the colonial university. These were the
principle of autonomy from Church and State; internal election of university officials; student participation in university governance; and the
State's financial responsibility towards the university.

A Partisan University

During the war of independence and in the early years of the new
Republic, the University became a partisan institution on the conservative

side and suffered intensely for that. The *Real y Pontificia Universidad de México* and the positivist *Escuela Nacional Preparatoria* are both relevant antecedents because they represent the traditions that gave birth to the new *Universidad Nacional* in 1910.

The early years of Mexican independent life (from 1821 to 1867) were characterized by intense conflicts between liberals and conservatives, by foreign interventions, and reform wars. The most relevant issues that were the object of conflict between liberals and conservatives were federalism *versus* centralism, the separation between Church and State, redemption of unproductive properties in the hands of the Church, and the nature of education. Liberals argued that the new nation's progress depended on the occupation of the Church's properties. They called for the abolishment of privileges for the church and the military. The liberals promoted the expansion of education to popular sectors of society, and its total independence from the Church (Mora 1963).

In this dispute between liberals and conservatives, the University retained its traditional stance on the side of the Church and the Conservative Party. The University became a party symbol, it was defended by the conservatives and constantly attacked by the liberals (Alvarado 1984; O'Gorman 1960). In this way, the fate of the *Universidad Pontificia* was linked to that of the factions in conflict.

Liberals closed the *Real y Pontificia Universidad de México* on two occasions (1833 and 1857). It was characterized as useless, non–reformable, and pernicious (Mora 1963). Mora labeled the University "useless" because nothing was taught and nothing was learned. The University was also considered "non–reformable," because any reform presupposed the ethical and moral base of the old establishment. Obviously, the University was useless and non–conducive towards the ultimate objectives of the establishment. The University was, furthermore, considered "pernicious" because it "gives place to the loss of time and the dissipation of the students" (Mora 1963). Based on Mora's recommendation, the government concluded that it was necessary to suppress the University. The University was reopened by conservatives in 1834 and 1863 only to be closed definitively by Emperor Maximilian in 1865 during the French invasion of Mexico.

The *Real y Pontificia Universidad de México* had been characterized by its political and academic conservatism during the colonial era. During the confrontation between liberals and conservatives the University strengthened this conservative stance and became openly partisan on the side of the most reactionary groups in Mexican society. In the final liberal victory against the French invasion, the Conservative Party, and the Church, the University and the *Colegios* were permanently closed and religious education was banned. In the construction of the new secular educational system (1867–1874) the unchallenged liberal government turned its eyes to a modern philosophy imported from France by Gabino Barreda: positivism, the philosophy of order and progress.[6] Barreda founded the *Escuela Nacional Preparatoria* (National Preparatory School, now a part of UNAM). This institution was to be the core of an educational system that would establish the "positive spirit" (Vázquez 1992).[7]

In 1876, a liberal faction led by Porfirio Diaz installed a long dictatorship that would last until 1910. Positivism continued to provide the ideological foundation for the group in power. The evolution of intellectual groups and ideas during this phase of Mexican history is very relevant in order to understand the composition of the central actors who recreated the National University in 1910. The liberal tradition that had allowed the bourgeoisie to emerge as a dominant group had become increasingly burdensome (Talavera 1973). The idea of *liberty as the means* was dropped as a metaphysical concept. Liberty was reinterpreted as the natural path of order. If order had been an essential concern of the victorious liberals in 1867, it had become the central issue for the emerging *liberal conservatives* that constituted the social base of the Diaz dictatorship (Zea 1966).

To promote the guiding values of positivism, the ruling political party called themselves *los Científicos* (the Scientists). The *Científicos* were the generation educated by Barreda in the *Preparatoria*. Their dominant ideas, however, had shifted from Comte's to Stuart Mill, Spencer, and Darwin's positivism. They reconciled their own interests with these authors' theories of individual freedom through the concept of *social evolution*: complete order would enable progress, and this in turn would allow for complete liberty (Zea 1974).

The *Científicos* were the object of critiques by the old liberal guard and by traditional positivists. Education policies as well were the object of critiques. Traditional positivists criticized the new education policies established in 1880, and defended the ultimate positivist project; the *Preparatoria Nacional* (Zea 1974). Liberals, in turn, had always been enemies of the Preparatory and the positivist education program, which they always characterized as unconstitutional (Zea 1974).

In the latter years of the *Porfiriato*,[8] a new variant of critiques against positivism emerged from the *Escuela Preparatoria* itself. Justo Sierra was Diaz's Minister of Instruction, a former positivist, a history professor in the *Preparatoria*, a *Científico*, and one of the developers of the idea of *social evolution* (Zea 1966). As early as 1874 Sierra carefully criticized Mexican positivism for its rigidity and routine (Salmerón 1966). Sierra's position was contradictory. He encouraged a broader philosophical perspective but never fully distanced himself from positivism. He provided the ideological foundations for the Diaz regime while he was concerned with the delegation of political liberties to the dictator (Zea 1966). This eclecticism became evident in the creation of the National University in 1910.

A small group of notable *Preparatoria* students and intellectuals, the *Ateneo de la Juventud* (the *Athenaeum* of Youth) provided a strong critique of positivism from a humanist and a religious perspective (Salmerón 1966). This group included Pedro Henríquez Ureña, Alfonso Reyes, Antonio Caso, and José Vasconcelos who were Sierra's disciples. Religious humanism reappeared against the discourse of scientific rationality and order. The *Ateneo* provided a group of very important intellectuals who would reject some of the values of positivism, and who were rooted in the eclectic position of *liberal conservatism*. One of these intellectuals, José Vasconcelos, would play a major role in the new educational projects of the revolution. All of them, but most significantly Caso and Vasconcelos, would become significant actors in the modern history of the National University.

The University Once Again

Justo Sierra reestablished the university in its modern form in 1910. For this purpose, Sierra brought together previously existing post–secondary institutions. These included the *Escuela Nacional Preparatoria* (National Preparatory School); the *Escuela Nacional de Jurisprudencia* (National School of Law); the *Escuela Nacional de Medicina* (National School of Medicine); the *Escuela Nacional de Ingenieros* (National School of Engineering); and the *Academia de las Bellas Artes* (Academy of Fine Arts) (Marsiske 1985). Sierra also created the *Escuela de Altos Estudios* (School of High Studies) (Alvarado 1984) to provide graduate and specialization studies for the other schools and to focus on the study of philosophy and the sciences. The new university was called *Universidad Nacional de México*.

The National University was the object of severe criticisms. Conservatives and Catholics attacked the university as positivist. Traditional liberals argued that the conservative university was being recreated (Garciadiego Dantan 1996). Orthodox positivists were also against its foundation claiming that this institution was guided by metaphysics and not by science (Villegas Moreno 1984).

Sierra's own contradictions between spiritualism and positivism synthesized the eclectic nature of the emerging university. The project brought together spiritual humanists like the members of the *Athenaeum*; positivists like Porfirio Parra (first Dean of the *Escuela de Altos Estudios*; and Catholics like Joaquín Eguía Lis (first Rector of the National University) (Garciadiego Dantan 1996).

Sierra had argued in favor of an "independent corporation" (Sierra in Pinto Mazal 1974) in his proposal to found a university in 1881. However, the law he put forward for the creation of the National University in 1910 established that the Minister of Instruction was the chief of the university. Justo Sierra argued that the National University could not situate itself in an ivory tower, far from the needs and expectations of Mexican society.

The University was under the direct influence of the President and the Minister of Instruction. A rector and a university council were in charge of the institution. The president appointed the rector. The government could add new schools. Academic program reforms had to be submitted by the council to the Ministry of Instruction for final approval. The same Ministry supervised major financial operations with the patrimony.[9]

The *Universidad Nacional* was established as a State project of the *Porfiriato*. In spite of Sierra's explicit rejection of any continuity with the *Real y Pontificia Universidad de México*, the new University inherited a strong tradition of autonomy, and full financial dependence from the government. The University was essentially a traditional institution and a supporter of Díaz's regime.

The University during the Revolution

Only a few months after the foundation of the National University, the revolutionary struggle against Porfirio Díaz began. The University suffered intensely during the years of military confrontations and the succession of revolutionary factions in government until 1917. University students and faculty participated very little in the different stages of the revolutionary process with a few notable exceptions.

A complex mixture of the social demands and equality values of the revolutionary armed struggle and some elements of positivism and universalistic humanism would permeate the first educational projects of the populist governments that emerged from the revolution. This mixture would not be exempt from tensions and conflicts that would shape the future of higher education in Mexico. When the first revolutionary governments established the direct subordination of the National University to the federal government (in 1914 and 1917), old ideas of independence and autonomy reemerged.[10]

In the years that immediately followed the armed struggle, the *Universitarios*[11] were split by the Revolution.[12] With the exception of Vasconcelos, the members of the *Athenaeum* were weary and critical of the Mexican Revolution. Vasconcelos was appointed Rector (in 1920) and later Minister of Instruction (in 1922). During that period, a group of disciples of Antonio Caso and the members of the *Athenaeum*, known as the *Siete Sabios* (the seven wise men) or the generation of 1915, started their careers as University professors. Alfonso Caso (Antonio's younger brother), Vicente Lombardo Toledano, and Manuel Gómez Morín, most famous among the *Siete Sabios*, enthusiastically followed Vasconcelos in his attempt to link the University with the demands of the Mexican Revolution.

The Autonomous University

The enthusiasm of a few *Universitarios* during the early years of the Revolution did not eclipse the demands for University autonomy. The attempt by the *Universitarios* to establish some distance from the populist State was recurrent.[13] However, the final step towards University autonomy stemmed from an apparently unrelated student conflict.

In 1929, opposition to new evaluation procedures and student demands for participation in the University Council and in the appointment of university authorities (Marsiske 1985), developed into a large movement. The negotiation between students and university authorities was unsuccessful. Mexican President Portes Gil accused the students of having political motivations behind their movement. This has become a recurrent practice of University and government authorities towards student movements until the present.

Portes Gil closed the School of Law. The students went on strike and were the object of repression by the police. Confrontations between students and the police increased and the movement gained strength in broad sectors of society. As the impact of the movement increased, the confrontation started to weigh against the Mexican government in light of the coming election where the government party would compete against Vasconcelos' presidential candidacy. Unexpectedly, the President responded to student demands with a proposal for a new law that granted autonomy to the National University.[14] This action by the government addressed a popular University cause and immediately gained student approval for the President.[15]

The new law provided limited institutional autonomy. It ran contrary to the students' autonomy project preserving ample space for presidential intervention in the appointment of Rectors.[16] At the internal level, the University Council was the center of political power and the site where decision–making processes took place. These were the essential elements of that legislation (Marsiske 1985 p. 58):

1. The University council would appoint the Rector from a group of three candidates proposed by the President.

2. The President had the right to veto resolutions and policies set by the university.

3. The Rector had to provide an annual report to the Federal Congress and the Ministry of Education.

4. The University depended on Federal subsidy and did not have the right to its own patrimony.

5. The President would oversee the University budget.

The Organic Law of 1929 put an end to the student movement but the students' demands for participation were not fully satisfied.[17]   A new Rector was designated in accordance with the new regulations. The university now became the *Universidad Nacional Autónoma de México.*

A new generation that would acquire political relevance in University struggles to come was established in this movement. It has been known as the *Generación del 29* (the 1929 generation). They became a symbol of University autonomy. However, the members of the *Generación del 29* would never acquire the political relevance of other promoters of University autonomy organized around Antonio Caso and the *Siete Sabios.*[18] For several decades, the latter group would maintain their dominance of the National University.

The difference between the political impact of these groups can be partially explained by two factors. On the one hand, the 1929 leaders demanded a strong student presence in University governance and this was not favored by Caso and the *siete sabios.* On the other hand, they were defeated in their support of Vasconcelos' presidential candidacy. When their strength in the movement decreased in the light of intense polarization in the 1930s, the 1929 generation's influence in University politics was reduced.

In this section, I have described the process through which urban middle class intellectuals had been able to establish a stronghold in the face of the Revolutionary State. As Mexican authoritarianism developed and the State pursued ambitious populist policies, University professionals were brought in to fill the requirements of the expanding State apparatus. While participating in the administration, many of them became disappointed by their limited influence and the direction of government policies.

Full Autonomy: The Organic Law of 1933

The distance between the *Universitarios* and the Revolution progressively increased. In some way, this detachment was symbolized by student and faculty involvement in Vasconcelos' presidential campaign against PNR's candidate Ortiz Rubio in 1929. While the majority of the University adhered to conservative positions, some groups pushed for a stronger commitment towards revolutionary policies. The relation between the University and the State apparatus became a matter of internal conflict, openly expressed over the appointment of University authorities.[19]

The conflict increased when the PNR put forward its project to establish socialist education. Conservatives reacted strongly against this project. In 1933, the University became fully involved in the national debate about socialist education. Rector Medellín, practically appointed by President Abelardo Rodríguez, and other University authorities, promoted the First Congress of Mexican University Members in order to debate the establishment of dialectic materialism as the guiding philosophy of Mexican higher education.

The *Universitarios* split in the face of this project. Lombardo Toledano, one of the most prominent *Siete Sabios* and Director of the National Preparatory School, defended the project against Antonio Caso, who was acclaimed as a prestigious humanist intellectual. Caso argued against the adoption of any particular philosophy and in favor of academic freedom. The First Congress voted for Lombardo's proposal.

Lombardo's supporters included a group of moderate liberals that had established strong ties with Revolutionary politicians. Most significant among this group were medical doctors Gustavo Baz and Ignacio Chávez (former and current director of the School of Medicine respectively). The National University was profoundly divided. Gómez Morín, another of the *Siete Sabios* and Ddirector of the Law School, became the head of conservative students. By using the arguments that Caso had presented in the debate, they were able to bring together a diversity of political forces and organize a strong reaction against the resolution. As the movement against Lombardo increased, Chávez and others withdrew their support. Lombardo and Rector Medellín were then ousted from the University.

Diverse authors have analyzed this confrontation between the University and the State apparatus from different perspectives (Bremauntz 1969; Guevara Niebla 1985; Mabry 1982; Mayo 1964). They all agree that the events that followed the University Congress signified a major confrontation between the University and the government. The National University exemplified an instance of conflict within the State. The government decided to let go of the University and defeat the conservatives through isolation and financial deprivation.

In October 1933, President Rodríguez and Secretary of Education Bassols put forward a proposal to grant full autonomy to the University. The new proposal was never discussed with members of the University. Congress unanimously approved the new law that deprived the University of its "National" denomination due to its lack of commitment to the State's popular education projects. The new law established that:[20]

1. The University would be now called *Universidad Autónoma de México* (UAM).

2. The University Council would be the highest authority of the University.

3. This University Council would appoint the Rector and directors of schools, faculties and research institutes.

4. The University Council would define the composition and rules of the *Academias de Estudiantes y Profesores* (Student and Faculty Boards), and

5. finally, the law established the right of the University to its own patrimony and to a unique donation after which the Federal Government would provide no additional subsidy.

In the absence of direct presidential intervention in the appointment of rectors, the University Council increased its political centrality within the University. Power conflicts over the direction of the University concentrated within this body. The University Council was the essential element in decision–making processes and exercised control over the rector and directors.

From 1933 to 1944, the University functioned under this Organic Law and three different statutes approved by the University Council in 1934, 1936 and 1938. Essentially the three statutes established that faculty and students would be equally represented in the *Academias* and University Council. The rector, deans, and directors were elected through direct vote in the University Council and could be revoked at any time.

Gómez Morín was elected Rector under the new law. From 1933 to 1935 the Autonomous University suffered a very difficult financial situation and was the center of external attacks that labeled the institution as conservative and anti–revolutionary. After Gómez Morín's resignation, the relation between the University and the government became more difficult with Rector Ocaranza (1934–1935). Under Ocaranza, the University became an organizing pole for other conservative educational institutions. Two systems that have become important components of UNAM until today, developed as part of this strategy of confrontation against the government. On the one hand, the University provided recognition, affiliation, and even financial support to conservative institutions like the *Universidad Autónoma de Guadalajara*. This organization became the system of *incorporated* schools. On the other hand, the Autonomous University created its own *Escuela de Iniciación* (initiation school) in response to the government's establishment of a secondary school system.[21] In fact, the University tried to become a parallel ministry of education and this situation could not be tolerated by the Mexican political system.

After several attempts to reach an agreement with recently inaugurated President Lázaro Cárdenas, Ocaranza was forced to resign his post at the head of the University. The relation between this institution and the Mexican government started to improve during the Rectorships of Chico Goerne (1935–1938) and Gustavo Baz (1938–1940). The 1936 and 1938 statutes attempted to address the social concerns of the government.

In this section I have shown that the National University created in 1910 inherited a tradition of conservatism and institutional autonomy from the *Real y Pontificia Universidad de México*. With few exceptions, the founders of the new University maintained a critical distance from the emerging Revolutionary State. This relation between the University and the

Mexican State was institutionalized when the government granted the University autonomy in 1929 and 1933.

The University was dominated by an ideology that has been identified as liberal conservatism, a mixture of humanist and spiritual values that characterized the most prominent members of the *Athenaeum* of Youth and the *Siete Sabios*. As the State's educational policies became more radical in the mid–1930s, the University assumed the role of articulating the struggle against socialist education at a national level. The University however, could not survive without the financial support of the government. Very soon the most radical conservatives were displaced by more progressively oriented liberals who attempted to reestablished connections with the State, insuring the survival of the University without formally altering its conservative traditions.

During this period, the University was involved in a struggle with the leadership of the Mexican Revolution at two levels. On the one hand, the University itself was the site of confrontations between socialist education and academic freedom. On the other, the University as an institution became a fundamental actor in resisting the government's socialist education policies. This confrontation synthesized two opposing views about the social role of higher education. It represented a struggle between those that demanded social commitment for the solution of practical problems of development *versus* those for whom the University was only responsible for the pursuit of knowledge in an abstract sense.

The conflict between the University and the State was also the struggle between urban middles classes that had been sidelined by the populist policies of the Mexican State and the leadership of the Revolution. It was in every sense a political conflict involving definitions about society and the University. Like other conflicted relations in the Mexican political scenario, it would enter a new phase in the ensuing transformation of the Mexican State.

DEVELOPMENTALISM AND NATIONAL UNITY

The University survived the confrontation with the State apparatus. Not only that, in very little time the struggle between University and government changed into a flourishing relationship. This process cannot be understood without addressing the profound political changes that occurred within the Mexican State by the end of the 1930s, and corresponding transformations at the University.

The pace of radical reforms and social mobilization that characterized the first years of Cárdenas' presidency started to decline after 1938. Internal opposition within the army and the political structures had not been strong enough to counter the broad support of organized peasants and workers to the Cárdenas Administration. However, the expropriation of the oil industry in 1938 generated a new economic crisis that eventually produced a shift in the State's reform policies.

In spite of the attempts to develop a national industrial base and internal markets, the Mexican economy was extraordinarily dependent on foreign capital. In response to the expropriation, the US applied a boycott to the Mexican oil industry, discouraged the approval of loans to public or private debtors, and stopped the purchase of silver (Meyer 1981a). Economic problems due to these external factors (pressures from petroleum companies, the US State Department, and other foreign governments) were increased by internal economic pressures such as production cutbacks, and price increases (Hamilton 1982). According to the latter:

> ...direct economic intervention by foreign capital combined with both indirect and direct forms of intervention by Mexican capital to limit the options of State action. The aggravation of the economic crisis and economic and political pressures from foreign capital influenced a shift in internal policy and a de–emphasis on working–class and peasant mobilization for reform and structural change (p. 235).

"El Viraje de los Años 40"

The selection of Ávila Camacho as the PRM presidential candidate in 1939 marked the transition from socially oriented development to a more orthodox capitalist program. A fast process of industrialization based on foreign capital investment and salary contention replaced import–substitution economic policies, emphasizing national development and internal consumption. Land distribution decreased notably. This change of direction has been called *el viraje de los años cuarenta* (the sharp shift of the forties).

By 1940, a new era of urban industrialization and economic growth had begun. From 1940 to 1966, the Mexican GDP grew 368%.[22] The average annual growth–rate of GDP for the same period was larger than 6%.[23] From 1940 to 1956, direct foreign investment grew more than 600%.[24] The dependency on US investments, however, also increased from 62% to 78% of the total foreign investment for the same period.[25]

Mexico underwent a rapid process of urbanization and industrialization (Meyer 1981b). From 1940 to 1970, population growth averaged 3.04% annually. The rural population grew at an annual rate of 1.6% while the urban population grew far above that average, at a rate of 5.6% during the sixties (Meyer 1981b). The urban population reached 17,700,000 out of 34,920,000 in 1960 (González Casanova 1970).

This process of urbanization and industrialization was, however, accompanied by significant marginalization and under–employment (Meyer 1981b). Economic growth did not imply a reduction of social, economic, and cultural inequalities. In 1939, the workers' share of the National Income was 30.4%.[26] This share decreased steadily until it reached 21.4% in 1946.[27] In 1960, wages and salaries still represented only 31%.[28] As late as 1968, 5% of the families in Mexico held almost 30% of total regular income and 15% of the families held 60% of the total amount (Meyer 1981b). Literacy rates, among other indicators, symbolized the failure of the development project and the social discourse of the Revolution after 1940. In 1960, more than 50% of the rural population and 24% in urban areas were illiterate (González Casanova 1970).

In spite of the unequal distribution of wealth and the increased dependency on the US economy, the growth of the Mexican economy became the pride of the regime. It was called *el milagro mexicano* (the Mexican miracle) (Carmona 1970). Notwithstanding the enormous social differences, as well as the disparities between the discourse of the Mexican Revolution and the reality of millions of impoverished rural and urban inhabitants, the social structure of the country held together. The political system was able to provide a period of stability in which the *milagro mexicano* took place.

Stabilization of the Political Regime

Cárdenas had set the conditions for this stage of economic development with the consolidation of a stable political system. The historical authoritarian characteristics of the Mexican State were strengthened with the political changes produced during *Cardenismo*. When Ávila Camacho took office in 1940, the authoritarian political regime had acquired its most salient features: uncontested presidential power, absence of electoral competition, corporatism, and pragmatic ideology.

In the midst of World War II, Ávila Camacho added the final touches to the political system with the exclusion of the military as a formal sector within the party in 1940. The war in Europe and the Pacific provided a fertile situation for the substitution of the class warfare discourse for the ideology of national unity (*unidad nacional*) and class collaboration. These changes were formalized with the transformation of the *Partido de la Revolución Mexicana* into the *Partido Revolucionario Institucional* (PRI) in 1946.

It was not until the late 1930s that the national bourgeoisie that had developed under the protection and guidance of the Mexican State acquired enough strength to actually become a relevant political player. While small business representatives were included in the official party through the popular sector organization, big business organized itself through commerce and industry chambers. Membership in these organizations was mandatory and constituted the vehicle to receive benefits and exercise influence upon the State.

Through this corporatist arrangement, vast sectors of the Mexican society were integrated into the political system. The political network established strict limits to social mobilization and citizen participation. The legitimate political scenario was bounded by these limits. As many social and political movements were able to experience, political participation outside these restrictions was faced with a repressive response by the State.

Education for Development

The development project of the Mexican government after 1940 also required changes in the educational system. The "socialist education law" promoted by Cárdenas was still in place. Under the new industrialization project,

> the school could not continue to be an instrument of social combat for the peasant community, the union, or the neighborhood; the new generations of Mexicans could not continue to be educated according to principles that promoted social antagonisms (Guevara Niebla 1980 p. 57).

By the end of the Cárdenas presidency socialist education had lost most of its momentum. The Ávila Camacho government abandoned socialist education even before Article 3 of the Constitution was amended. New educational policies were geared towards the consolidation of the *unidad nacional* ideology and the national project of industrialization. The popular education system of the *normales rurales* (rural teacher education schools), *las escuelas técnicas* (technical schools), and the *Instituto Politécnico Nacional* (National Polytechnic Institute) were marginalized, abandoned, and even harassed by the new regime (Martínez Della Rocca 1983; Raby 1974).

Educational policies, developed during the early 1940s, set the main features of Mexican education until this day (Sotelo Inclán 1982). Education was heralded as the mechanism for social transformation; it replaced the old ideology of class struggle and became an essential component of the system (Guevara Niebla 1980).

Socialist education had been based on an intuitive assumption that schooling is determined by and in turn reproduces the class structure of society. Guevara (1980) explains that the new education philosophy portrayed schooling "as autonomous from the social classes, as sustained by the old spiritualist ideal that saw the transmission of knowledge as an end in itself" (p. 61). In addition to this, education was increasingly perceived in human capital terms as directly related to economic growth and development.

In 1941, Congress approved a new Federal Law of Education. This law modified in practice the socialist education article still in place in the Constitution. Finally, socialist education was banned from the Constitution in 1945. The new amendment to Article 3 stated that education would be scientific, democratic, and national; lay and free of any fanaticism or prejudice. It established that all the education provided by the State would be free, and that primary education should be compulsory. This article remained in place with no substantial modifications until 1993.

Many authors (Carmona 1970; González Casanova 1970; Guevara Niebla 1980; Meyer 1981b) have stated that the change of direction in 1940 constituted a reconfiguration of the historically dominant block. The social bases of the regime were no longer workers and peasants, though their acquiescence was guaranteed by the corporatist political arrangement. Urban middle sectors and bureaucrats now occupied their place. Along with the national bourgeoisie, they would become the main beneficiaries of the following regimes.

Education became a major piece in the articulation of this new hegemony. Liberal intellectuals that had resisted and even opposed the revolutionary regimes would become the supporters and ideologues of the new "revolutionary stage." The old antagonism between the State and these intellectuals was closed through active government policy. Liberal intellectuals were attracted to become part of the government. The Mexican government created new institutions such as *El Colegio Nacional* in 1943, and the *Instituto Nacional de Bellas Artes* in 1946 to promote or recognize intellectual and cultural activities.

The Mexican government promoted reconciliation with liberal intellectuals. One of the most important actions was the attempt to produce a radical change in the relations between the State and the *Universidad de México* (Guevara Niebla 1980). It is in this context that the *Universidad Nacional Autónoma de México* lived what many call its golden years, from 1945 to the early 1960s.

A NEW HEGEMONY

The reorientation of State policies at the end of the 1930s produced many changes within the National University. These changes were not the product of gradual evolution or adaptation to the new political environment. The reorganization of political forces within the National University generated new confrontations among former allies. The establishment of a new hegemony occurred when the most conservative sector of the institution was defeated in a joint action by the government and University liberals.

The relation between the University and the Mexican State had been informally reestablished during the Rectorship of Chico Goerne (1935–1938). Federal subsidy for the University was reinstated in 1937. By 1944 it had already doubled in real terms.[29] Beginning in 1940, the relation between the *Universidad de México* and the government radically improved as a consequence of new State policies. As stated in the previous section, new government projects focused on the expansion and improvement of urban middle classes. State demands for professional education translated into increasing opportunities for the *Universitarios* and additional resources for the institution. Educational policies that liberal conservatives within the National University perceived as radical threats were abandoned. The participation of notable members of the University in the new State administration symbolized the reestablishment of relations between *los Universitarios* and the government.[30]

The composition of the political forces within the National University changed in response to the new situation. With the end of the confrontation between the University and the government the old alliance between the liberals and the religious right, which had resisted the radical projects of the revolutionary governments until 1940, also ended. Liberal intellectuals adapted very quickly to the new opportunities. Like at no other time before, many of them became part of the government in different areas and at different levels of responsibility.[31]

The most conservative and militant sectors of the religious right had a harder time coping with the new reality and they remained within the *Universidad Nacional* in an attempt to maintain this stronghold *vis-à-vis* the government. When provisional Rector De la Cueva finished the last two years of Baz's Rectorship in 1942, the right wing made a bid for this post.

The Last Stand of Radical Conservatives

In the June 18 election within the *Consejo Universitario*, the conservative candidate, Brito Foucher,[32] defeated Salvador Azuela, a former student leader in the 1929 struggle for autonomy.[33] Brito Foucher had been director of the School of Law where he played a major role in organizing the conservative students against Lombardo Toledano and Rector Medellín in 1933 (Mabry 1982).

Brito was famous for his violent methods and lurid style. He intervened directly in the elections of student association representatives (*sociedades de alumnos*). He organized armed student gangs to maintain control over opposing students[34] and challenged the latter to "fight on any field" while threatening "if the blood flows it will be the students' fault" (Guevara Niebla 1980 p. 63).

Brito's conservative radicalism was unacceptable to liberal and left–wing members of the University, as well as to the government. It became problematic also for moderate Catholics.[35] In an attempt to strengthen his control over the Council and the University as a whole Brito established restrictive methods for the election of student and faculty representatives.[36] He also forced the election of his candidates as directors for several schools and institutes. Students and faculty alike strongly challenged the election of directors in the veterinary and commerce schools. The election in the Preparatory School was, however, the most glaring case of the new political confrontation between liberals and conservatives within the University.[37]

Because of Brito's imposition, the *Escuela Nacional Preparatoria* went on strike and the confrontation developed into a struggle between student supporters of candidates Soto y Gama and Yáñez. The strike extended to other schools like Law and Veterinary. Brito's student gangs attacked the striking students in the Veterinary School. Several were badly hurt and one student was killed. Protests against Brito increased. Thousands of students demonstrated, demanding his removal from office. A large number of faculty members from Law, Medicine and other schools and institutes withdrew from their posts. Many among them would play a major role in the subsequent future of the University.[38] In the light of this enormous internal opposition and pressure from President Ávila Camacho, Brito resigned as rector of the University on July 28, 1944.[39]

The Emergence of a New Historical Alliance

President Ávila Camacho and University liberals led by Alfonso Caso took advantage of the situation to consolidate the dominance of this latter group over the Institution. By will or chance, a moderate expression of a historical political trend within the University, now also embedded within the State apparatus, was provided with an enormous power to shape the political organization of UNAM. The process through which the institutionalization of this political relation occurred has not been fully addressed by other historical or political studies of the University. Let us look at these historical developments.

Brito's departure did not end the conflict. A few hours before he presented his resignation, many of the professors who had withdrawn in protest and the students that supported them challenged the authority of the University Council and organized a *Directorio Universitario* (University Directorship).[40] The right wing coalesced around the University Council.[41]

Each group appointed its own "Rector" and they were unable to reach an agreement for several days. In contravention of University laws, both parties demanded recognition from President Ávila Camacho and the bestowing of government funding. After consulting with Secretary Torres Bodet, and Director Alfonso Caso, both from the Ministry of Education, President Ávila Camacho intervened on August 7, 1944 (Torres Bodet 1969). He called for the formation of a provisional board constituted by former rectors of the University who in turn would elect a new rector. The *Consejo Universitario* and the *Directorio Universitario* had no alternative but to accept Ávila Camacho's intervention although some considered that it went against University laws, and it constituted an intrusion contrary to the autonomy of the institution.[42]

Appointment of Rector Caso. The *Junta de ex–Rectores* (board of former Rectors), or *Junta de Avenimiento* (reconciliation board) as Ávila Camacho had originally called it, included the six living ex–rectors since the University became autonomous in 1929 (obvioulsy excluding Brito).[43] The *exRectores* appointed Alfonso Caso as Rector.[44] The appointment was no accident. Alfonso Caso was part of a long and respected University tradition established by his brother Antonio. With Gómez Morín, he was one of the *Siete Sabios*. Like the other members of that group he had been detached from the struggles of 1929 (Mabry 1982) but was a firm supporter of the concept of autonomy.[45] During the confrontations around socialist education from 1933 to 1938, he played a discreet role as a supporter of academic freedom actively opposing University authorities that were close to President Cárdenas.[46]

Alfonso Caso was also a close collaborator of President Ávila Camacho in the Ministry of Education. Secretary of Education Torres Bodet argued in his memoirs (1969) that

> [m]any thought the *Secretaría de Educación* had interfered in the University altercation.... Wasn't I, under the advice of Alfonso Caso, who suggested the procedure to which the Reconciliation Board owed its life, to the President? Hadn't the Board appoint the person who had given me that advice, as Rector?

> Everything seemed knit by a magical thread. And, however, there was nothing of interested or personal in those circumstances (p. 221).

Regarding Alfonso Caso's motives, Torres Bodet explained that

> the suggestion made to [him] by Alfonso Caso obeyed a good faith plan: to help General Ávila Camacho to not assume the responsibility of solving, on its own, a controversy that was not of his competency (p. 222).

According to Torres Bodet, Caso did not want to be Rector. This is probably true since a few months later Caso adamantly refused his nomination to become the first Rector in the era of the new organic law.

An instrument for institutionalization. In accordance with the task entrusted to them by the President, the Board of former Rectors also established some Provisional Bases for the operation of the University.[47] Through these Bases, Alfonso Caso was given an enormous amount of power. The Provisional Bases mandated the Rector to personally appoint directors for all the schools and institutes, as well as a secretary general and an administrative team. The Rector had to reorganize the University Council along guidelines provided in the Provisional Bases. The new University Council would dictate the regulations for the integration and operation of the *Academias*. Most importantly, the new Council was instructed to formulate a new *Estatuto Universitario* (University Statute) before December 31, 1945. Finally, the bases also established the creation of a Treasury Committee composed of Alejandro Quijano, Evaristo Araiza, and Roberto Casas Alatriste.[48]

The guidelines provided by the former rectors stated the composition of the new *Consejo Universitario*. It was to be composed of the rector; the directors of faculties, schools, and institutes; by one representative of professors and one of the students for each faculty or school; as well as one representative of the staff.[49] The composition of this new University Council altered the tradition of shared governance that had begun in 1929. The mandate for the formation of this body ruled out parity between students and faculty. This decision was based on the idea that the University had to be freed of politics and that student participation was the main cause of politicization. This was to become one of the major issues in the discussions to come.

Following the directives set by the Provisional Board, Rector Caso chose García Maynez, who had worked for him in the Ministry of Education, as Secretary General. He also appointed 25 directors of faculties, schools, and institutes.[50] The majority of these newly appointed directors in the schools and faculties were part of the university liberals that had established connections with the federal government at different levels.[51]

Based on the same idea of de–politicizing the election of faculty and student representatives to the *Consejo Universitario*, the former rectors established eligibility requisites and regulated the elective process. In a document approved by a meeting with the newly appointed directors, Caso went beyond those guidelines.[52] Drawing from Brito Foucher's regulations, Caso put together a complex elective mechanism under his direct control.[53] Faculty and student representatives to the University Council were practically handpicked by Rector Caso and the secretary general.

The Rector and his appointees constituted almost half of the University Council. There were 15 faculty and 15 student elected representatives. Each of these sectors constituted one fourth of this governing body. The composition of the *Consejo Universitario*, the appointment of *directores*, and election procedures of faculty and student representatives ensured Alfonso Caso's control over this body. The instrument for the institutionalization of the emerging dominant formation within the University and the new relationship between this institution and the State apparatus was now in place.

"De–politicization" of the University

The political reorganization of the National University was undertaken in the name of a crusade for the de–politicization of the institution. The emergence of this discourse is particularly relevant for the understanding of current political processes within UNAM. Since 1945, this argument became one of the cornerstones of the hegemonic discourse in the

University. In this section, I show how this argument was constructed and utilized as a legitimating device, in the establishment of a new political arrangement at UNAM. Caso constructed a multifaceted discourse tying together traditional University values like autonomy and academic freedom with new concepts about the internal social fabric of the University and the relationship with the federal government.

In October 1944, the University Council was installed. In his inauguration speech, Caso described the tasks lying ahead of the *Consejo*.

> We can now face the grave problem for which you have been appointed: to provide our University with a new constitution that will allow it to take a normal life, organizing it in such a way that disorders will not be, as they have regrettably been in multiple occasions, the characteristic of university life (González Oropeza 1980).

The University Council was to be a constitutive legislative body. However, Caso went beyond the mandate of the former rectors to reform the University Statute. Following the suggestions made by the *Directorio*, he intended that the Council approve a proposal for a new Organic Law that could eventually be sanctioned by Congress.[54] In the second meeting of what was now called the *Consejo Universitario Constituyente* (Constitutive University Council), Caso appeased traditional fears of unwelcome State intervention through the legislation of the University's Organic Law.

> For the first time in the history of the University, the Executive has addressed the University requesting that this institution state its aspirations to take them into account and convert them into an Organic Law of the University. This attitude by the President of the Republic is, in my opinion, the best demonstration of the friendship and interest that he holds for university affaires.... [H]e has asked the University to formulate its points of view in writing with the purpose of him being the bearer of these points of view (González Oropeza 1980 p. 66).

Caso continued:

> As *universitarios* we have been given the opportunity to present our ideal of university organization and I believe that we, the *universitarios*, need to take advantage of this opportunity that has been offered to us, in this way the University would be ideally organized (p. 66).

Finally, he explained that based on this situation he had decided not to submit a proposal for a new university statute. Instead, he had turned in a proposal for a new Organic Law to the statutes committee of the

Constitutive Council.[55] This implied that the time for deliberation and approval of the new law had been shortened in order for the legislature to approve this proposal before the end of the legislative period on December 31, 1944 (González Oropeza 1980).

In different statements, Caso set the ideological foundations of the new reform. He stated: "the principle of teaching and research freedom (academic freedom) has to be consecrated, next to the principle of autonomy, as an essential postulate for the very existence of the university as an institution" (Caso 1944 p. 7). After the Caso–Lombardo debate in 1933 the dominant view in the University held that this institution was "a community of culture" (Caso 1944 p. 3) in which the main objective was the pursuit of scientific knowledge. The assumption about the neutrality of science, a legacy from the strong positivist tradition in the University, provided the basis for considering the university as a technical institution (Jiménez Mier y Terán 1982). Further on, if neutral science constituted the ultimate goal, the university should necessarily be a

> community of faculty and students that pursue not antagonistic, but complementary goals, that translate into a fundamental end, considered from two different, but not opposing, points of view: *to teach and to learn* (Caso 1944 p. 9).

According to Caso, there were no antagonisms between faculty and students and ideological differences should not create adversaries within the University. Playing on the extended concern over the latest confrontation within the University it was easy to generate a broad consensus around the idea that politics should have no place in this institution. From this view, it was evident that political interests were the main cause of problems within the university. Rector Caso argued,

> The real cause of university conflicts rests in that certain authorities, certain professors, and certain students do not want to fulfill their obligations. Unfair authorities, incompetent and uncommitted teachers, students that aspire to obtain certificates or titles instead of knowledge: but these evils can not be cured by giving our University a political organization, as if dealing with antagonistic social groups. Its remedy rests in a healthy and rational technical organization (González Oropeza 1980).

He continued:

> It is not a secret for anybody that the main cause of disorganization of UNAM has been the constant conclusion of these two forms of organization: the political and the technical. University authorities have always had this double character of political authorities, that require popularity

and the support of groups, and on the other hand, the character of technical authorities that need to solve teaching and research organization problems from a purely objective point of view. The struggle between political and technical has prevented the University from realizing its objectives, and indisputably has been decreasing the quality of teachers, their teaching, their programs, and consequently, the preparation of students (González Oropeza 1980).

The implication of Caso's discourse was that student participation and shared governance, introduced with ill–disposed purposes by the framers of the 1933 law, had brought politics into the University. Implicitly, and against the evidence of most of the conflicts since 1933, the faculty as a body was relieved of responsibility in those political conflicts. The existence of opposing and even conflicting views about the University was negated. Personalized and dishonest political interests manipulating students had to be extirpated from the University. Altogether, these ideas became in themselves one of the great foundational myths of the 1945 Organic Law. The students were framed as the big losers in this process.

The discourse of power. In the previous section, I reviewed the ideological concepts that provided the foundation for the political reorganization of UNAM. Since 1944, these arguments have constituted the dominant political discourse within the University. These concepts can be summarized in four arguments put forward by Alfonso Caso. The University was characterized as a *technical institution* with the unique objective of creating and transmitting knowledge. This objective constituted the common purpose of all members of the institution and the unique legitimate interest of the *Universitarios*. Consequently, the University was considered as a *homogeneous community* with no conflicting interests. The absence of conflicting legitimate interests justified the need to *eradicate politics* as the representation of extra–university interests. Access to University governance would not be based on internal politics but only on *individual merit*. It was assumed that any *Universitario* who would hold an administrative responsibility would be driven by the common interest, and would necessarily represent the aspirations and views of all the members of the community.

The "Technical" Reorganization of UNAM

The power structure of the University was also based on this distinction between technical and political issues. This section shows that the University was reorganized in order to ensure the preeminence of executive authorities over collegial bodies. The former held real decision–making power. The latter were considered technical bodies dealing with a limited set of issues under the direction of the rector or directors. The political structure of the University was organized into a circle of power where the

Governing Board and the Rector occupied the center of the decision–making process. Student and faculty representation were reduced to a minimal expression and, for any practical purpose, excluded from the decision–making spheres at UNAM.

Most historical accounts have described the establishment of the 1945 governing structure at UNAM as a consensual process. Only a few studies have reflected on the confrontation that took place between student representatives and Rector Caso. This section will provide historical evidence of the fact that, since its very origin, the new structure of UNAM was challenged by the students who criticized the concentration of power in the organization of the University.

On November 22, 1944, Alfonso Caso turned in a preliminary plan for a new Organic Law to the statute committee. The project was argued based on the ideas described in the previous section. The most salient features of the proposal were:

1. The University was defined as a public corporation, a decentralized institution of the State.

2. The University authorities would be a newly created *Junta de Gobierno* (Governing Board), the University Council, the Rector, the *Patronato* (Trustees), the directors of faculties, schools and institutes; and the *Consejos Técnicos* (Technical Councils) which replaced the *Academias* of schools and faculties.

3. The composition of these *Consejos* and the University Council was changed along the line of the provisional bases set by the former Rectors. Parity between faculty and students in these bodies was terminated. The attributions of these collegial bodies were reduced *vis-à-vis* the directors and the Rector (Jiménez Rueda 1955).

4. The *Patronato* was an independent body in charge of the administration of the university endowment.

5. The *Junta de Gobierno* would be responsible for the appointment of directors (selected from sets of three proposed by the Rector), and the designation of the Rector. The Junta would also intervene in the case of a conflict between authorities and appoint the members of the *Patronato* (trustees).

In spite of the wide acceptance of the anti–student and anti–political discourse, student representatives reacted strongly against the loss of parity in the University Council. It was surprising that, notwithstanding the mechanism put in place to control their elections, the student's response was almost unanimous against the composition of the *Consejo Constituyente*. On December 6, 1944 they demanded a vote to overturn that issue and lost 29 against 12.[56] Student representatives from eleven, out of thirteen schools, abandoned the meeting in protest.[57] According to the minutes of the session Caso responded harshly to the students arguing that "this was a purely political maneuver," that this attitude by the student councilors "revealed that they were driven by other persons." Finally, Caso "denounced the existence of a secret society within the University."[58] The discourse against "political agents" had been put in use.

The Governing Board. The Governing Board has been considered as the essential component of the political arrangement at UNAM. The discussion about this board was one of the most important debates in the establishment of the current governance structure. Its existence was argued in terms of de-politicizing the University and guaranteeing autonomy. In real terms, it signified the localization of legitimate University politics and an element of political continuity for the dominant groups. Since 1945, the control over this body has ensured the political domination over UNAM. It is important to understand the formal operation and composition of this structure and its relation to the rest of the organization at the University in order to comprehend the historical development of politics at UNAM.

Most of the debate around Caso's project was centered on the Governing Board. It was to eliminate politicking around the designation of directors and Rector as well as preserve the autonomy of the University in the face of the government. Perceptions about the role of the Governing Board differed slightly among directors and faculty representatives. Some supporters viewed the new governing body as "the power organism of the functions of the Institution."[59] Others thought of it as "out of the way of every conflict, of every struggle, of every interest, be it academic, political or confessional."[60] While most of the members of the Council agreed that the Board should not be a representative body,[61] there was general accordance with the idea that it should be diverse in ideological and disciplinary terms.[62] The Constitutive Council extensively discussed election methods in order to guarantee this diversity.

The discussion about the Governing Board was long and it involved political as well as technical issues. It took place during several sessions of the University Council. Student representatives returned to one of the sessions with an alternative Organic Law project. All of their initiatives were defeated. Students centered their critiques on the reduction in the weight of student representation to the *Consejo Universitario* and *Consejos Técnicos*. They also argued against the creation of a Governing Board that would reduce the Council to a secondary role and abolish faculty and students participation in the appointment of university authorities.[63] Finally, the student representatives abandoned the Constituent University Council again, in disagreement with the proposal that was going to be approved.[64]

According to this law and the corresponding University Statute (approved by the Constitutive Council in March of 1945) the Board would be composed of 15 members. The Constitutive Council would designate them. Five years after the appointment of the first fifteen members, the University Council would be able to substitute one Board member each year,[65] as well as fill those vacancies motivated by death or reaching the age limit. The Board itself would fill the vacancies created by resignations.

SUMMARY: AUTHORITARIANISM IN THE UNIVERSITY

Congress approved the proposal of the Constitutive Council and the new Organic Law was published on January 6, 1945. The new governing structure of the university was complete. The University Council, constituted by appointed directors (50%), as well as elected student and faculty representatives (25% each) would elect long–term members to the Governing Board. The Board would designate the Rector who, in turn, would be the president of the University Council. The Rector would play a major role in the appointment of directors by proposing a set of three candidates to the Governing Board. This body would finally designate directors from the Rector's proposal. The directors would constitute the majority of the University Council.

The 1945 Organic Law and the University Statute formally established the levels of authority as follows: Governing Board, University Council, Rector, Board of Trustees, Directors of Schools and Institutes, and Technical Councils (one for the social sciences and the humanities research institutes, one for the natural and exact sciences institutes and one in each school). In reality however, the Rector concentrated a large amount of power over the University Council, the Board of Trustees, and the Directors. The Governing Board played a significant political role through the appointment of rector and directors. Beyond the real functions assigned to them by the Organic Law, the Governing Board became a fundamental site of decision–making and power in addition to the Rectorship and its administration.

University directives were optimistic. The new governing structure, and particularly the Board, would "solve serious conflicts within the University ... [it would] put an end to politics"[66] within the institution, and it would guarantee the "technical nature" of university governance. The Governing Board would preserve institutional autonomy by preventing the government and political interests from intervening and exercising any influence in the appointment of the university Rector and the directors of schools, faculties, and institutes.[67]

Beyond the official discourse, after this reorganization, the governance structure of the University now mirrored the arrangement of the Mexican political system. These were the essential traits:

Personalized power. Personal or executive authorities (Rector and directors) were placed above collegiate organisms (*Consejo Universitario* and *Consejos Técnicos*). The Rector was designated *jefe nato* (natural boss). He presided over the Council as described above, and he exercised a direct influence in the composition of the *Consejo,* through the nomination of directorship candidates. The Rector wielded enormous power over the directors through the control of their possible reelection and over each school's budget. Through the Council, he could also influence the composition of the Board.

Lack of effective competition. Given established election methods, the Rector could influence student and faculty elections through the directors. The whole structure was reproduced at the faculties and schools where the directors exercised vast power over the *Consejos Técnicos.*

Limited participation. Faculty and student collegial organizations did not have any attribution in the discussion or decision of academic policies and no influence in the appointment of professorships or directive positions. Faculty collegial organizations were not even mentioned in the Organic Law, while student associations or federations were deemed "totally independent from the authorities" of UNAM.

Ideological ambiguity. The emerging hegemonic arrangement was founded in two distinct and powerful traditions: autonomy and academic freedom. These traditions developed through a historical process that we have already described. In the development of the new order, the neutral and apolitical nature of the institution was elevated, in conjunction with autonomy and academic freedom, to become one of the fundamental values of the University. Additional concepts integrated an ambiguous ideological assembly that provided legitimacy to the new political arrangement. The former goal of consecrating "all the collective forces towards the alleviation and improvement of the life of men that were forgotten and hurt by yesterday's legal norm,"[68] was replaced by the essential purpose "of being integrated to the service of the country and the humanity."[69] The University was in this way responsive to the official discourse of *unidad nacional.*

The Mexican government did not have to intervene directly to exercise their influence in the reorganization of the University. The motivations and projects of a group of liberal intellectuals integrated with the State apparatus, who had been able to organize a new hegemony within the institution, were in tune with the discourse, style, and demands of the Mexican government. Torres Bodet (1969) expressed this situation with much symbolism:

> "How well did the government maneuver!" the critics of that time thought. And they were mistaken. Or, at least, they were mistaken if, by saying this, they tried to suggest that the government had used the disorder for its own benefit. On the contrary, things went well because we

never acted neither to promote disorder nor to benefit from its uncomfortable consequences. There was never, in our measures, a maneuver purpose. We intervened only to not intervene, and so that the University could solve its controversies in a dignified and independent form (Torres Bodet 1969 p. 223).

The outcome of this reorganization of UNAM was a combination of governmental design and of unpredicted outcomes of the internal political dynamics. The final product, the new political organization of the University, was satisfactory for both internal and external dominant political actors. The new political arrangement symbolized the pact between the Mexican State and urban intellectuals. They had been awarded a political space with relative autonomy in exchange for loyalty and responsiveness towards the State. In the next chapters, I will show that this relationship was not exempt of conflict and that University autonomy was limited and frequently fettered by governmental interventions.

The new political arrangement within the University was combined with the dependability of political relations between this institution and the State and with the increasing stability of the Mexican political regime. Authoritarianism had consolidated in the University and in the broader political system. Dominant groups within UNAM had high expectations for the new era after the end of politics.

NOTES

[1] I am using an analogy with the concept of *primitive accumulation of capital*, the process through which the cycle of capital reproduction was initiated according to Marx (1967 pp. 713–716).

[2] Throughout this work, I will use the concept of institutionalization following the Weberian notion of the fixation of informal societal relations into particular arrangements of norms and structures.

[3] Political bosses.

[4] Kings were patrons of the University. They were supposed to provide protection, enforce the University statutes, and sanction rules created by the University's legislative bodies (González González 1987). The King did not intervene in the appointment of officials and professors, or in any other aspect of university governance. Viceroys were also patrons and compelled to support decisions made within the University.

[5] The amount and sources of these appropriations changed several times during the colonial period (Menegus Bornemann 1987 p. 101).

[6] Barreda was a disciple of Comte in Paris. Upon his return to Mexico he attempted to spread the ideas of this new philosophy and made a strong effort to teach

the liberals to be the bearers of the "positive spirit." He argued for the assumption, by the liberals, of the motto *liberty, order and progress* (Zea 1966). Barreda put together an ecclectic mixture of liberalism and positivism. For him, the struggle for liberty was part of a metaphysical stage. Liberty constituted the means, order the base, and progress the end (Barreda 1973).

[7] In an attempt to provide general and encyclopedic knowledge the new Preparatory included, among others, courses in arithmetic, logic, algebra, geometry, calculus, cosmography, physics, chemistry, botany, zoology, universal and Mexican history, German, French, and English (Gortari 1980).

[8] *Porfiriato* has been the denomination for Porfirio Díaz's dictatorial regime from 1877 to 1910.

[9] *Ley Constitutiva de la Universidad Nacional de México* (Universidad Nacional Autónoma de México 1985a).

[10] After Justo Sierra's original proposal of an autonomous university, there were many demands for autonomy. In his 1912 report Joaquín Eguía Lis, first Rector of the National University argued that this institution "would be an autonomous entity within the Nation's government" (Eguía in Appendini 1981, p. 60). In 1914 a group of university professors organized by Ezequiel A. Chávez, former Minister of Instruction, wrote a proposal for the independence of the National University (in Pinto Mazal 1974, p. 71). In 1917 Rector Macías and Félix Palavicini proposed new amendments in the same direction (pp. 51–62). In 1923 the Mexican Student Federation presented a new proposal to the Senate and the Congress. The proposal was supported by all the members of both chambers but was never put to vote by the Congress (p. 115).

[11] Members of the University.

[12] Garciadiego Dantan (1996) provides an excellent historical description of the University and its actors during the armed phase of the Revolution and the early revolutionary governments.

[13] In his first initiative to create a national university in 1881, Sierra had argued for the necessity of autonomy. A group of faculty led by Antonio Caso and other former members of the *Athenaeum* put together a project for the independence of the University in 1914. Six signatories of this proposal would later become Rectors (Miguel Schultz, Antonio Caso, Mariano Silva y Aceves, Ezequiel A. Chávez, Alfonso Pruneda, and Genaro Fernández MacGregor) and five more would become members of the Governing Board at UNAM (Federico Mariscal, Alejandro Quijano, Ricardo Caturegli, Antonio Castro Estrada, and Joaquín Gallo) (Pinto Mazal 1974 p. 74). Two additional autonomy projects were presented to Congress by the Minister of Iinstruction as well as by University students and faculty in 1917. The document by students and faculty was again promoted by former members of the *Athenaeum* and by the 7 *sabios* (pp. 81,82). In 1923, the *Federación de Estudiantes de México* presented Congress with a new initiative for autonomy. In spite of having support of many members of Congress, this initiative was never approved (pp. 109–112).

[14] Portes Gil suggests that the students never demanded autonomy for the University. According to his version, the initiative to grant University autonomy was his. Interview with former President Emilio Portes Gil (in Wilkie, Monzón de Wilkie, and Beteta 1969 p. 559).

[15] Interview with former President Emilio Portes Gil (in Wilkie, Monzón de Wilkie, and Beteta 1969 p. 559).

[16] Students had demanded that the Rector be appointed by the presidents from within threesomes provided by the University Council. Portes Gil's law worked in the opposite direction. The University Council would appoint the Rector from within threesomes provided by the president.

[17] The Student Strike Directory objected to many of the articles in the new law. The students demanded more institutional autonomy and participation rights (in Pinto Mazal 1974 pp. 151–161).

[18] Alejandro Gómez Arias is widely recognized as the most important leader in the 1929 strike. He exercised a strong influence in the student movement at UNAM for many years and he was a University Council member on several occasions. However, he never became Rector or member of the Governing Board. Only two leaders of the 1929 strike, Salvador Aceves and Ricardo García Villalobos ever got to the Governing Board.

[19] See Mabry's (1982) description of internal struggles over the appointment of rectors in 1929 and 1932.

[20] In the *Ley Orgánica de la Universidad Autónoma de México. 19 de octubre de 1933* (México, Congreso, and Diputados 1933).

[21] In his memoirs, Ocaranza (1943) describes these two components of the University strategy against socialist education. Fernández MacGregor (1969) who became Rector ten years later also described the system of incorporated schools and its origin as part of the struggle against the State's educational policies.

[22] Source: Calculation based on data from Ibarra (1978 pp. 100–101).

[23] Source: Calculation based on data from Ibarra (1978 pp. 100–101).

[24] Source: Calculation based on data from González Casanova (1970).

[25] Source: González Casanova (1970).

[26] Source: González Casanova (1970).

[27] Source: González Casanova (1970).

[28] Source: González Casanova (1970).

[29] Source: González Cosío (1968).

[30] Rector Gustavo Baz (1938–1940) was invited by Ávila Camacho to become part of the new government as the head of the new *Secretaría de Salubridad y Asistencia* (SSA, the Secretary of Public Health and Social Welfare).

[31] Among the most notorious cases were those of Manuel and Antonio Martínez Báez (president of the National Banking Commission and Undersecretary at the SSA), Alfonso Caso (Director of Higher Education in the Ministry of Education). Equally notable were Gabino Fraga (Supreme Court Justice), Jesús Silva Herzog (Financial Director in the Ministry of the Treasury), Pedro Martínez Tornel (Undersecretary of Public Works), as well as José Torres Torija and Ignacio Chávez (Directors of Juárez General Hospital and the National Institute of Cardiology respectively). From the compilation of biographies produced for this research.

[32] Brito Foucher had been the president of the *Federación de Estudiantes Universitarios* (University Students Federation) in the early twenties (Garciadiego Dantan 1996). In 1935 he had led an armed expedition of Catholic university students to the state of Tabasco into a confrontation with anti-clerical governor Garrido Canabal. This "punitive expedition" had a terrible outcome. Governor Garrido Canabal's henchmen killed four students. A vigil over the students' corpses was organized at the University back in Mexico City. It was lead by Rector Ocaranza who stated that the students had fallen in a struggle in favor of "university ideals." For details on these events see Martínez Assad (1979) and Mabry (1982).

[33] Azuela was considered liberal and progressive (Silva Herzog 1974) and he was supported by Baz and his group (Mabry 1982).

[34] Brito's student supporters were part of right–wing student organizations such as the *Asociación Católica de la Juventud Mexicana* (Catholic Association of the Mexican Youth); the *Unión Nacional de Estudiantes Católicos* (National Union of Catholic Students); fascist groups like *Lex* (in the School of Law), *Bios* (in Medicine), and *Labor* (in the School of Engineering); the Jesuits and students from private Catholic schools called *los conejos* (the rabbits) (Guevara Niebla 1986; Mabry 1982).

[35] Like Alfonso Noriega who resigned his post as Secretary General of the University and assumed the Directorship of the School of Law.

[36] At Brito's initiative, the University Council approved the *Reglas para la elección de Consejeros Universitarios* (Rules for the election of University Council members) on June 5, 1942 and the *Reglamento para el funcionamiento de las Academias de Profesores y Alumnos y de las Sociedades de Alumnos* (Regulations for Faculty and Student Academies and Student Associations) on March 9, 1943. According to these rules, the *director* of each school and a representative of the University Council would supervise student and faculty elections. Only the students from the last academic years and highest averages could be elected. Elections would be held within the classroom where students would publicly cast their votes when called by the professor and under the supervision of the director and the University Council representative.

[37] Brito supported former *zapatista* revolutionary Soto y Gama, now transfixed into one of the most conservative representatives of the religious right (Guevara

Niebla 1986). University liberals supported Agustín Yáñez who was perceived as the candidate of the government (González Oropeza 1980; Guevara Niebla 1986; Mabry 1982). Brito managed to get Soto y Gama elected but Yáñez protested the elections.

[38] Among the most relevant resignations we note those of Alfonso Noriega (director of the School of Law), Lucio Mendieta (director of the Institute for Social Sciences Research), Raúl Cervantes Ahumada (secretary of the National Library), former Rector Fernando Ocaranza, Agustín Yáñez, Leopoldo Zea, Luis Garrido, Antonio Carrillo Flores, Manuel Gual Vidal, Salvador Aceves, Raul Fournier, Manuel Martínez Báez, Alfonso Millán, Juan Manuel Terán Mata, and Antonio Martínez Báez.

[39] For a detailed description of this conflict see González Oropeza (1980), Mabry (1982), and the newspaper reports published in *El Popular* (in Guevara Niebla 1986).

[40] This group established a *Directorio Universitario* (University Directorate) declaring themselves the legitimate leaders of the University. Manuel Gual Vidal, Fernando Ocaranza, Alfonso Noriega, Raúl Fournier, Agustín Yáñez, Octavio Medellín, Juan Gómez Piña, and Alberto Trueba Urbina among others formed part of the *Directorio*. For a broader list of participants in the *Directorio* see Guevara Niebla (1986) and González Oropeza (1980). The *Directorio* called for the integration of a *Consejo Constituyente* (Constitutive Council) that should elect a new Rector and reform the legal statute of the University. Gual Vidal and Noriega, representing the liberal and the moderate Catholic trends respectively, contended in this election. Manuel Gual Vidal was finally elected.

[41] This group also included others like José Vasconcelos, who had protested against Brito but considered the Council the legal authority; among these were several directors appointed during Brito's Rectorship. A few days after Britos' resignation the *Consejo Universitario* appointed José Aguilar Álvarez as rector.

[42] Raúl Cervantes Ahumada, member of the *Directorio* openly stated his disagreement with the fact that the Board of former Rectors received its authority from president Ávila Camacho. He suggested that the Constitutive Council, created at the *Directorio's* initiative, should call for the creation of the Board of former Rectors and provide some guidelines for the operation of this board in an attempt to save the autonomy of the University (González Oropeza 1980).

[43] It was therefore integrated by García Téllez, Gómez Morín, Ocaranza, Chico Goerne, Baz, and De la Cueva. This board expressed a variety of positions in the political spectrum. García Téllez was furthest to the left, very much attuned to the radical program of the Cárdenas administration. Chico Goerne was a moderate Catholic who had helped close the breach between the University and the government before the *viraje* in 1940. Baz and De la Cueva were the most evident representatives of the university liberals who had been able to integrate into the political system and the new government projects. Gómez Morín, founder and directive of the *Partido Acción Nacional* (the right wing party), was repre-

sentative of moderate Catholics that maintained a critical stance *vis-à-vis* the political system. They constituted a loyal opposition that frequently collaborated with the government. Ocaranza had been very close to Gómez Morín and succeeded him as Rector with Antonio and Alfonso Caso's support in an attempt to prevent Chico Goerne from being appointed.

44 Not much is known about the internal workings of the Board of former Rectors. Latter developments suggest that Baz, De la Cueva, Ocaranza, and Gómez Morín were able to exert more influence in the final decisions of this body.

45 On July 28, 1917, Alfonso Caso and others signed the *Memorial de profesores y estudiantes a la Cámara de Diputados* demanding that Congress award autonomy to the *Universidad Nacional* (in Pinto Mazal 1974 pp. 75–82).

46 Alfonso Caso had been active in his opposition against García Téllez and against the election of Chico Goerne as rector. Mabry (1982) describes how Alfonso Caso, and others, maneuvered within the University Council against García Téllez's policy (p. 90). Caso also worked intensively to get Ocaranza elected as rector in an attempt to stop Chico Goerne from reaching that post (p. 145).

47 Ávila Camacho's proposal explicitly stated that "in one week the Board will be able to elect a new Rector and reestablish the organization of the University, making the arrangements that it deems more adequate..." (González Oropeza 1980).

48 From the "Bases aprobadas por la Junta de ex-Rectores de la Universidad Nacional Autónoma de México para el Gobierno Provisional de la Institución" (Universidad Nacional Autónoma de México. Comisión Técnica de Estudios y Proyectos Legislativos 1977).

49 Ibidem.

50 The complete list of the directors appointed by Alfonso Caso can be consulted in González Oropeza (1980 pp. 99, 100).

51 The most clear examples of this group were Antonio Carrillo Flores (Law), Ochoa Ravizé (Commerce), González Guzmán (Medicine), Martínez Tornel (Engineering), and Gilberto Loyo (Economics). Another group of directors concentrated on the natural and exact sciences institutes represented the emerging research community at the University. Most of them had been detached from the political conflicts in the University. With few exceptions, like José Vasconcelos (National Library), the majority of the directors shared a liberal and moderately Catholic ideology.

52 Reglamento de la cuarta base aprobada por la Junta de ex-Rectores de la Universidad Nacional Autónoma de México, para el gobierno provisional de la Institución (Universidad Nacional Autónoma de México. Comisión Técnica de Estudios y Proyectos Legislativos 1977).

53 In the election of faculty representatives, professors of each school would vote in partial meetings by year or specialization area. The votes from each partial meeting would be added to elect the school representative. All the partial meet-

ings took place in the University Council meeting hall and were presided by Rector Caso himself. In the case of students only those belonging to the second to last year of studies (last in the case of the *Preparatoria* and *Iniciación Universitaria*) whose grade average was above 8 (in a 0 to 10 scale) were able to elect or be elected *Consejero*. Elections would also take place in the University Council hall under the supervision of Secretary General García Maynez (Universidad Nacional Autónoma de México. Comisión Técnica de Estudios y Proyectos Legislativos 1977).

[54] In August 1944, the *Directorio* presented a declaration of principles that stated the need to reform the Organic Law. See excerpts of this document in González Oropeza (1980 pp. 39, 40).

[55] This statutes committee was appointed in the first meeting of the University Council. It included Antonio Carrillo Flores, Agustín Yáñez, and Ignacio González Guzmán (Alarcón 1979). Carrillo Flores had been a prominent member of the *Directorio's* statute committee (González Oropeza 1980).

[56] Resumen de la sesión del Consejo Universitario Constituyente, December 6, 1944 (Alarcón 1979).

[57] The students that abandoned that session belonged to the schools of *Medicina, Ciencias, Leyes, Filosofía y Letras, Comercio, Odontología, Ciencias Químicas, Arquitectura, Música, Preparatoria*, and *Iniciación Universitaria*. The faculty representative for *Odontología* also abandoned the session for the same motives. Resumen de la sesión del Consejo Universitario Constituyente, December 6, 1944 (Alarcón 1979).

[58] Sesión del Consejo Constituyente Universitario, December 6, 1944 (González Oropeza 1980).

[59] Martínez Báez, faculty representative of the School of Law, during the December 8, 1944 session of the Constitutive University Council (González Oropeza 1980).

[60] Mario Sousa, faculty representative of the School of Economics, during the December 8, 1944 session of the Constitutive University Council (González Oropeza 1980).

[61] Mario Sousa and Martínez Báez during the December 8, 1944 session of the Constitutive University Council (González Oropeza 1980).

[62] Calderón Caso, faculty representative from the School of Dentistry and Antonio Caso, Rector, during the December 8, 1944 session of the Constitutive University Council (González Oropeza 1980).

[63] Acta de la Sesión del Consejo Universitario Constituyente, November 29, 1944 (González Oropeza 1980).

[64] Acta de la Sesión del Consejo Universitario Constituyente, December 15, 1944 (p. 209).

[65] The order of these substitutions would be established by draw. After all the original members had been substituted, the University Council would replace the most senior member of the board each year.

[66] González Guzmán, director of the School of Medicine, during the December 14, 1944 session of the Constitutive University Council (González Oropeza 1980).

[67] Alfonso Caso, Rector, during the December 14, 1944 session of the Constitutive University Council (González Oropeza 1980).

[68] *La Nueva Universidad*, October 19, 1935 (in Ocaranza 1943 p. 476).

[69] Estatuto General de la UNAM, Artículo 3^{ero}, March 9, 1945 (Universidad Nacional Autónoma de México 1995).

CHAPTER 4

The End of University Politics

The previous chapter analyzed how Alfonso Caso and the group of liberal intellectuals that he represented were in a privileged position to shape the University governing structure in accordance with their own ideas about the institution and favoring the exercise of this group's influence. This chapter's focus is on the initial composition and the historical evolution of forces within the Governing Board. The analysis is based on original data on the political actors within this most powerful body. The analysis of this data in a historical perspective will show that, contrary to what University authorities insistently argue, the new organization of UNAM did not eliminate but rather redefined the political arrangement and practices of the University.

Given the strength of the discourse of de–politicization at UNAM, it is important to show that University governance is founded on political alliances and restricted competition within the dominant groups for the directive positions in this institution. In this chapter, I will identify the actors and political groupings within the dominant sectors of the University. In this second moment of institutionalization of power, Caso and the University Council he had appointed designated the first fifteen members of the Board. This was a competition among those already at the top of the University structure.

Historical evidence shows that, in spite of the cohesive nature of the *Universitarios* in the position to elect or be elected, very quickly two different expressions competed for the control of the *Junta* and the appointment of rectors. These groups were differentiated on the basis of minor discrepancies over issues of student access to the University, the social role of the institution, the allocation of resources, and the political styles of interaction with faculty and students.

Daniel Levy (1980) has argued that UNAM has a significant degree of autonomy. The history of government intrusion in the appointment and removal of University Rectors challenges this view. There exists evidence of presidential intervention in the *Junta*'s designation of rectors. These interventions vary in the mechanisms and degrees of influence exercised by the President over the Governing Board. This study shows that in no case during the period from 1945 to 1966 did the Board appoint a Rector without complete agreement by the President. Candidates' "connections" with the presidency appeared in many occasions to be even more relevant than internal strength or consensus among the Board members. Presidential intervention, or the lack of it, was part of the balance that enabled rectors to survive student protests. This historical study will also provide evidence of presidential responsibility in the ousting of three university rectors.

The "golden years" of the University during the most stable phase of Mexican authoritarianism did not imply an end of politics outside the realm of legitimate competition of the elites. The ways in which student mobilization changed in nature and evolved during this historical period made the student movement a key actor in political conflicts at UNAM. Different types of political expression existed outside the legitimate political channels. Most of these occurred in the form of student movements of one ideology or the other. This chapter shows that the period between 1945 and 1966 is not representative of the best political traditions of the student movement. Weakened in the face of a government supported authoritarian structure, many student organizations evolved into opportunistic groups at the service of one university or government official or another. A few exceptions were of interest as representative expressions of the student movement with legitimate social demands and political claims. By the end of the historical period reviewed in this chapter, the student movement had moved towards the left and had begun the construction of independent representative organizations in what became a preamble of the 1968 student movement.

In summary, the University did not de–politicize but rather that it changed its political practices in order to strengthen the domination of liberal groups. It will become clear in this study that the new governance structure in no way brought an end of politics to UNAM. However, it restricted political competition to a "selected" group of *Universitarios* who had acquired the "merits" and had the necessary political connections within the University and with the Mexican government. The groups recognized themselves and their adversaries as a meritocracy and in this way legitimized the lack of capillarity of the political system.

THE INSTITUTIONALIZATION OF POWER

On January 22, 1945 the same University Council chosen by Caso appointed the first Governing Board. Caso and his allies again exercised an enormous power in appointing the first members of the board. This power would be extended for almost 15 years. This was the second phase of the *primitive accumulation* of power.

Since the election of the first fifteen members of this body, lawyers and physicians held an absolute majority of the *Junta*.[1] The first Governing Board was homogeneous though slightly divided in two fractions. A coalition of lawyers and medical doctors dominated the board. These two groups were relatively consistent in their views. Moderate liberals controlled this body very early. Fraga, De la Cueva, and Martínez Báez were a closely knit group in this trend. Quijano had been their professor and recruited them as members of the law school faculty when he was director in 1925.[2] Chávez established the relations of this group with Torres Torija and Ayala González.[3]

Since the very origin of the Governing Board, some of its actors acquired significant influence and power due to their political centrality and their professional and personal ties with other members of the *Junta*. A political diagnostic of the Board shows that very soon Ignacio Chávez emerged as the most powerful actor in this body. He integrated the physicians and lawyers through his lifelong friendship with Martínez Báez and Fraga[4] as well as the strong ties between Baz, Chávez's closest friend, and De la Cueva. Ignacio Chávez also bridged the relation with Sandoval Vallarta and Caturegli as members of the technical and scientific areas. Chávez was also a very good friend of Alfonso Reyes.[5] Probably more relevant than his internal relations were his external linkages with Gustavo Baz,[6] President Ávila Camacho[7] and other highly placed members of the political apparatus as well as his prestige as a cardiologist and an organizer.

Ocaranza and Gómez Morín were further to the right of this faction, representing Catholic organizations within the University. They were close to Antonio and Alfonso Caso and maintained links with mobilized Catholic student groups. Ocaranza and Gómez Morín had been adversaries of Chávez and Baz when the former two headed the School of Medicine and the Rectorship respectively. Board member Jesús Silva Herzog, former Dean of the School of Economics, was situated to the left of all the other members in ideological terms. He did not belong to any of the previous groups. However, most of the time he acted in accordance with Chávez and his friends for practical purposes.

The End of Politics?

The political effects of the new structure were not immediately felt. In this chapter, I show that political confrontation between different University fractions was deeply entrenched in University life. After the approval of the University Statute, Caso resigned to the Rectorship. The Governing Board had a difficult time in selecting a new rector. Finally, they were able to convince Fernández MacGregor, Board member Quijano's law partner,[8] to accept the nomination. Fernández MacGregor had been away from the University since he resigned in 1922.[9] The *Junta* had to interpret the requisites set by the new statute loosely to allow for Fernández MacGregor's eligibility.[10] Fernández MacGregor was perceived as a member of the Baz and Chávez group.[11]

Caso was replaced on March 24, 1945. At his departure from the Rectorship, Caso thought that UNAM was still in a lamentable state. In a private conversation with the incoming rector, Caso described the major problems faced by the institution. According to Fernández MacGregor (1969), Caso said that the main problems were economic poverty, low quality of teaching and teachers, lack of discipline, and politics. He said that the University budget was too small for the large amount of enrolled students. In his view, the lack of discipline was caused by the moral relaxation of the Mexican people, a consequence of the revolutionary movements, and by a misunderstood concept of autonomy.

Fernandez MacGregor (1969) provides an account of Caso's view of the political problem:

> Ultra–conservatives and leftists understand that the *Universidad Autónoma* is a very important position for their ends, and have attempted to get hold of it to impose their ideas. For both factions, academic freedom is just a façade; they wave that principle in all university mutinies; but in fact both parties would finish it if any of them triumphed definitively. The first that contemplated the possibility of getting hold of the University was a social action Catholic group, supported by the largest mass of students and for most of the professors that belong to that religion. ... [This group] managed to get one Rector to put the university, founded on its autonomy, not outside the State but **against the State** (1969 p. 387, emphasis by the author).

From this citation, it is clear that beyond the official discourse Caso recognized that the National University was a site of political struggle between competing forces and ideologies. According to Fernández MacGregor, Caso provided him with a systematic political analysis of the University at that time. This depiction of Alfonso Caso's diagnosis might not have been completely accurate. I summarize it here because it certainly reflected Fernández MacGregor's perceptions of the political struggles within the University. According to Fernández MacGregor's account of the description provided by Caso, the *Preparatoria* represented a huge political problem. It was overpopulated and professors were badly paid and strongly unionized. Student's youth made them prone to manipulation. *Jurisprudencia* was the site of strong ideological struggles and almost totally dominated by ultra–conservatives. This same party controlled *Filosofía y Letras*. Ultra–conservatives also held *Odontología* and *Arquitectura* but these were not excessively problematic because of their small size.

Ingeniería, also controlled by the rightwing, usually did not get involved in political movements. *Ciencias, Ciencias Químicas,* and *Comercio y Administración* were, in general, quiet and manageable. In *Enfermería y Obstetricia* professors and female students were troublesome "due to the social class to which the majority belong." *Medicina Veterinaria* was the site of confrontation between two local opposing fractions. This was also the case of *Música*. *Economía* was "a communist cell." Finally, *Medicina* represented the greatest problem of the University because its population was too large, most students came from a "low social class," and there was a fight within the faculty.[12]

The Return of the Right

University groups that had been excluded from the new political scenario of the University did not give up immediately. New conflicts emerged and very soon, Fernández MacGregor would have the opportunity to confirm Caso's fears. He lasted in office less than one year.

In October of 1945, a new student movement started in the School of Medicine against director González Guzmán, a member of Chávez's group, protesting a new examination plan.[13] Rector Fernández MacGregor supported González Guzmán and seemed to reach an agreement with the students. Student protestors came back and seized the school building. The *Conejos* and the FEU[14] tried to extend the movement to other schools, criticizing the Rector for allowing known leftists in his administration. At Vasconcelos' initiative the University Council censured the students and supported the Rector and González Guzmán.

Students responded by occupying the main University and the Preparatory School buildings. Fernández MacGregor received support from President Ávila Camacho who refused to meet with the students. Backed by the Executive and the Senate, the Rector established sanctions including the expulsion of student protestors. In a meeting with the Governing Board Gómez Morín and De la Cueva criticized Fernández MacGregor's handling of the situation. They were particularly critical of the Rector's request for the intervention of the Attorney General's office. The other members of the Board supported Rector Fernández. Because of this, Gómez Morín resigned from the *Junta*.

The strike ended on November 30, 1945. The problem, however, was not completely solved. The students requested that sanctions be forgiven. With presidential elections coming soon, government officials wanted the problem at the University to be over for good. President Ávila Camacho suggested that the Rector reduce the punishments imposed on the students. However, Fernández MacGregor would not go back on his decisions. In the light of this situation, Rector Fernández MacGregor presented his resignation to President Ávila Camacho on February 15, 1946.

The *Junta* knew of the resignation of February 20 and on that date appointed Salvador Zubirán to assume the post of interim Rector on March 1, requesting Fernández MacGregor to stay until that date. Reluctantly he accepted the Board's request. In one of his last actions as Rector, he presided over a University Council session in which Alfonso Caso was appointed to the Governing Board replacing Caturegli. Caso was now a member of the *Junta* he had created.

A few days later, students occupied University buildings again. According to Fernández MacGregor, Zubirán and Chávez asked him to call on the loyal students to recover the buildings before Zubirán's inauguration.[15] The Rector refused to do this and against the *Junta*'s opinion, Fernández MacGregor publicly announced his going on leave on February 28, 1946.

Interpretations of this process differ in some respects. Chávez's biographer, Romo Medrano (1997), recorded some newspaper articles that accused Chávez, Baz, and Zubirán as instigators of Fernández MacGregor's downfall. It is true that at the end of the student strike students called to have Chávez appointed Rector (Mabry 1982) but there is no evidence that this was instigated by Chávez or his followers. The movement started against the director of Medicine, González Guzmán, another of Chávez's friends and collaborators who received full support from Fernández MacGregor. At the end, however, Zubirán was to become the next Rector of UNAM. He was the third partner of Chávez's closest clique: *los chavistas* or *bazichavistas* as many called them.[16]

This historical episode provides some interesting elements for the analysis of University politics. I have already mentioned the fact that political resistance outside the legitimate political arrangement was the origin of new University conflicts. Student discontent had been expressed around an academic issue, however, it had clearly targeted the dominant group in the University. The Rector was only able to cope with student unrest when he had complete support from the President. As soon as eAvila Camacho addressed other political considerations and his support towards the Rector decreased, the latter was forced to resign.

The conflict also evidenced discrepancies within the political structure of the Board and the Rectorship. Board member Gómez Morín, who was linked to the most conservative groups at UNAM, resigned from the *Junta*. Fellow conservative Ocaranza would soon follow. Differences between Chávez and Fernández MacGregor also became apparent in this conflict revealing different political styles in dealing with student opposition.

Universitarios and the Government

Miguel Alemán, the presidential candidate of PRM, was elected with 77.9% of the votes. He took office on December 1, 1946. His election symbolized the shift in power from the military to civilian political enclaves

(Camp 1996). It also symbolized another thrust towards political and economic conservatism. During his administration, the pace of industrialization was increased. Private industries received full support from the government. In the same period, the inequality of income distribution grew significantly (Meyer 1981b).

Miguel Alemán had received a law degree from the National University in 1928. He was called *el presidente universitario* (the president from the university). Alemán radically changed the paths of government recruitment and fixed patterns that are prevalent until this day (Camp 1995b). His administration included 75% of office holders with a University or post–professional degree,[17] 50% of which were from UNAM.[18] Alemán recruited 24% of his collaborators among his university generation, 29% of these were professors at UNAM.[19]

The *Universidad Nacional* benefited enormously from Aleman's good disposition. Federal appropriations for the National University grew almost 2.5 times from 1946 to 1952. Aleman's most important contribution to UNAM was the granting of a large piece of land and a significant amount of funds for the construction of a new University City. This support was a major relief for the university. Overpopulation was one of its largest problems. Student enrollment reached 20,963 students in 1946. The number of students had doubled during the last ten years. By 1952, at the end of the *sexenio*, the student population had grown to 28,292 an increase of 35%.[20]

The political implications of this process were very important. The University was now tightly linked to the government through a group of professors and Board members who were at the same time high–level government officials. That these individuals shared responsibilities and allegiances blurred the boundaries between the *Junta* and the government. Autonomy was more relevant as a discourse and a university value than a reality in the relationship between the University and the government.

Salvador Zubirán had become interim Rector in March 1946 only a few months before Aleman's coming to office. The Governing Board appointed him permanently on February 20, 1947. Zubirán had been a professor in the School of Medicine since 1925. He was Undersecretary in the Ministry of Health, under Gustavo Baz, until 1943. Zubirán's close relation with Baz and Chávez dated from their student days in the School of Medicine back in 1915.[21]

During his provisional Rectorship, on October 3, 1946, the Governing Board recruited Antonio Carrillo Flores to replace Gómez Morín who had resigned in February of that year. Carrillo Flores maintained his post in President Alemán's administration. A few months later, on December 30, 1946, Pedro Martínez Tornel, director of Engineering appointed by Caso, replaced Ocaranza who resigned from the Board. Martínez Tornel had been secretary and Undersecretary of Public Works during the Ávila Camacho administration.[22]

Students Glance towards the Left

New conflicts emerged over academic issues and tuition increases. This historical description reveals that the governing structure of the University was notoriously limited in its capacity to deal with demands from sectors outside the legitimate political arrangement. It shows that student demands were frequently met with authoritarian responses by the administration. This episode evidences how the lack of effective political channels produced violent political confrontations. It is also one of many situations in which students would demand a political reorganization of the University.

Zubirán resigned in 1948, a consequence of student protests against tuition increases and for academic reforms.[23] The movement started when Law students demanded academic reforms to the University Council. This body responded that most of these demands were acceptable. Trying to set an example, Zubirán establish sanctions to student protestors because they had framed their demands outside of the procedures established by University regulations. Law students went on strike and kidnapped Zubirán, demanding his resignation. The police rescued Rector Zubirán.

In the next few days, several confrontations between students and the police took place. Police brutality and violence against the students increased. Students from other schools reacted against the government's repression and went on strike too. Students from the Preparatory School demanded the reversal of tuition increases. Others demanded the reestablishment of shared governance and elimination of the Governing Board.

The media and Catholic organizations, like the *Unión Nacional de Padres de Familia* (National Parents Union), labeled the movement as a communist plot and supported Zubirán. There is no doubt that this time progressives and leftwing students led the movement. In spite of the accusations, student support for the movement increased. Even the Catholic–controlled CNE and conservative schools like *Comercio y Administración* joined in the strike. The most surprising support, however, came from the *Federación Nacional de Estudiantes Técnicos* (National Federation of Technical Students, FNET) representing the students of the *Politécnico* and other technical schools founded by Cárdenas.

Alemán intervened on both sides of the conflict. His private secretary met with the students while the president defended the Organic Law and called students to stop the strike. On April 23, 1948 Alemán met with members of the Governing Board and promised them full support. Later that same day, Zubirán resigned after telling the same members of the Board that Alemán had asked him to do so.[24]

The most interesting features of this conflict are that it started a slow transition of the student movement towards the left, and the solidarity exchanged between students from the *Politécnico Nacional*, and striking students at UNAM.[25] Students once again demanded the elimination of the Governing Board and rejected the 1944–45 Organic Law. This had almost exclusively been a demand of conservative students against the new alliance of moderate Catholics and liberals who dominated UNAM. As these dominant groups became more integrated with the government when the conservative Alemán administration was shifting the country more to the right, they also became the target of left–oriented students who were detaching themselves from the government. Finally, it is important to note that again, a reversal in presidential support precipitated the resignation of a University Rector.

The Organic Law Survives

Challenges against the 1945 Organic Law continued from left and right. The historical events described in the following section show that the organization of the University survived thanks to constant interventions by President Alemán at a high cost for University autonomy. President Alemán and his successor Ruiz Cortines repeatedly interfered in the appointment of University rectors and became a fundamental factor in the consolidation of political groups, within the political structure of UNAM.

After the Zubirán downfall, students continued the strike demanding participation in the election of the new Rector. The *Junta* closed the university in response to the students' demands. At this point, the student coalition split. The conservative CNE appointed Soto y Gama as Rector. The strike committee controlled by the left rejected Soto y Gama and proposed three candidates to the *Junta*. This body convinced Serra Rojas, one of the strike committee's candidates, to accept the Rectorship. Serra Rojas changed his mind and rejected his appointment a day later.[26] The *Junta*'s alleged "consultation to the community" had lasted fifty days when the Board required President Aleman's help in order to appoint Luis Garrido as new Rector of UNAM.[27] Board member Quijano, Garrido's friend, was again instrumental for this appointment.[28]

Luis Garrido was a contemporary of the *Siete Sabios* and a student of Antonio Caso. He supported Vasconcelos' presidential campaign in 1929. After getting his law degree, Garrido worked for the government of Michoacán as prosecutor attorney and head of the state Supreme Court. He was Dean of the Law School in the *Universidad Michoacana* under Rector Manuel Martínez Báez. Back in Mexico City, he worked for the city government and the Foreign Ministry. Garrido was a professor at UNAM since 1929. He taught several courses, including Marxism, in the schools of Law, and Economics.[29]

Garrido took hold of the Rectorship, in the only building unoccupied by the strikers, on June 1, 1948. Conservatives who now led the movement ratified Soto y Gama as their Rector with Vasconcelos' support. A few days later Soto y Gama withdrew apparently scared by government threats. The movement weakened and finally the students negotiated the end of the strike with Garrido.

The rest of Garrido's Rectorship was relatively peaceful in spite of student unrest due to student conflicts in Morelia (1949) and the *Politécnico* (1952). In spite of being a firm supporter of Caso's Organic Law, he allowed students to express freely and demonstrate without ever exercising a heavy hand.[30] He obtained benefits for the staff and supported their right to unionize. His tolerant attitude had previously created a confrontation with Chávez who insisted that the student leaders, that had ousted his friend Zubirán, be expelled.[31] Instead, Garrido removed the director of the Law School in order to pacify the University.

Alemán supported the new Rector. The construction of the new University City began in 1949. Garrido was able to preside over the inauguration of the *Ciudad Universitaria*. When he concluded his term in the Rectorship, Garrido was reelected at Alemán's request. Board member Silva Herzog revealed that President Alemán requested that the *Junta* re–appoint Rector Luis Garrido in 1952, and we "assented to his kind request" (Silva Herzog 1974, P. 117).

In his memoirs, Garrido recalls permanent conflicts of the *Junta*'s designation of directors for schools and institutes.[32] He was supportive and respectful of the Board. In 1952, President Alemán entrusted Antonio Carrillo Flores to write a new Organic Law for UNAM. When presented with this project, the Rector stated his "complete opposition." The new initiative was never sent to Congress.[33]

During Garrido's Rectorship the *Junta* recruited 5 members due to resignations. Through these recruitment the Board filled four positions (two selections were substitutions for the same slot), one fourth of this body. Three of them were close to Chávez. Manuel Martínez Báez (medicine) was his childhood friend.[34] Francisco De P. Miranda had always been part of his group in the School of Medicine.[35] Silvio Zavala, who replaced Garrido's appointee and friend Castro Leal,[36] was a historian and a friend of Chávez.[37] Rector Garrido presided over the appointment of 3 board members by the *Consejo Universitario*. Roberto Casas Alatriste (Commerce) was a good friend of Garrido and Quijano.[38] León Salinas (Engineering) had been a government official on many occasions[39] as well as director of the Engineering School. The University Council also ratified Jesús Silva Herzog's appointment to the Board.

A few months after the dedication of the University City, Garrido voluntarily resigned the Rectorship. Ruiz Cortines, the new President, and the Governing Board asked him to complete his period but he refused to do so. Before leaving the Rectorship, he discussed his successor with Ruiz Cortines. Nabor Carrillo Flores, *Coordinador de Ciencias* (Provost for Scientific Research) during Garrido's Rectorship, appeared as the strongest candidate. According to Garrido (1974), Ruiz Cortines said that he had good reports about his aptitude, so much that he though about using him as an expert to study the problem of the Texcoco lake, but that, on the other hand, he did not like having two brothers in highly relevant posts at the same time: Antonio Carrillo Flores had been appointed Secretary of the Treasury.[40]

Ruiz Cortines asked Garrido if he knew González de la Vega, the attorney general during Alemán's administration, who could be a good candidate. Following the President's wishes, the *Junta* offered the Rectorship to González de la Vega, who was Garrido's friend and colleague. He accepted the nomination but set some conditions that were impossible meet. In light of this situation, Garrido insisted on Nabor Carrillo's candidacy in an interview with Ruiz Cortines. Nabor Carrillo was finally appointed Rector.[41]

Competing Alliances

Nabor Carrillo took office on February 13, 1953. Carrillo had been *Coordinador de Ciencias* during the Rectorships of Caso, Fernández MacGregor, Zubirán, and Garrido. He represented a significant part of the emergent scientific research establishment, especially from the areas of mathematics and physics. His group shared with Chávez's an interest in the development of the sciences and their infrastructure at UNAM. Although presidential intervention shadows the view of internal competition over the Rectorship, it seems clear that *garridistas*, *chavistas*, and *carrillistas* agreed on Nabor Carrillo's designation. This agreement would decline during Carrillo's second period in the Rectorship.

Discrepancies within the dominant block had increased. Two competing factions started to develop. These factions were heterogeneous and not easy to differentiate in the political spectrum. At the time of Carrillo's designation, Chávez held at least one third of the Governing Board.[42] His was the most cohesive group in this body. Interestingly enough, in this occasion the *chavistas* did not seem to have their own candidate.[43] Diverse elements contributed to Carrillo's appointment. Still weakened by Zubirán's resignation, Carrillo must have been an acceptable candidate for Chávez's group. Their weight in the government had been reduced when the president changed and they did not seem to have a real possibility of influencing Ruiz Cortines' decision.[44] On the other hand, Carrillo's influence increased through his brother, a close collaborator of the President. In case presidential intervention had not been enough to impose a decision on the *Junta*, it also shaped the outcome by encouraging an alliance between Garrido's followers and Nabor Carrillo's friends, as well as other members of the Governing Board.

Carrillo's first period at the head of UNAM was concentrated on moving the University from its old locations in the center of Mexico City to the new University City. This process finally began in 1954. At that time, the National University had increased its student population to 32 thousand students.[45] In the same year, there were 5,372 faculty members,[46] perhaps twenty of these (less than one percent) were full time.[47]

Notwithstanding the President's intervention in the appointment of Rector, Silva Herzog, former member of the *Junta*, stated that "Ruiz Cortines respected university autonomy scrupulously" (Silva Herzog 1974 p. 128). He continued, "in those years there was not even a minimal hostility between the University and the Government. If anybody says anything to the contrary, it is because of ignorance or is knowingly lying" (p. 128).

It is true that UNAM students remained distant from the massive student movements that were taking place at the *Politécnico Nacional*, the *normales* (teacher's schools), and the rest of the technical education system.[48] The most important was the strike at the *Politécnico* in 1956. Students demanded the approval of a new organic law for the IPN (based on a project written by a faculty and student committee); increase of federal funds for the *Instituto*; curricular reform; increase in the number of scholarships; and other demands.[49] Others schools followed, and the movement involved more than 100 thousand students. Ruiz Cortines granted a few demands but a few days later the student leaders were put in jail and the army occupied the student dorms and dining halls, remaining there until 1958.[50]

The leadership of UNAMs student federations did not want to get involved with the *politécnicos* because leftists led their movement.[51] In spite of this, the conflict at the IPN would affect the University too. Dorms and dining halls included in the original project were never opened at *Ciudad Universitaria*. Mexican public higher education students would never enjoy the benefits of university housing and dining.

The student movement at UNAM had degenerated since 1948 into a multiplicity of small bands related to different politicians and university authorities. The use of *porros* (organized student gangs) had become common practice in the University. During Carrillo's Administration, these groups had expanded notoriously and it was claimed that most of them were paid and organized from the Rectory.[52]

During Nabor Carrillo's first period at the head of UNAM, Chávez and Baz strengthened their presence on the Board. First, the University Council appointed former rectors Baz and Garrido; as well as architect José Villagrán and former student leader Salvador Azuela. Chávez resigned from the *Junta* in 1953. According to the Organic Law, he would be eligible for the Rectorship two years later. The Board designated historian Edmundo O'Gorma, to replace him. Later the Council elected lawyer Trinidad García, whose son was married to Chávez's daughter;[53] Fernando Orozco, former director of Chemistry; Alfonso Noriega, former leader of the *Directorio*; and Pedro de Alba, another *chavista* from the School of Medicine.[54]

By 1957, eight members of the *Junta* were close to Chávez and Baz (himself a member of the Board). There are two possible explanations for the growth of *chavistas* in the board at the expense of Rector Carrillo's own group. First, it is possible that at the beginning both groups did not see each other as antagonistic to the extent of trying to block Chávez's followers from the getting to the Board. Second, Rector Carrillo probably did not have enough strength, within the University Council, in order to further his own candidates. Both explanations need to be supported and qualified. While the Board's own designations were balanced, University Council appointments were, in most cases, for *chavistas*. On the other hand, Carrillo was reelected in 1957 with no apparent opposition from Chávez and his followers. These developments suggest that the expansion of *chavismo* in the Board during Carrillo's first period was probably an outcome of a combination of both explanations.

Carrillo assumed the Rectorship for a second time in February of 1957. By 1959 all the schools and institutes had transferred to the University City. The University had grown at an incredible rate reaching almost 58 thousand students in 1960.[55] Faculty reached almost 6 thousand members.[56] Manual workers and staff reached an estimated number of 4 thousand.[57] Federal subsidy for UNAM increased 269% in real terms during the 8 years in which Carrillo was Rector.[58] Growth at every level was unprecedented.

Most of Carrillo's second term took place during the presidency of Adolfo López Mateos. In 1958, López Mateos was elected president. He had obtained a law degree at the National University in 1934. In his youth, he had been the leader of the Socialist Labor Party and he became deeply involved in Vasconcelos' presidential campaign. Later he developed a long career within the official party as a speaker for Alemán and Secretary of Labor under Ruiz Cortines. López Mateos had many connections within the University, particularly in the School of Law. During his administration, the University would continue to receive enormous support from the government.[59]

These facts are revealing of the relation between the Governing Board, the Rector, and the Mexican government. It is important to note that one of the groups within the dominant block, the *chavistas*, was able to increase its control over the Governing Board in spite of their differences with the Rector. This suggests that although the latter held undeniable influence in the election of Board members by the University Council, the weight of professional groups played a major role in the composition of the Board. The medical group has always been very powerful and its political influence in the Board was already significant in the early fifties. In spite of this, the most important factor in the designation of University rectors continued to be the intervention by the President.

A New Era for the Student Movement

Carrillo's second period was essentially peaceful with the exception of the student rebellion called *Movimiento de los Camiones* (Passenger Bus Movement) under the Ruiz Cortines' Presidency. This movement developed in the midst of the large social and political movements of teachers as well as telegraph, railroad, and electrical workers. Guevara Niebla (1986) describes that students from UNAM hijacked hundreds of buses and brought them into the University City protesting bus fee increases. In addition to their rejection of fee increases, students demanded higher wages for bus drivers, expropriation of transport by the municipality, and dismemberment of the bus–owner alliance. After one of their leaders was run over by a bus, students assaulted several bus depots. Confrontations between students and riot police took place all over Mexico City. Many students were hurt and public opinion began to support the students. The Army was dispatched to patrol the capital.

Railroad workers supported the students at UNAM. The *Politécnico*, the *Normal Superior*, and the *Nacional de Maestros* adhered to this struggle establishing the first alliance between students of these institutions.[60] Students continued hijacking buses and threatened to burn them if the Army attempted to go into the University City. Two hundred thousand students participated in a huge demonstration in the center of Mexico City.[61] President Ruiz Cortines intervened and fee increases were reversed.

This movement is relevant for this study in that it shows two important facts about the University. On the one hand, during the whole movement Carrillo acted very carefully and did not resort to repressive measures against the students. He never confronted the student movement and played an active mediating role with the government. In this way, the Rector distanced himself from traditional practices that depicted the students as agitators, provocateurs, or simple criminals. On the other hand, it is important to note that this was the first student movement at UNAM, since 1933, to be directed against the government. This was also the first time that students from both expressions of the public education system had been able to establish an alliance. According to Guevara Niebla (1986) this experience opened a new era and a new popular orientation for the student movement at UNAM.

Scientists Part Ways

During Carrillo's second period, the relations between his group and the *chavistas* deteriorated significantly. The two groups had different views about science, research, and the nature of the University.[62] Nabor Carrillo's followers were more aware of social issues. They were more flexible and tolerant. Though very prestigious in diverse fields, its members were more concerned with understanding the problems of science and teaching to a wide audience, than on publishing and interacting at an international level. Teaching was a fundamental activity for this group of scientists. Its most notable members were Manuel Sandoval Vallarta, Nabor Carrillo, Javier Barros Sierra, Carlos Graef Fernández, and a group of mathematicians including Alberto Barajas and the Adem brothers.[63]

The second group was more elitist. It was fundamentally oriented towards basic research. Even at that time, their essential concerns about the University were quality, efficiency, and productivity. The group was centered on Chávez, Zubirán, and Baz. It had a lot of influence in the biomedical sciences, the public health system, and the government's health research centers (Cardiology Research Institute and the Nutritional Diseases Research Institute). This group included Ayala Guzmán, González Ayala, González Herrejón, and Manuel Martínez Báez among others.[64]

The tensions between these two groups, labeled here as *populists* and *elitists*, became an open political confrontation during the selection of the rector that was to follow Carrillo. Many candidates were mentioned during the selection process. At the end, however, the Governing Board only considered five. The real contenders within the Board were Efrén del Pozo, Agustín García López, and Ignacio Chávez.

Del Pozo had been Carrillo's Secretary General for eight years. He was one of the founders of the Institute for Biomedical Research at UNAM.[65] Del Pozo had been accused by the *chavistas* of handling corrupt relations with student and faculty groups used to insure support for Carrillo's policies.[66] Agustín García López, a lawyer, had been Secretary of Public Works during the Alemán Presidency. Luis Garrido[67] and Casas Alatriste supported García López. Chávez had been Director of the school of Medicine in 1933 and a member of the Governing Board since its foundation until 1953. He had been closely related to presidents Ávila Camacho and Alemán. With Ruiz Cortines, Chávez and his group had lost much of their political influence. López Mateos, however, renewed their privileged linkages with the government.[68]

The designation of Rector in 1961 was one of the most heavily contested processes UNAM has ever witnessed. This designation was also one of the very few occasions in which the internal workings of the Governing Board have been made public. The Board had a majority of members in favor of Chávez.[69] Regulations require a minimum of ten votes for one candidate in order to appoint him Rector.

By the time of the designation, Chávez had eight votes. These included his friends Baz, García, Martínez Báez, González Herrejón, Fraga, and Zubirán. Orozco and Silva Herzog completed his lineup. *Chavistas* would work hard for the missing votes. Silva Herzog played a major role by convincing Casas Alatriste, the night before the meeting, to vote for Chávez.[70] According to Board member Vázquez, at the beginning of the meeting Baz said he had met with President López Mateos that same morning: the

President had told him that he would respect the Board's decision. The message was clear, Chávez's supporters had gotten presidential acquiescence. After two rounds Chávez still held nine votes, Del Pozo had three, García López, Fournier, and Agustín Yáñez had one vote each. Silva Herzog convinced Noriega that Yáñez did not really want the Rectorship. In the third round, Chávez finally got the ten votes. Board members Millán, O'Gorman, and Vázquez, immediately challenged different parts of the process.[71]

Reactions within the university community were equally heated. Attacks against Chávez came from the left and the right. In the next few days, students occupied the Rectory building and the University radio station. Del Pozo criticized the occupation but in spite of this some versions held him and Carrillo responsible for the protests against Chávez.[72] Mabry's analysis of these events seems more reliable when suggesting that García López's supporters led the movement against Chávez.[73]

One month later, student opposition had weakened. At Garrido's insistence, Chávez was able to deliver his inauguration speech in the school of Sciences between tear gas bombs and student protests.[74] A few weeks later, he had been able to reduce the movement out of existence and control the students.

Michis and Chavistas

With Chávez's occupation of the Rectorship, the most powerful political group in the history of UNAM was able to establish a significant control of University politics. This group symbolizes the articulation of politicians within the University and in the State apparatus. The analysis of diverse historical periods will show the extent of this political network and the influence of this group as an incarnation of a dominant University tradition.

Chávez was born in *Michoacán* in 1897. He was a student of the *Colegio de San Nicolás* until 1915. In that school, he became a friend of Antonio and Manuel Martínez Báez, Salvador González Herrejón, and Gabino Fraga. In the later days of the Revolution, some members of this group moved together to Mexico City to enroll in the National University. Here they became known as *los Michis* (diminutive for those who came from the state of Michoacán). Chávez became a student in the School of Medicine where he met Gustavo Baz, Salvador Zubirán, and Abraham Ayala González.

Governor Múgica, a friend of Chávez's father, appointed him as rector of the *Colegio de San Nicolás* or *Universidad Michoacána de San Nicolás*. In 1922, Múgica resigned as governor and Chávez abandoned the Rectorship. He left his friend Manuel Martínez Báez at the head of the *Michoacána*.

Back in Mexico City and after completing postgraduate studies in France, he played a major role in developing specialized services in

Cardiology and Nutrition at the General Hospital. These services would later become departments and eventually the National Institutes of Cardiology and Nutrition. Chávez's prestige as a cardiologist increased nationally and internationally. With doctors Aceves, Ayala González, Martínez Báez, Miranda, González Guzmán, and González Herrejón, they became the strongest group within the hospital. By 1932, *los Michis* were the only candidates to direct that hospital. When their control over the hospital was challenged by President Ortiz Rubio (in 1932), Chávez and his group held ground and eventually triumphed after Ortiz Rubio's resignation.

This victory allowed Chávez to become director of the school of Medicine at the National University in 1933. The situation of the country and the University during this period was reviewed in the previous chapter. Chávez's participation during the conflict over socialist education is revealing of his pragmatism. He supported Lombardo Toledano and Rector Medellín until it became clear that they were going to be defeated. Then he switched sides and demanded their resignation.[75] In spite of this, Chávez would not survive as director of the School of Medicine. Using his lack of tolerance and his academic reforms as a pretext, right–wing students ousted him under the indifference of Rector Gómez Morín and rival Ocaranza.

Chávez's prestige continued to rise. In 1939, during Cárdenas' Presidency, he was appointed director of the *Hospital General*. Chávez promoted many positive reforms in this institution. Ocaranza's group, however, criticized these reforms and forced Chávez's resignation a few months later. In 1943, with Ávila Camacho's and Baz's support, Chávez founded the *Instituto Nacional de Nutrición*, his most important contribution and a major advance for Mexican medicine. In that same year, he became one of the founding members of the *Colegio Nacional*. In 1945, he became one of the original members of the Governing Board at UNAM.

Chávez was always a polemic, public figure. On many occasions, both the left and the right criticized him. According to Silva Herzog, Chávez considered himself a non–communist left–winger.[76] His political pragmatism makes this claim difficult to ascertain. He was always close to power and was friends with a variety of politicians from different tendencies. These ranged from Cárdenas to Alemán. Most people agree that he was a liberal, but also note that he was profoundly elitist and intolerant.[77]

UNAM in the Sixties

At the beginning of his Rectorship, in 1961, UNAM had grown enormously. Enrollment had reached 66,870 students, of which 22,455 (33%) entered the University in that year.[78] Almost 40% of the total were part of the Preparatory School. Faculty had grown slower to reach 6,214 in 1961. Full professorships had been established in 1940 but part–time teachers still constituted most of the faculty. In 1961, there were only 209 full and half–time professors.[79] Government subsidy had grown steadily and

UNAMs budget increased in real terms. Even considering enrollment growth, the University budget continued to improve.[80]

Nabor Carrillo had already expressed concern over student enrollment growth.[81] Along similar lines, Chávez addressed this concern in his first statement as Rector: "Problems capable of clouding our optimism lay ahead of us. The largest of these, what lies at the root of others, is that of school overpopulation."[82] In a very revealing statement he continued:

> That human flood of sixty thousand youngsters that pours upon the university, compromises everything, chokes everything. If we do not find the formula, tomorrow they will be eighty thousand, one hundred thousand. It is good that as Mexicans we can not feel pain but, on the contrary, rejoice of this increase in the number of those who reach higher degrees of education; but as university members, as educators, we can not do less than look, with strong concern, almost with fright, at this plethora that chokes us and threatens to transform individual education into a mass, impersonal, technified, antihuman education.[83]

Chávez put forward an ambitious program. In his view, it was possible to enhance the quality of university studies by controlling student enrollment as well as tightening academic requisites and establishing disciplinary measures for students. In accordance with this perspective, he introduced the entrance exam (*examen de admisión*) that produced a good number of student protests. Chávez argued that students that were not competent enough to become part of the University should be received by a system of public and private technical schools.[84]

His most important academic reform was the extension of the academic program at the Preparatory School to three years. He also promoted a teacher–training program. During his administration, the University Council approved curricular transformations in several schools.[85]

Chávez expanded the number of full–time faculty and reformed the organization of academic work through a new Statute of Teaching Personnel. Similarly, he put together a Statute for Research Personnel that provided guidelines for the reorganization of the research institutes and activities.[86] These statutes created discomfort among faculty in the institutes and provoked a conflict with professors at the Preparatory School who organized the *Sindicato de Profesores de la UNAM* (Preparatory School Teacher's Union –SPUNAM).[87] The latter would become one of the antecedents of faculty unionization in the 70s. Chávez rejected any possibility of unionization. According to him, the University is a community with no conflicting interests, and labor relations within the institution were not those of employers and employees.[88]

The University Council also approved a statute for Administrative Personnel. In his relation with administrative staff and manual workers,

Chávez acted within the most traditional patterns of Mexican politics. He provided some significant benefits to this sector and bargained with the *Sindicato de Empleados y Obreros de la UNAM* (Employee and Workers Union–SEOUNAM) while restricting organization rights and subordinating the organization to Rectorship control.[89] The relation was terribly patronizing.[90] When the Statute was discussed, Chávez rejected the workers' demand that it recognize their right to organize as they wished, claiming that a workers' union would threaten the autonomy of the institution.[91] This argument represented the opinion of many members of the University Council[92] and would become a major issue in the 1970s. University employees however considered that the new Statute, and the recognition of the Workers Association that it established, represented an important step for this sector. They were thankful to Chávez and even supported his reelection in 1965.[93]

However, the most conflictive relations continued to be with the student organizations. A few weeks after the movement against Chávez's appointment withered, some student leaders tried to bring the different student federations together into one organization, the *Federación Universitaria de Sociedades de Alumnos* (University Federation of Student Associations–FUSA). Following the corporatist tradition of the Mexican political system, these student leaders requested Chávez's support and recognition. Chávez promoted his own faction within the FUSA. Rival groups to the left and right of Chávez's proteges criticized the FUSA leadership from within and outside the organization.

Student confrontations riveted the country during the 1960s.[94] UNAM was no exception. Chávez had to face student movements in 1961 when rejected students protesting against the entry exam occupied the Rectory building;[95] and in 1962 when Law School students rejected Cesar Sepúlveda's designation as Law School director.[96] The rector always applied harsh discipline against student opposition leaders.[97] The "three year plan" for the *Escuela Nacional Preparatoria* provoked a new student reaction. Preparatory students rejected this plan and demanded Chávez's resignation. University security and riot police confronted students. When the movement died, a consequence of internal divisions, the leaders were expelled for one year.[98]

The events reviewed above show that during Chávez's administration the authoritarian features of University governance were exacerbated. The personal political style of Rector Chávez loomed over every aspect of University life. Significant attempts were made to establish corporate control of student and staff organizations. Sanctions were applied to political adversaries. Policies were adopted and enforced through the personal will of the Rector. Chávez made intense use of traditional ideological values and relied heavily on the de–politicization discourse in order to deal with political conflicts and internal opposition.[99]

The Crisis of Authoritarianism

A few weeks after new President Gustavo Díaz Ordaz assumed office the *Junta* reelected Chávez in a competed election, but without major conflicts. Three candidates arrived at the final round: Chávez, Javier Barros Sierra, and Efrén Del Pozo. In the first round, Chávez got only six votes. In the second, Chávez and Barros Sierra were tied with seven votes each. Inexplicably, in the third and final round, Chávez got twelve votes. He was appointed rector for a second time. Perhaps Barros Sierra's words can shed some light on this process:

> In 1965 I had, partly due to information and partly to intuition, full certainty that doctor Chávez's reelection was perfectly sure, that is, totally independent of the outcome from a doubtful, incomplete, and rigged consultation of university opinion, because it was the State's will and concretely—to avoid abstractions—the government's, that this person would continue at the head of the University.[100]

In 1966 Law School students protested Sepúlveda's reelection attempt. Sepúlveda and Chávez suspended a group of students for distributing propaganda. One of the students was the son of the governor of Sinaloa. It is argued that this governor as well as other politicians fueled the Law school conflict by using gangs. Chávez countered with his University security force. Sepúlveda and Chávez refused to bargain when the students presented a petition. Law students went on strike. Economics followed a few days later demanding the abolition of Article 82 of the University Statute that enabled the administration to expel students for political motives. Participants and commentators accused that PRI politicians were deeply involved in this conflict, claiming that student protestors received money and protection from them. Chávez granted some of the students' demands but the movement did not end. A confrontation between security forces and students at the Rectory building spurred a violent reaction. The Rectory building was occupied and Chávez, surrounded by angry students, forced to sign his resignation. A few days later Chávez ratified his resignation and most of the university officials and directors, all of them appointed during Chávez's administration, resigned as an act of repulse and in solidarity with the Rector.[101] It seemed like Chávez and his followers were out of the University forever.

There seems to be no question about external involvement in the Rector's downfall. The linkages between some of the student leaders and high government officials, as well as PRI politicians, have been well documented.[102] While there is no evidence that Diaz Ordaz was directly involved in the ousting, it is clear that the President never intervened to support Ignacio Chávez. The fact that Díaz Ordaz did not like Chávez was evident in the following comment by Silva Herzog (1974):

> according to other sources, the president did not hide his hostile opinions towards Chávez with his state secretaries and other persons, were they relevant to the point or not. ... in an indirect way Díaz Ordaz intervened in this conflict in favor of student agitators; because surely his opinions were spread little by little by many of those who heard them and in this way they became known by the youngsters, who feeling themselves supported by the government, became more demanding and aggressive against the Rector until they came to the point of demanding his resignation (p. 148).

Former law–school student leader Rojas Bernal expressed the same idea many years later:

> Ignacio Chávez hoped for the president of the republic's support, but it never came. It is not that Díaz Ordaz acted against him, he only created a vacuum, and allowed the movement to develop (Rojas Bernal 1995).

It is often considered that while the Rector and Díaz Ordaz never had a good relationship, Chávez had so much internal support for his reelection that the President would have had to intervene very openly to stop him.[103] However, discrepancies between Chávez and Díaz Ordaz increased over the Rector's opposition to the expansion of student enrollment.[104]

The student movement did not end with the resignations. It extended to other faculties that in turn integrated the *Consejo Estudiantil Universitario* (University Student Council–CEU). This branch of the student movement criticized the violence employed by law student leaders and their connections with the government and the PRI. The CEU put forward a democratization program for the University. This program included three types of demands. A first set dealt with immediate student concerns like the elimination of admission exams and the establishment of free entry from UNAM's preparatory schools to its undergraduate programs. It also demanded the revision of the three–year plan for the *Preparatoria*; as well as the provision of student aid, university housing and dining, scholarships, and health services. A second set dealt with freedom of speech and organization issues. These included the elimination of University Statute articles that sanctioned student expression; respect for student's right to organize freely; and disappearance of the University security force. Finally, a third set dealt with democratic reform issues. Students' demands included the disappearance of the Governing Board, whose main attributions would be transferred to the University Council. They also demanded the establishment of shared governance and equal representation for faculty and students in collegial bodies; direct election of student and faculty representatives; and student participation in the appointment of rectors and directors.[105]

The student movement had come to a critical point in the history of UNAM. According to Guevara Niebla (1988), "with this struggle the historical cycle of student opportunism came to an end, and this would be the last occasion in which the School of Law would act as leader of University strikes" (p. 32). From this point on, the left (in its multiple political expressions) would become hegemonic and the movement would gain a great degree of independence *vis-à-vis* the government. CEU's program became a historical reference for the student movement. Guevara explains that this program synthesized two alternative traditions from the student movement: the liberal struggle for shared governance and democratic participation, and the popular demands for the improvement of material conditions and opportunities for students. A new component, the critical stance on social and political relationships and the struggle for political rights at the national level slowly started to emerge. In this way, the movement at UNAM was fed by and became part of the new student movement trends of the early 1960s.

The Governing Board was placed in a very uncomfortable position. It was put into question by one part of the student movement (the CEU) and threatened by the remains of the Law school leadership. Government officials tempered the latter[106] and opened the way for the Board to appoint a new Rector. The same Board who had selected Ignacio Chávez a little more than a year earlier designated Javier Barros Sierra as the new Rector of UNAM.

There is no information available about the internal workings of the Board for this nomination. In the previous selection process Barros Sierra had been very close to getting appointed, but this in itself does not explain if his designation was essentially an internal decision, a Presidential design, or a combination of both. Mabry (1982) reviews two alternative explanations: either Díaz Ordaz appointed a friend to replace Dr. Chávez whom he disliked; or the *Junta* needed a *Universitario* with strong ties to the government. Both explanations are flawed by the fact that Barros Sierra and Díaz Ordaz were not close at all; moreover, they had a very conflictive relationship since the time in which both were part of President López Mateos' cabinet.[107]

Barros Sierra had been one of the most important *carrillistas* during his stay at the University. He had strong connections with the research institutes and the school of sciences as well as broad support in one of the most important schools: Engineering. After Chávez's downfall, the *carrillistas* and their allies, progressives in the school of Political and Social Sciences and several social sciences research institutes, almost had a free way to the Rectorship. They also had a very important connection with Díaz Ordaz's government. Antonio Carrillo Flores, once a member of the *Junta* and the former Rector's brother, was now Foreign Secretary and a very good friend of Díaz Ordaz.[108] These conditions might have influenced Díaz Ordaz to promote, or at least allow, Barros Sierra's appointment. It might have seemed a good opportunity to get rid of an uncomfortable adversary.

As soon as Barros Sierra assumed the Rectorship on May 5, 1966, he progressively addressed student's demands. Barros Sierra established free transit (*pase automático*) for students from the *Escuela Nacional Preparatoria* who obtained their preparatory degree to enter undergraduate programs at UNAM's schools and faculties and uncapped student enrollments at every level (baccalaureate, undergraduate, and graduate).[109] He ended financial support and recognition to the FUSA's and provided the *comités de lucha* (student combat committees) with information and support to eradicate gangs in a joint effort with the administration. Articles 82 and 84 of the University Statute were removed and University security was eliminated. In sum, Barros Sierra granted most of the students' demands except for those related to the democratization of UNAM. Like all the rectors before him, he shared the ideas underlying the Organic Law of 1945 and the governing structures it sanctioned.[110]

However, the governing style was very different from Chávez's. Chávez had believed in establishing discipline even through the use of an aggressive security force, the use of sanctions and the control of students through their organizations. In contrast, Barros Sierra sought to encourage student and faculty participation within the limits established by the Organic Law. During his period, the University Council was a site of unprecedented activity and participation. The Council appointed a committee for the analysis of curricular innovation. In addition to curricular reforms, Barros Sierra's academic program addressed the reorganization of academic work.[111] Semester programs replaced the old annual structure. Courses were reorganized into an academic units system. Numeric grading was replaced by a reduced–range letter evaluation.

Since 1951, there had been no tuition or fee increases at UNAM. Implicitly this had become a significant part of the corporatist relationship between the students and University authorities, as well as between the former and the Mexican State. Embedded in this pact was a tacit paternalistic relationship between the students and the government and an understanding that student protests would not exceed the limits of the University.

However, the Mexican government was now willing to break the pact, established with young members of the urban middle class, on many fronts. In 1968, the Secretary of the Treasury, Ortiz Mena, proposed that the University charge the students for the full cost of their education. The government would award scholarships to students through a special institute and, in this way, it would indirectly fund the University.[112]

Barros Sierra fervently opposed any attempt to increase student tuition. His refusal was based on two arguments. On the one hand, the government's proposal would limit the autonomy of the University and would place it under the control of this funding agency. On the other, it would increase inherent inequalities among students and limit the opportunities for those with a lower socioeconomic background. Not only that, Barros Sierra insisted on the need to create equal opportunities for students by granting scholarships.[113] In fact, scholarships were almost tripled during Barros Sierras' period.[114]

At the political level, Barros Sierra also produced some significant changes. According to Barros Sierra himself, when he became Rector among "the fifteen members [of the governing board] there was a majority of government officials of different hierarchies."[115] When he left the Rectorship in 1970 this situation had been reversed. Barros Sierra explained that when he became Rector a majority that revolved around Dr. Ignacio Chávez composed the Governing Board. That situation had been accomplished through many "years of constant labor that took two prestigious physicians to the Rectorship of the University."[116] Physicians and lawyers, many of whom were originally from one State (Michoacán), dominated the Board. In general "it can not be said that this body acted impartially and with serenity in the face of specific conflicts."[117]

Overall, Barros Sierra generated a new climate within UNAM. It was based on ideas of broad participation; social commitment; tolerance and free political expression; as well as a real exercise of University autonomy. Under his guidance, the University administration tried to comply with the new government requirements for the production of professionals and technicians and still follow the internal design of the *Universitarios*. His attempt to reform UNAM would soon be hampered by a historical confrontation between students and the Mexican government. The 1968 student movement that was about to begin would simultaneously bring the "golden era" of the University to an end, and deal a severe blow to the authoritarian political system.

SUMMARY: THE POLITICS OF DE–POLITICIZATION

The redirection of government policies in the early 1940s brought about a new era in the relationship between the National University and the Mexican State. Rapid industrialization and urbanization expanded opportunities for the *Universitarios*. Educational requirements of the new regime redefined the role of the University. Ávila Camacho fostered the coalescence of a new dominant alliance within the *Universidad Nacional* and its articulation with the government under a discourse of national unity. The 1945 Organic Law institutionalized this new relationship between the University and the State, as well as the dominance of an emergent coalition.

Ideological and Structural Foundations of the Political System

The construction of this new hegemony was founded on the principles of autonomy and academic freedom that emerged from significant histori-cal episodes of the confrontation between the University and the State that were analyzed in the previous chapter. In the light of the new circum-stances, the nature of these historical processes was reinterpreted. Student political mobilization, the mechanism through which university intellectu-als' highest aspirations of autonomy and academic freedom had come to place, was now constructed as the origin and expression of the troubles of the *Universidad Nacional*. The University was reinterpreted as a commu-nity with a unique purpose, the search for truth and knowledge, and there-fore deemed as necessarily technical and deprived of politics.

Of course, politics were not eliminated from the National University. The political rules were redefined and the space for legitimate participation in the running of the University was reduced. The political arrangement sanctioned by the 1945 Organic Law mirrored the most essential charac-teristics of the Mexican political system. Power was concentrated on a few executive authorities. Collegial bodies were subordinated to these executive positions. Participation and political competition were extremely limited. The new political arrangement was founded on loosely defined ideas of an autonomous community, brought together with no other legitimate inter-est but the free pursuit of knowledge, where authority and access to deci-sion-making opportunities were based uniquely on merit. In sum, the governance system at UNAM presented the most relevant features of authoritarianism.

The Reduced Political Spectrum

The political arrangement at UNAM was self–feeding and contained. It was self–feeding because it provided an efficient mechanism for the repro-duction of the *primitive accumulation of power* concentrated most signifi-cantly in the Governing Board. It was contained, because the only legitimate competition took place within the dominant social formation that had ben-efited from this original accumulation of power. The analysis of the origins of accumulation shows how dependent was this process upon the figure of Alfonso Caso, who had almost unlimited influence in the formation of the University Council and therefore the election of the first Governing Board.

This study shows that legitimate competition during the "golden years" took place essentially between two broad and vaguely defined political alternatives that shared this common history and were part of the domi-nant block since the creation of the Board. The competition between these groups was precisely over the control of the Governing Board, and through this, over the appointment of Rectors and consequently the University Council.

These competing groups were roughly identified as *chavistas* and *carrillistas*. I have labeled them *elitists* and *populists* respectively. Chávez, Baz, and Zubirán articulated an alliance with strong roots in the bio–medical disciplines and professional groups. During most of this period, they relied on privileged relations with the state apparatus enhancing their strength and political centrality. Through political connections, personal ties, and regional contacts they were able to incorporate a significant group of lawyers who were part of the core of this alliance.

The alternative was probably a looser system of alliances. Different components coalesced around Luis Garrido, Nabor Carrillo, and later Javier Barros Sierra. This alliance included progressive sectors in the emerging area of the social sciences with personalities like Pablo and Henrique González Casanova, Luis Villoro, Horacio Labastida, and others.

The original dominant block included a few representatives of more conservative positions like Ocaranza and Gómez Morín. They were very marginal and ended up resigning from the Board. Other political expressions in the University on both sides of the political spectrum were practically excluded from any opportunity of participation and most certainly from exercising any influence in the competition within the political structure. The explosive expression of these sectors, fundamentally through student mobilization, was an uncomfortable presence that shook the political structures on several occasions. Student protests frequently altered the balance between the two competing alliances within the political structure as well as their power dynamics.

Issues Within the Dominant Block

Competition within the dominant block was constrained to a limited set of issues. All its members obviously agreed on the maintenance of the political arrangement sanctioned by the Organic Law. They commonly rejected demands for shared governance and for broadening political participation. They shared similar views about the need to develop a scientific research system, increase the quality of University studies, and the importance of having a professional faculty core.

While they were responsive to government demands for a professionally oriented University, they differed in their approach to the social responsibilities of the institution. *Chavistas* focused more on preserving and enhancing the elite characteristics of the University. *Carrillistas* and their allies were more sensitive to social demands for access and the expansion of educational services. Chávez and Barros Sierra represent the two extreme positions when dealing with the problems of increasing student enrollment and demands for participation.

Political Dynamics of the Governing Board at UNAM (1945–1966)

Largely, this chapter dealt with the dynamics of the competition for the Governing Board. In previous sections, I have focused on two different processes related to this body: the appointment of Board members, and the appointment of Rectors. A combination of both allowed the identification of some patterns of political behavior.

In all of the cases, there is evidence of government intervention, of different degrees, in the appointment of Rectors. This seems to be the single most important explanation for the designation of one Rector or another. The reelection of Garrido, as well as the selection of González de la Vega and latter appointment of Nabor Carrillo, exemplified the lack of independence of the Board *vis-à-vis* the President. In spite Chávez's control over a large majority of members on the Board in 1957, Carrillo was reelected with Ruiz Cortines' support. Fernández MacGregor and Zubirán's resignations also show the small degree of autonomy from the government.

The fact that Chávez and Baz were able to build a majority of Board members even during Carrillo's administrations is revealing. It shows that while the Rector carries much weight in the nomination of Board members by the University Council, there are occasions in which he does not exercise absolute control. It is difficult to perceive this phenomenon by analyzing Board selection within the Council. There, the Rector "never loses."

According to the minutes of the University Council, in most elections for the Governing Board there was only one candidate. It is evident that the bargaining process takes place outside the University Council. The dominating presence of lawyers and physicians on the Board, as well as the continuity of some slots that seem reserved for different professional groups, suggest that these professional entities drove the selection of Board members.[118] It seems evident that even indirect student and faculty participation in selection of board members through the University Council was extremely limited.

From 1945 to 1965, the Governing Board included 54 members, all of whom were male.[119] The University Council made the majority of the appointments during Alfonso Caso's and Nabor Carrillo's Rectorships (15 and 14 respectively). During Chávez's Rectorship 8 members were appointed, and he exercised enormous influence in 8 out of 10 board–member designations made by the *Junta* when he was part of that body. During this same period, the composition of the Board by disciplines was clearly dominated by lawyers and physicians.[120]

Governing Board members by academic discipline 1945–1966
(years on the governing board)

Unknown	5	1.52%
Social Sciences	0	0.00%
Business Administration	15	4.55%
Architecture	21	6.36%
Medical and Biological Sciences	73	22.12%
Law	115	34.85%
Economics	22	6.67%
Exact Sciences	13	3.94%
Humanities	25	7.58%
Engineering and Chemistry	41	12.42%
Total	330	100.00%

Source: University Biographies

This account of the historical evolution in the political composition of the Board shows the vast influence that Ignacio Chávez and his political group had over the Governing Board. In this work, I have not analyzed the appointment of directors of faculties, schools and institutes. While evidence of the government intervention in the appointment of directors exists, it seems safe to assume that the *Junta* exercised more autonomy in these designation processes. Given that the *Junta* appoints directors of schools and institutes, each of the groups in the Governing Board exercises a direct influence over the composition of one half of the University Council[121] and in the control of schools and institutes. Since the University Council appoints members of the *Junta*, the influence over the Council in turn expanded the possibilities of determining the composition of the Board.

Government and Students: External and Internal Balances

The dominant groups within UNAM relied heavily on the Mexican government to counter student assaults upon the political structure of the University. When this did not occur, as in the cases of Fernández MacGregor, Zubirán, and Chávez, rectors were not able to maintain their positions. At the same time for most of this period, the Federal Government contained UNAM's student unrest. The government imposed upon the University authorities two constitutive elements of the corporate pact between UNAM's students and the State: tuition control and unlimited enrollment. These two elements, in addition to the opportunity of professional employment, assured for many years the compliance of University students with the Mexican government. They were also part of the delicate political balance and stability of the institution. Tuition increases and restrictions of student enrollment were usually among the underlying causes of student mobilization.

Authorities at UNAM attempted to put in place the instrumental component of corporate control over the students. Sponsorship and financial control over student groups on the one hand, and the attempt to legitimize and subject student confederations on the other, were for many years the alternative forms of relations between university authorities and students. Student politics adapted to these forms and to the emerging process of political recruitment by the PRI and the government. A tradition of student corruption and opportunism permeated student organizations and their movements with few exceptions until 1966.

It was precisely the emergence of a new student movement and the lack of presidential support that put an end to Ignacio Chávez's Rectorship and with it to what many consider the golden era of UNAM. The expansion of student enrollment had become a most prominent factor in the life of the University. The academic and political consequences of that expansion marked all the University administrations after Chávez. In this context Barros Sierra's administration and the 1968 student movement, discussed in the next chapter, closed a cycle of power relations at UNAM. The next chapters analyze how these relations evolved during the critical phase of Mexican authoritarianism.

NOTES

[1] Five appointees, Gabino Fraga, Alejandro Quijano, Manuel Gómez Morin, Antonio Martínez Báez, and Mario De la Cueva, belonged to the school of Law. De la Cueva replaced Antonio Caso who declined his membership on the Board. Four more, Abraham Ayala González, Ignacio Chávez, Fernando Ocaranza, and José Torres Torija, were from the School of Medicine. Alfonso Reyes belonged to the School of Philosophy, and Jesús Silva Herzog to Economics. Finally, Mariano Hernández Barrenechea was from Engineering; Manuel Sandoval Vallarta from the Physics Institute; Ricardo Caturegli from the School of Chemistry; and Federico Mariscal from Architecture (University Biographies).

[2] Mendieta y Núñez (1956).

[3] Ayala González was one of Chávez's friends since he arrived to Mexico City to study medicine. Together they promoted specialization services at the *Hospital General* since 1925. Chávez and Ayala founded the medical review of that same hospital (Romo Medrano 1997 pp. 61–107).

[4] Chávez, Antonio and Manuel Martínez Báez, Fraga, and Salvador Gutiérrez Herrejón were schoolmates and friends from the *Universidad Michoacana de San Nicolás de Hidalgo* before 1922. They traveled to Mexico City together to enroll at the University in different disciplines. They remained a close group for most of their lives. They were known to others as the *michis* in reference to their common origin in the state of Michoacán (Ibidem.).

[5] Alfonso Reyes, the *michis*, and others had a permanent gathering in one of Mexico City's famous cafés. Chávez invited Reyes to visit Morelia. They considered each other great friends (p. 45).

[6] Chávez's biography provides ample information on the close relationship between Chávez, Baz, and Zubirán. It also presents evidence of how they were identified by many as a very homogeneous political group with strong ties to high government officials (see Romo Medrano 1997).

[7] Chávez was President Ávila Camacho's personal physician. Chávez and Baz were also very good friends with Ávila Camacho's successor President Miguel Alemán (Romo Medrano 1997 p. 132).

[8] See Fernández MacGregor (1969 p. 274).

[9] Ibidem.

[10] Fernández MacGregor writes that he did not complete 10 years as a teacher before his resignation and therefore he did not fulfill one of the requisites established in the University Statute to be eligible as a rector (1969 p. 386).

[11] Romo Medrano (1997 p. 179).

[12] I have summarized Fernández MacGregor's account of the political diagnosis of the University provided to him by Alfonso Caso (pp. 387–388). Quotations in this paragraph are also taken from Fernández MacGregor's memoirs. Caso is not explicitly cited in these pages, consequently none of these expressions can be attributed to him.

[13] Three different accounts of this conflict can be consulted. These are Fernández MacGregor (1969), Guevara Niebla (1986), and Mabry (1982).

[14] Right wing student organizations led by Catholic groups.

[15] Fernández Mac Gregor (1969).

[16] Chávez's biography provides ample information on the close relationship between Chávez, Baz, and Zubirán. It also presents evidence of how they were identified by many as a very homogeneous political group with strong ties to high government officials (see Romo Medrano 1997).

[17] Camp (1995b p. 85).

[18] Ibidem. p. 98.

[19] Ibidem. p. 97. Some of the most notable *Universitarios* participating in his administration were Francisco González de la Vega (Attorney General), Antonio Martínez Báez (Secretary of Economics), Antonio Carrillo Flores (Director General of NAFINSA, the government's financial bank), Alfonso Caso

(Secretary of Government Properties), Andrés Serra Rojas (Secretary of Labor), Manuel Gual Vidal (Secretary of Education), Alfonso Noriega Cantú (Director General of Education), and Antonio Dovalí Jaime (Undersecretary of Public Works).

[20] For data on student enrollment see table compiled by the author in Appendix 2.

[21] (see Romo Medrano 1997).

[22] Dates provided by Camp (1995a) suggest that Martínez Tornel occupied these posts in the Ávila Camacho government while being director of the Engineering School.

[23] For detailed descriptions of this movement see Mabry (1982) and Guevara Niebla (1986).

[24] See Silva Herzog (1974 p. 96) and Mabry (1982 p. 199).

[25] Guevara Niebla (1986) argues that there was an unusual coalition within the student movement. He also argues that this movement was a turning point that it started a new era of "crisis, corruption, and close relations between official politics and the students" (p. 39). I think that these characteristics were already present in the student movement and would reappear and probably increase in different periods after this movement. However, the student movement against tuition increases and for academic reforms represented the first time in which the student social left acted independently, and probably against the government acquiring its own identity and with it the capacity to lead the students of UNAM for the first time.

[26] Silva Herzog (1974 p. 97).

[27] Romo Medrano (1997 p. 181).

[28] Even though Quijano was older than Garrido, they had been colleague professors in the Law School. They were also close friends and got together for an informal weekly breakfast, "*la mesa de Sanborn's,*" which included Casas Alatriste and others (Garrido 1974 p. 205).

[29] Ibidem.

[30] Ibidem., p. 289.

[31] See Garrido (1974 p. 267) and Mabry (1982 p. 203).

[32] Garido (1974 p. 271.

[33] Ibidem., p. 341.

[34] See footnote 1, supra.

[35] Ocaranza (1943 p. 321).

[36] Castro Leal was a friend of Garrido and Quijano (Garrido 1974 pp. 191, 205). He was most probably designated at Quijano's request.

[37] Romo Medrano (1997 p. 192).

[38] See footnote 25, supra.

[39] León Salinas had been Undersecretary of Commerce in 1917, President Carranza's Private Secretary in 1919, Undersecretary of the Treasury in 1923, and interim director of *Banco de México* (Federal Reserve) in 1946. See Biographies database compiled by the author.

[40] (Garrido 1974 p. 356). It is important to remember that Antonio Carrillo Flores was also a member of the Governing Board.

[41] Garrido (1974 p. 357).

[42] Board members in this group were Manuel and Antonio Martínez Báez, Ignacio Chávez, Gabino Fraga, and Abraham Ayala González.

[43] There is no evidence that Chávez and his group had a candidate for the Rectorship.

[44] Gustavo Baz and Antonio Martínez Báez, former secretaries of Health and Commerce respectively, had been replaced in 1952 by incoming president Ruiz Cortines. The group's influence had been increased by Chávez's and Baz's personal friendship with presidents Ávila Camacho and Alemán. They did not enjoy that frienship with the new president.

[45] See Appendix 2.

[46] See Appendix 3.

[47] Silva Herzog (1974)

[48] Mabry (1982).

[49] Guevara Niebla (1986 p. 50).

[50] For detailed descriptions of the 1956 student movements see Guevara Niebla (1986) and Mabry (1982).

[51] Mabry (1982 p. 209).

[52] Romo Medrano (1997 pp. 220–221). Guevara Niebla (1986) explains that the student movement after the ousting of Zubirán went into a long period of transition where the old conservative ideologies of the student body were shaken and a new era of opportunism and corruption came about. The influence of external official political groups became overwhelming during this period.

[53] Romo Medrano (1997 p. 135).

[54] See Ocaranza (1943) and Romo Medrano (1997).

[55] See Appendix 2.

[56] See Appendix 3.

[57] Estimation based on data for manual workers and staff from 1965 to 1988 as well as student and faculty growth.

[58] See Appendix 5.

[59] From 1958 to 1964, López Mateos' presidential term, federal subsidy for UNAM would increase in 122% in real terms. See Appendix 5.

[60] Mabry (1982 p. 211–213).

[61] Newspaper *El Popular* (in Guevara Niebla 1986 p. 56).

[62] (Peimbert Sierra 1999).

[63] Ibidem.

[64] Ibidem.

[65] According to Eliezer Morales Aragón, Del Pozo took care of all the operative aspects of Carrillo's Rectorship. Henrique González Casanova and Horacio Labastida assisted him in this task (Morales Aragón 1997). These three individuals constituted a closely-knit group since their student days. Henrique González Casanova would later become a member of the Governing Board and long-lasting counselor for several rectors. He is the brother of Pablo González Casanova who would become director of the Political and Social Sciences School and Rector of UNAM.

[66] Romo Medrano (1997 pp. 220, 221).

[67] Ibidem., p. 223.

[68] Gustavo Baz was at the time governor of the state of México, López Mateos' own state (See University Biographies database). Chávez was López Mateos' friend and the new President's sister was the doctor's personal secretary. (Romo Medrano 1997 p. 228).

[69] It is said that Chávez always commented that he would only attempt to run for the Rectorship when he held at least 8 votes within the Board.

[70] Silva Herzog himself describes his conversation with Casas Alatriste the night before the final meeting (Silva Herzog 1974 p. 139).

[71] O'Gorman had insisted on a longer period of consultations with the community and protested against the Board's lack of interest about university members' opinions (Vázquez 1961). Millán protested Fraga's membership in the Board (Ibidem). A few days after the designation Vázquez resigned form the Governing Board (Ibidem). According to the Organic Law, Fraga should have left the board almost one month before the designation was made.

[72] Romo Medrano 1(997 pp. 224–253).

[73] Mabry (1982 p. 220).

[74] Garrido (1974) and Mabry (1982).

[75] Mayo (1964).

[76] Silva Herzog (1974 p. 140).

[77] See the author's interviews with Peimbert, De la Peña, and Villoro. Villoro's opinions are particularly noteworthy since he was Chávez's Private Secretary at UNAM.

[78] See Appendix 2.

[79] Ramírez and Domínguez (1993)

[80] UNAM's budget per capita calculated by the author based on information in Appendices 2 and 5.

81 Carrillo stated that the explosive growth of the university population was a matter of deep concern for his administration. He said that a special committee had been put together to address this problem and its sequels. He hinted at a possible solution through the development of state universities (Carrillo in Silva Herzog 1974 p. 133).

82 Ignacio Chávez, Inauguration Speech, February 13, 1961 (Universidad Nacional Autónoma de México 1985b).

83 Ibidem p. 19.

84 Ramírez and Domínguez (1993).

85 Ibidem.

86 Ibidem.

87 Pulido (1981 p. 47)

88 Ramírez and Domínguez (1993).

89 The relation between Rector Chávez and UNAM's workers' organizations was not exempt of problems. However, Chávez obtained access to state health services as well as other benefits like housing, union officers leave of absences, etc. for University employees (Pulido 1981).

90 Pérez Arreola (1998).

91 Ramírez and Domínguez (1993).

92 Ibidem.

93 Pérez Arreola (1998).

94 (Mabry 1982). Guevara explains that student insurgency was spurred by three factors: the crisis of professional occupations, the crisis of higher education, and the clash of values with the older generation (Guevara Niebla 1988 pp. 24, 25). Other authors (Martínez Della Rocca 1986) recall the impact of third world liberation struggles and particularly the Cuban revolution as a determinant factor in student revolts. For a description of student movements in Mexico during the early 1960s see Mabry (1982), Martínez Della Rocca (1986), and Guevara Niebla (1988).

95 Guevara Niebla (1988 p. 27).

96 Ibidem.

97 Five students form the Law School were expelled in 1962 (Mabry 1982 p. 224).

98 Mabry (1982 p. 225).

99 Ramírez and Domínguez (1993).

100 Barros Sierra (1972 p. 33).

101 (Flores Zavala 1972 pp. 3–43). It is important to look at the list of the resignations because many of them played a major role in the following two decades in the history of the National University. Among the University officials who resigned were Roberto Mantilla Molina (Secretary General), Ignacio González

Guzmán (provost for Scientific Research), Mario de la Cueva (provost for the Humanities and Social Sciences), Rosario Castellanos (director for Information and Public Relations), Manuel Martínez Baez (director for Teacher Training), Eduardo Cesarman (office of the registrar), Enrique Velasco Ibarra (Private Secretary). The following directors of schools also turned in their resignations: César Sepúlveda (Law), Antonio Dovalí Jaime (Engineering), Donato G. Alarcón (Medicine), Horacio Flores de la Peña (Economics), Manuel Madrazo Garamendi (Chemistry), Carlos Pérez del Toro (Commerce), Enrique González Pedrero (Political and Social Sciences), Fernando Prieto (Sciences), Pablo Zierold (Veterinary), and José Briseño (Preparatory School). Institute directors Guillermo Haro (Astronomy), Fernando Salmerón (Philosophy Research Institute), and Roberto Llanas (Mathematics) also resigned (Flores Zavala 1972 p. 42–43). Romo Medrano (1997 p. 418) presents a list with a few discrepancies. It includes Guillermo Soberón (director of the Biomedicine Research Institute), Fernando Alba Andrade (Physics Research Institute), and lists Arturo Elizundia Charles as director of the School of Commerce.

[102] One of the leaders, Leopoldo Sánchez Duarte, was the son of Leopoldo Sánchez Celis, governor of the state of Sinaloa. Sánchez Duarte received support in the way of money and armed gangs (Flores Zavala 1972 p. 7; Mabry 1982 p. 227), Romo Medrano (1997) reviews accusations about other public officers intervening in the conflict. These include some comments by Chávez himself accusing Díaz Ordaz of direct involvement in these events (Romo Medrano 1997 pp. 412–424).

[103] Villoro (1999).

[104] Martuscelli (1997); Soberón Acevedo (1997)

[105] See the *Programa de acción revolucionaria del Consejo Estudiantil Universitario* (Revolutionary Action Program of the University Student Council) in Flores Zavala (1972 pp. 43–45).

[106] Rojas Bernal (1995).

[107] A well known anecdote of unconfirmed origin states that at one occasion during a Cabinet meeting Díaz Ordaz and Barros Sierra tried to go through a door at the same time. In a sarcastic tone Díaz Ordaz told Barros Sierra that *sabios* (wise men) should lead the way. Barros Sierra responded wittily "no way my friend, it is *resabios* (vestiges) that should go first."

[108] Gil Mendieta, Schmidt, Castro, and Ruiz (1997).

[109] See Barros Sierra (1972 pp. 38,39).

[110] Ibidem., p. 43).

[111] Domínguez (1986).

[112] Barros Sierra (1972 pp. 54–59). This proposition put forward in the late 1960s is very similar to today's voucher proposals.

[113] Barros Sierra (1972 pp. 54–59).

[114] Domínguez (1986).

[115] Barros Sierra (1972 p.116).

[116] Ibidem., p. 117)

[117] BIbidem., p. 117)

[118] University Biographies database.

[119] Some individuals have been appointed two times to the Governing Board. I have taken each of these instances as different memberships.

[120] This information is based on the University Biographies database.

[121] Directors constitute 50% of this body. See previous chapter.

Democratization of the University
The University in the Crisis of Authoritarianism (Part I)

The student movement of 1968 opened a new political cycle in Mexican history. At the national level, the outcome of the student movement was a profound legitimacy crisis for the authoritarian political regime. The years that followed this landmark event were characterized by intense social insurgency. Independent social movements, unions, and peasant organizations emerged. A myriad of political parties and groups were created. Movements for the freedom of press and association became very prominent. The emergence of diverse urban and peasant guerilla movements all over the country evidenced the extent of this legitimacy crisis.

With the selection of Luis Echeverría to succeed President Díaz Ordaz, the authoritarian political regime assumed a populist discourse and project in an attempt to recover its political legitimacy.[1] At the same time, the government practiced a hard containment policy based on corporatist control and the use of repression. Some examples of this face of the political regime were the new student massacre in 1971; the government's intervention against the newspaper *Excelsior* in 1976; the violence against democratic electrical workers that same year; and the repression against guerrilla movements during the 1970s and early 1980s. The legitimacy crisis of the authoritarian regime would not signify a process of political democratization for many years. The government combined a limited political opening (*la apertura política*) with the most violent traits of State authoritarianism expressed in a systematic violation of human, civil, and political rights.

Presidencialismo was exacerbated both by the need to tighten the political system and the State party after the events of 1968, and by Echeverría's personal political style.[2] Given the political centrality of UNAM, relations between this university and other State institutions had always been mediated by the presidential figure. After 1968, this situation became more radical. The University became a matter of the utmost political importance for the regime and a permanent issue in the presidential agenda. Struggles within other State institutions were in most cases isolated from the University.

On the one hand, democratization attempts within the PRI barely touched upon UNAM. Attempts to rid unions and peasant organizations of corporate control by the State party became a reference for activist groups within the University, but struggles in both arenas were isolated from each other with few exceptions. On the other hand, the government drew from all its political resources in its interaction with UNAM. There is no evidence of party factions competing against each other in the University arena. While many politicians actively participated in public attacks upon the University, the most progressive members of the PRI were silenced during the campaign against González Casanova and the attempt to democratize UNAM.

In this chapter I present a brief account of the 1968 student movement and examine the beginning of a new political cycle at UNAM. The first of two consecutive periods in the political history of the University are analyzed in depth in the following pages. This analysis focuses on the relationship between the University and the national political system. It looks at the evolution of the dominant discourse within the University, the shifts in political alliances, and the characteristics of the political arrangements as they developed in an environment of permanent political confrontation.

Immediately after the review of the 1968 student movement, I analyze the political role of the Rector and other University authorities during this conflict. I provide historical evidence of Barros Sierra's alternative interpretation of University traditions of autonomy and the social role of the institution. I will show that the *Universidad Nacional Autónoma de México* was shaken both by the dynamics of internal groups in the aftermath of 1968, and by the duality of populism and violence of the authoritarian regime.

In the brief historical account upon which Daniel Levy grounded his study of University autonomy, he called the period after the 1968 events the "reconciliation." Levy states that "Echeverría would be more preoccupied with reconciliation than control" and that he "perceived the necessity to stabilize the political system through reconciliation with the university" (Levy 1980 p. 33). However, a careful historical study of the University from 1970 to 1977 shows that there was no such reconciliation. There is no doubt that Echeverría tried to close the breach between the *Universitarios* and the State, but he was also concerned with establishing control over the University as a source of opposition. This chapter will show that a relative degree of government tolerance towards internal democratization, political activism, and the progressive modernization of UNAM combined with an urge for political control and intervention by diverse means in University affairs. The study of this process is fundamental. The extent and limits of University autonomy cannot be fully understood if we fail to recognize multiple instances of presidential intervention like the ones analyzed in the present chapter.

I will show that in a first phase, a populist political opening prevailed and González Casanova's democratization project was tolerated. In a second phase, the government's attitude towards the University hardened, the government contributed to González Casanova's ousting, and the conservative reaction led by Guillermo Soberón was promoted, protected, and supported by the political system.

This chapter and the one that follows provide an original historical reconstruction of the political confrontations involving UNAM from 1970 to 1980. Studies about UNAM usually refer to some of these events but they are rarely analyzed in depth. There are a few chronologies and documentary compilations about the staff and academic union struggles.[3] However, there are no systematic historical accounts of the University and its political conflicts during the 1970s. This historical study attempts to fill this vacuum.

The analysis is based on media accounts, original interviews, and official documents. It makes extensive use of these chronologies and documentary compilations. It is a political history that focuses on the analysis of the project for University democratization and aperture led by González Casanova, and that of conservative restoration, led by Guillermo Soberón (in the next chapter). It looks at the ways in which political practices within the University were modified without formally changing the organizational structure and the legal foundations of the University. The Organic Law of 1945 prevailed. In the case of González Casanova, University autonomy and academic freedom were interpreted as the foundations for the exercise of full political liberties and a permanent critique *vis-à-vis* the Mexican State.

González Casanova insisted on the need to expand faculty and student representativeness to collegial bodies and decision–making processes and sought to democratize the procedures for the selection of University authorities. During his administration, the idea of the University was constructed as an agent of social change. The growth in student demand for enrollment was faced as a cultural challenge and an opportunity to extend the reach of the University to diverse social sectors and multiple regions.

This chapter provides historical evidence of the ways in which political conflict shaped the dominant discourse and the organization of the University. It will show that the distinction between political practices within the legitimate political system and the actions of organized faculty and students for democratic participation and University reform were blurred. Internal and external political activities and projects by student and faculty organizations were also integrated and difficult to differentiate. Solidarity from campus organizations to popular movements became a constant. Academic reform discussions always had social responsibilities as a reference point.

Historical evidence shows that although power was not really decentralized, the Governing Board was diversified in terms of political composition and disciplinary representation. The University council became a
proactive body holding intense debates and promoting profound transformations such as the *Colegio de Ciencias y Humanidades*.

Finally, I show that the democratization project did not take root; that
González Casanova was not able to establish a hegemonic process due to
permanent attacks from the government and internal conservative forces.
The confusion and lack of political stability that prevailed in the country,
and consequently in the University, was used to legitimize a conservative
restoration when the PRI regime and traditionalist sectors within UNAM
coincided in their objective to stop González Casanova's project. The discourse about the University changed radically. University traditions of
autonomy and academic freedom were now used to discredit democratization attempts. Instead of political liberties and critical attitudes, they came
to symbolize an aspiration for order and stability.

1968 AND THE UNIVERSITY

By 1968, Mexico had reached a population of 47,952,040.[4] The average
annual growth–rate of GDP from 1960 to 1968 was 6.8%. The average
growth rate per capita between 1963 and 1971 was 3.6%.[5] However, social
and economic inequalities had increased and vast sectors of the population
lived under extreme conditions. In 1966, 1% of the families received 12%
of the total income, the bottom 50% received 15.4% of this amount, and
the lowest 20% only 3.6%.[6] The authoritarian regime had been able to
contain social unrest for many years. The López Mateos and Días Ordaz
administrations, however, had relied increasingly on the army to cope with
worker, peasant, and student protests. The most notable examples had
been the repression against *Politécnico* students in 1956; teachers and railroad workers in 1958 and 1959; university students in Morelia in 1963;
and the physician's movement in 1965.[7]

A large number of student movements took place all over the country
between 1966 and 1968. Universities in the states of Guerrero, Durango,
Sinaloa, Michoacán, and Sonora, as well as the School of Agriculture in
Chihuahua were the sites of violent confrontations between students and
the police or the army. The army occupied the universities of Michoacán
and Sonora, as they had previously done at the *Politécnico*.[8] The most significant, and in some way the synthesis of these movements, took place in
Mexico City between July and December of 1968. It has been known since
as the *Movimiento de 68*.

The attempt to gain international recognition based on the economic
success of the *Mexican Miracle* and the stability of the authoritarian political regime; had driven to Mexican government to request, and obtain, the
right to organize the 1968 Olympics. For the first time, these Games would

take place in a third world country. Mexico became an object of international attention increasing the government's concern to project an image of social stability and internal order. In a context of economic growth, increasing social inequality, and growing discontent the government sought to enhance it international legitimacy among the nations of the world. This situation intensified the authoritarian features of the political regime. Political compliance within the system and allegiance to the President became more critical than ever. Intolerance towards political dissidence increased, constraining even more the government's ability to deal with a social opposition like the student movement of 1968.

"El Movimiento"

The events of 1968 have been broadly described and analyzed by many authors and from different perspectives.[9] In the following section, I provide a summary of the most relevant events related to this student movement. I have based this summary on Guevara's (1978) account of the conflict between July and December 1968.[10] Given the interest of my present study, I focus on the impact of the student movement on internal University politics during the days of the student movement and after its tragic conclusion.

The trail of student insurrections and social unrest in universities all over the country intensified from 1966 to 1968. At the beginning of 1968, the National University itself witnessed strong confrontations of left wing and democratic students against violent gangs. A few months later, students from the humanities schools at UNAM demanded the liberation of political prisoners from the previous railroad and teachers' struggles. By the end of July all of these atomized struggles consolidated into in the most important student movement in Mexican history.

The 1968 student movement started as a reaction against police brutality and the occupation of one of UNAM's Preparatory schools and an IPN *Vocacional* by the army and the police.[11] The occupation of the *Preparatorias* by the military brought about a large number of protests. In an unprecedented action, Rector Barros Sierra declared a day of mourning on July 30 and called for a massive gathering of *Universitarios* in the University City the next day. On August 1, Barros Sierra and the members of his Administration led a huge demonstration protesting against the violation of university autonomy by the government and demanding respect for democratic rights.

Barros Sierra's actions had a very important effect on the movement. The Rector's presence during these three days provided legitimacy for the student movement and discredited the government's version of a "communist plot." This brought a temporary decline of the repressive actions against students. Finally, and probably against Barros Sierra's own desire, it encouraged other University schools to join the strike providing the foundations for the creation of the movement's directive body: the *Consejo Nacional de Huelga* (CNH).

After the protest led by Barros Sierra, the student movement grew in numbers and legitimacy. Under the direction of a representative committee, the *Consejo Nacional de Huelga* (CNH)[12] *Politécnicos* and *Universitarios* presented six demands that symbolized the struggle for civil and political liberties.[13] In addition to these petitions, students called for public and open negotiations challenging the President's authority and credibility.[14]

All through August the movement expanded at the national level. Schools and universities all over the country adhered to the strike and became part of the CNH. Faculty support was organized in the *Coalición de Maestros* (higher education teacher's coalition). On August 15, the University Council adopted some of the students' demands.[15] The movement permeated other sectors of society using communication brigades canvassing Mexico City with their anti–authoritarian message. The government made limited attempts to establish negotiations, but students' conditions for dialogue were never fully met. In a victorious atmosphere of growing strength and sensing the possibility of a successful negotiation with the government, the movement reached its peak on August 27 when half a million people marched to the *Zócalo*.[16]

A few days later Díaz Ordaz addressed the students in a speech in Guadalajara and in his "state of the nation address." In these speeches, the President dealt with the student movement in the traditional ways of the authoritarian regime. On the one hand, he characterized their movement as a conspiracy involving foreign and obscure internal forces. This "conspiracy" had "the evident and restated purpose of creating a climate of social unrest… by the most angered and confronted political and ideological trends and the most varied interests, in curious coincidence or unconcerned coexistence."[17]

According to Díaz Ordaz, these were the same "internal and external forces that have continued to join up trying to make the conflict worse, to extend it, involving other groups, and to hinder its solution."[18] Citing the powers awarded to him by the Constitution, the President threatened to make use of the armed forces, that is the infantry, the navy, and the airforce, for internal security purposes. He then stated, "we would not like to be in a situation of taking measures that we are unwilling to take, but we will if it is necessary; whatever our duty is we will do; wherever we are forced to go, we will go."[19] On the other hand, Díaz Ordaz ambiguously offered to intervene and provide a "solution." "My hand is extended to you in friendship" he had said previously in Guadalajara. In the next days students replied through their brigades: "the President's hand should be tested for gunpowder traces."[20]

Attacks upon the movement and repression increased again after Díaz Ordaz's address.[21] Within that climate, the army occupied IPN and

UNAM's campuses denounced by the government as subversive centers. The attack upon UNAM was not restricted to its campus. PRI congressmen and public officials orchestrated a harsh campaign against Rector Barros Sierra, forcing him to resign. Students from all the institutions supported the Rector and compelled the Governing Board at UNAM to reject his resignation. Barros Sierra stayed in office but unexpectedly called on the students to return to classes.

The student movement had put the government in an unprecedented situation. It challenged the strongest political traditions of the authoritarian regime and the symbols of power. According to Monsiváis (Zermeño 1978) the student movement challenged the essence of the *Presidencialista* regime. Traditional tactics of leadership corruption, encouragement of internal divisions, terrorizing, and presidential patronizing had failed to subdue the students. In the face of growing international attention and less than two weeks away from the inauguration of the Olympic Games, the Mexican government decided to stop to the student movement for good.

While repression continued in the streets, the President opened negotiations with student leaders.[22] However, the negotiations were only a diversion and presidential goodwill only an illusion. The illusion would be cruelly torn a few hours after the first meeting between Presidential and CNH representatives when the Mexican army, the police, and paramilitary corps slaughtered participants at a CNH meeting in Tlatelolco on October 2, 1968. The number of deaths as well as details about the government's decision to attack the student gathering and military operation still remain a mystery; and have been long time objects of contention.[23] The day after the student massacre most newspapers published official government versions stating that 25 persons had died in Tlatelolco.[24] In its first public statement after Tlatelolco, the CNH declared that there had been more than 100 deaths. Other versions, including British newspaper *The Guardian*, argued that more than 300 participants were killed.[25]

The majority of CNH representatives were captured and the most important student leaders were locked in army prisons and tortured by army and government intelligence for many days and then in jail for years. The movement entered a defensive stage but students still refused to end the strike. Persecuted and terrified by government repression, divided, and deteriorated, the new leadership within the CNH called an end to the strike on December 4. The CNH was disintegrated two days later without assuming any organizational program or providing political directives for students in their return to schools. The student movement had suffered a tremendous defeat.

University Authorities and the Student Movement

From the very beginning, the student movement of 1968 developed into a profound rupture between the University and the Government. Barros

Sierra's performance during the 1968 events was truly exceptional. No public official or a University Rector had ever assumed such a critical stance *vis-à-vis* the President and the government.[26] His initial response to the army's invasion of University locales was grounded on the strong tradition that conceived the university as an independent corporation. This conception had been upheld by his grandfather, Justo Sierra, in 1881,[27] developed into a spiritualist, humanist tradition, enforced by the 1929 student generation, and embodied by the Caso brothers.

As if responding to a premonition, in 1966 Barros Sierra had called the University Council to approve a statement about University autonomy. Barros Sierra's declaration on autonomy had gone beyond the concepts of the University's self–determination to establish its own academic programs, legislate its regulations, and administer its own resources that were already established in the Organic Law. In this declaration, he also stated that

> University self–determination has to be respected; internal academic, administrative, and political problems have to be solved, exclusively, by members of the university. In no case is the intervention of external agents admissible, and on the other hand, full exercise of autonomy requires that university enclosures be respected.[28]

A few paragraphs later Barros Sierra concluded that

> There is a violation of [university] autonomy when the State restricts the academic independence of the University or prevents it from ruling itself internally, by any means, but also when a private corporation, a political party, a group, and in general any entity or external force intervenes in the life of the University, by altering, or obstructing the performance of its tasks or limiting, in one way or another, the liberties that sustain it.[29]

The ideas of this declaration shaped Barros Sierra's dignified attitude towards the government as well as his initial relationship with the student movement; exemplified by his leading the demonstration and by warning students against the actions of external provocateurs.[30] Very soon Barros Sierra went beyond the defense of the corporation and assumed a broader commitment to the student cause. According to Guevara Niebla (1978), Barros Sierra

> defended the institution not only in the old spiritualist terms, but fundamentally in *political* terms: in his perspective the University was, in addition to a Temple of Knowledge, a space of liberty within the country, the unique terrain in which democratic rights had full validity...(p. 19).

This attitude was clearly expressed when, sensitive to student exigencies and the public statements of multiple faculty gatherings, he proposed that the University Council vote to demand respect for University autonomy, the end of government repression, and reparations for the damages caused by the armed forces to university buildings. In addition to this, the University Council, at Barros Sierra's initiative, voted to support the CNH's demands.[31]

Barros Sierra's positions were not exempt from criticism within the University. On the one hand, the students had not been able to overcome their traditional distrust of University authorities. The Rector's initial defense of autonomy helped coalesce students around the CNH and establish some common ground between the administration and the movement. His call to "reestablish normal academic activities," a carefully crafted statement in response to government pressures, created discomfort among the students and was massively rejected. When the Rector presented his resignation, after the occupation of the University by the army, he blamed the government and ambiguously signaled other *Universitarios* that had misused the institution. The students resented the statement, but in spite of this, the movement demanded that the Governing Board not accept Barros Sierra's resignation.[32] Despite these differences, the figure of Barros Sierra acquired a historical dimension in the eyes of the students.[33]

On the other hand, Barros Sierra faced expressions that were more conservative, within the institution. Perhaps one of the most evident of these differences was the public statement by law school faculty that protested the army's intervention against the *Preparatoria* but rejected the notion that this implied a violation of autonomy.[34] President Díazß Ordaz used that statement to justify the army's intervention "in an attempt to **preserve** the autonomy of the institution."[35] Both statements would be very relevant in framing the relations between the University and the State in the years to come.

A second confrontation occurred when Barros Sierra resigned the Rectorship. Under the pressure of students and faculty, the Governing Board rejected the resignation. According to Barros Sierra, the *Junta* drafted a first response in which, although they did not accept the resignation, they implicitly accused Barros Sierra of allowing University discipline to be disrupted by students. Barros Sierra stated that, "before and after that occasion it was demonstrated that there were some members of the Governing Board that faithfully echoed the government's thoughts and desires."[36] Barros Sierra rejected that draft and the *Junta* had to write a new statement declaring that they would not accept his resignation.

In the Aftermath of the Tlatelolco Massacre

Barros Sierra issued a new call to return to classes in November 1968. After the CNH officially ended the strike, students slowly returned to classes at the beginning of December. The University was completely demoralized. Attendance in classes was very low during the first months of 1969. The student movement entered a declining phase. In spite of this situation the struggle for the liberation of student political prisoners continued.

The minutes of the University Council show that this body tried to resume its normal business as early as December 20, 1968. With the exception of Rector Barros Sierra's decision to provide institutional support for students' legal defenses and allow students in jail to register for courses and present examinations, not a minor thing, the governing bodies proceeded with the designation of new directors and members of the Governing Board. The process of curricular reforms was reinitiated but the broad community participation that characterized this process before the student movement had already been broken. Barros Sierra continued being Rector until the end of his period in 1970. In spite of vast support from the *Universitarios*, he did not accept a re–appointment for a second period.[37]

By the end of his administration in April of 1970, student enrollment at UNAM had reached 107 thousand students, a 38% increase since 1966.[38] Faculty grew 21% during the same period, reaching a total of 9,400 teachers and researchers.[39] Barros Sierra introduced new administrative procedures and reorganized staff and manual work. Administrative personnel increased to 9,126, almost 28% more than in 1966.[40]

Under Barros Sierra the University Council replaced seven members of the Governing Board. The *Junta* chose four more members during the same period. This body became more diverse with its members being from nine different academic disciplines.[41] The weight of the professions that had traditionally controlled the Board (law and medicine) was notably diminished. The relation of forces between *chavistas* and Barros Sierra's allies was almost equivalent.[42] The student movement, however, had shifted the University towards the left, restricting the political possibilities of the more conservative *chavistas*.[43] This situation was clearly reflected in the designation of Pablo González Casanova as the new Rector of UNAM.

THE DEMOCRATIZATION OF UNAM

Since the beginning of 1970, Luis Echeverría, the new PRI presidential candidate, was already in control of the government. Echeverría was the former *Secretario de Gobernación* (Minister of the Interior) during Díaz Ordaz's presidency. By the time the new Rector was appointed Echeverría's populist discourse and style had impacted the Mexican political environment.

Pablo González Casanova was designated Rector in April, 1970. He was the first Mexican to obtain a Ph.D. in Sociology and was considered a renowned social scientist at the world–wide level. Pablo González Casanova's family had a long tradition in the University. His father (also Pablo González Casanova), a moderate Marxist and famous linguist, had been a professor until 1935. The elder González Casanova had rejected

Lombardo Toledano's project in 1933. He had also been a good friend of the Caso brothers.[44]

The new Rector had been director of the School of Political and Social Sciences as well as the Institute for Social Science Research at UNAM. He had also been a prominent member of the University Council for many years. Pablo González Casanova was identified as a democratic socialist and part of a progressive group of social scientists that included Enrique González Pedrero, Víctor Flores Olea, and Francisco López Cámara (appointed to the Board by Barros Sierra).[45] This group had strong ties with Luis Garrido, Nabor Carrillo, and Barros Sierra. At the time of the new Rector's designation by the Board, González Pedrero was a personal advisor for Echeverría during the presidential campaign.[46]

New Relation of Forces

There is no doubt that Pablo González Casanova served as the most progressive Rector ever appointed by the Board. He enjoyed broad support from faculty and students. Student assemblies did not openly propose candidates because they did not agree with the existence of the Board itself; however, they were able to build a large consensus around the idea of having an internal candidate become the next Rector.[47] Several "external" candidates, including former *universitarios* Yáñez and Carrillo Flores, Días Ordaz's Ministers of Education and Foreign Affairs respectively, declined the nomination a few days before the designation.[48]

Only two candidates were left —González Casanova and Madrazo Garamendi, director of the School of Chemistry. It became known that González Casanova won after the second round but the votes from this session were not made public.[49] In the election of Flores Olea as director of the School of Political and Social Sciences a few weeks earlier, the progressives had barely obtained the required minimum of eight votes.[50] In the days between this vote taking place and the Rector's election, two key elements of Chávez's group were replaced when Fournier reached the age limit and Aceves Parra, Díaz Ordaz's minister of health, surprisingly resigned from the Board.[51] According to Villoro, who would later be appointed to the Board during González Casanova's administration, the election was difficult for the progressive candidate.[52] Conservative sectors of the *Junta* coalesced around Madrazo who had been a weak and gray candidate until that moment.[53] Echeverría's approval of González Casanova helped to diminish internal opposition against the latter who was perceived as a leftist. Echeverria was a populist and González Casanova would help him project his image and reestablish a connection with the *Universitarios*.[54]

If the new relation of forces within the Board and González Casanova's connections with incoming President Echeverría were not enough, the political climate of UNAM after 1968 pushed in the direction of increased participation, tolerance, and democratization of University life. Media reports show that there was a large amount of pressure and attention focused upon the activities of the *Junta*.[55] In spite of enormous difficulties generated by the atomization and decomposition of the movement after Tlatelolco, students had started to reorganize along two lines: liberation of students incarcerated in 1968 on the one hand, and academic reform and democratization of the University on the other.[56]

An Alternative Vision of the University

University reform was also a major issue for the new University administration. Chávez and Barros Sierra had put forward two different transformation programs. These programs took place within the parameters of the Díaz Ordaz administration's most developed project for higher education.[57] President Echeverría's populist project did not pose a definite plan for post–secondary education. He focused on the political objectives of recuperating legitimacy among urban intellectuals, shattered during 1968, and at the same time effectively controlling the universities as opposition centers to the PRI regime.[58] Because of Echeverría's attempts for reconciliation between government and University, federal funding for UNAM increased significantly during the two years of the González Casanova administration.[59] The government encouraged the expansion of student enrollments in higher education at the national level.

Consequently, González Casanova enjoyed strong financial support and faced fewer external constraints. While external conditions enhanced his transforming vocation, González Casanova met a contradictory situation at the internal level. On the one hand, students and faculty were eager to participate in changing the University. On the other, the institution was plagued with internal conflicts, violence, and distrust. As explained earlier, both were the legacies of the 1968 events.

González Casanova assumed the Rectorship with a strong commitment to University reform, and he addressed the problems of the University explicitly. In his inauguration speech, he summarized a transformation project along the following lines:

1. Democratization of education understood as "the opening of higher studies to increasing numbers of students," and also as allowing "a larger participation of faculty and students in University decisions and responsibilities."

2. Training of new teachers and researchers as well as bringing University faculty up to date in the new developments of scientific and humanistic knowledge, and

3. Integration of teaching and research activities as well as promotion of inter–disciplinary academic programs at every level in an

attempt to increase educational quality, motivate students, and renovate knowledge.

González Casanova shared with the previous rectors his respect for the 1945 Organic Law and the principles of autonomy and academic freedom. Like Barros Sierra before him, he assumed that these concepts were intricately related to political liberties within the University.[60] On various occasions, González Casanova expressed the idea that University problems could not be solved using repression or the intervention of the army or police forces.

Regarding the presence of politics within the University he went beyond Barros Sierra to recognize that the University was a site of ideological struggle:

> Never expect... our university to resign to its autonomous decisions regarding the designation of authorities, the allocation of resources, and the organization of its academic activities; do not think that the ideal university can ever be a site of full consensus, in our times implying the disappearance of the right to think and the right to organize oneself. In the university there has always been and there will always be the right for ideological struggle and organization, to think rationally along different ideological perspectives, and for the organization of rational beings in accordance with their philosophical, cultural, and social goals.[61]

González Casanova conceived of the University as an agent for social change and a privileged space where social freedom and political liberties were exercised.[62] Students had to be taught and respected, so that they could be "able to learn and to do, able to act for a better University and a better Mexico."[63]

For the new Rector, students were part of the strength and the object of existence of the University. Consistent with his view about the institution, and along the lines set by Barros Sierra, the new Rector expressed his views about the expansion of student enrollment.

> All the statistics indicate that secondary education will continue to grow at high rates, higher education too, and we must contemplate this fact with optimism and without fear, because being fearful of secondary education and higher culture growth in the new technical and scientific modalities is being fearful of a more developed Mexico and we the members of the university have to be the first not fearing the development of the nation.[64]

These ideas allowed González Casanova to view the students within the university as actors in their own right. Moreover, they constituted a fundamental force for University reform. True to these principles, González

Casanova respected and encouraged the creation of independent student political organizations.[65]

An Ambitious Program for University Reform

González Casanova's first steps as Rector were forceful. A few months after assuming office a set of permanent committees that would gather student and faculty opinions and study the problems of university reform were put in place.[66] In November of 1970 González Casanova presented a thorough critique of the traditional university, based on the classic professions of law, medicine, and engineering, and provided the first ideas of the new reform. This document shows the Rector's concern about the conservative nature of the professional schools and sheds light on the reform strategy that he implemented a few months later. The basic ideas of this document can be summarized as follows:[67]

1. The traditional model of the University, centered on the classical professions, is in crisis due to the rapid transformations occurring in contemporary society. The University has to be reoriented towards the production of scientific and technical knowledge as well as the critique, by the social sciences and the humanities, of the social and economic arrangement of our times.

2. The University has to be brought out from the cloisters and linked to the sites of production, health care, and family.

3. The traditional role of faculty has to change in two directions: on the one hand, by addressing new issues, and assuming new research and teaching activities; on the other, by extending the benefits of knowledge and culture to broader audiences.

4. Increasing enrollment demands have to be met through a reorganization of academic activities and by using modern technologies that expand the capacity of the institution.

In December of 1970, at González Casanova's initiative, the University Council approved the *Estatuto del Personal Académico* (Faculty Statute). González Casanova recognized the increasing process of professionalization of teaching and research, and through this document, he established the procedures, categories, and levels for faculty hiring, as well as the organizational structure of academic work.

In January of 1971, the Rector presented the University Council with the proposal to create a whole new system, parallel to that of schools and faculties: the *Colegio de Ciencias y Humanidades* (College of Sciences and Humanities–CCH). González Casanova was convinced that the traditional structure of the University was extremely conservative and that reform efforts would be more beneficial if oriented towards the construction of this parallel system. The CCH attempted to establish a connection between the three educational levels of UNAM (baccalaureate, undergraduate, and graduate) as well as the three essential activities of the institution (teaching, research, and outreach).

The first phase of the project was the foundation of the CCH baccalaureate. Its vocational and academic undergraduate degrees as well as graduate programs, run in conjunction with the research institutes, would be developed in following stages. The overall plan was incredibly ambitious. It included the creation of new decentralized campuses, a national system of academic units that would allow transfers from different institutions, and the establishment of a national evaluation system. In sum, the project extended the reach of the National University, expanded its capacity, and it reestablished UNAM's centrality and preeminence in the higher education system. CCH's baccalaureate was approved in January of 1970. The rest of the project would never come to life.

The Conflicted University Arena

The University environment in which González Casanova was trying to develop his reform project was extremely problematic and complex. As I noted earlier, the political system faced an intense crisis of legitimacy expressed in many fronts. Opposition parties demanded new electoral rules and spaces for participation, corporate organizations and the media were the objects of democratization attempts. Guerrilla groups emerged in several States. The government acted to reverse this situation through the implementation of populist policies in search of legitimacy, and by strengthening its control over political institutions and social organizations. This control increasingly involved the use of repression and military force.[68]

The University was also plagued by political tensions. The student movement was split into many factions and different political orientations. While many activists abandoned the University and focused on external social struggles, others tried to establish or continue academic reform projects within their schools. Students focusing on reform were not attuned to the Rector's initiatives. González Casanova called for extended participation in decision–making processes and in the direction of the University. However, he never suggested or allowed for the possibility of changing the governing structures, or the Organic Law in which they were founded, and that limited student and faculty intervention in running the institution.

Students emphasized the need for new governance structures and the democratization of the University. For the Rector, democratization was based on the creation of student and faculty representative bodies acting within the limits of the Organic Law. Students demanded structural change that the Rector was not willing to address. Instead of creating a common purpose for university reform, mutual misunderstanding of each other's dynamics and possibilities opened a breach between the progressive Rector and the progressive students.

Rector González Casanova's most difficult problems did not stem from his political conflicts with the student movement.[69] During the few years of his Rectorship, the presence of externally–controlled violent gangs and provocateurs of dubious origin constantly haunted him. In relation to this source of conflict against student organizations and the University as a whole, he assumed a clear stance as early as September of 1970.[70] In this declaration, the Rector established a clear distinction between gangs and legitimate student organizations. He rejected the intervention of police forces or the use of student groups to get rid of the gangs; and he denounced this phenomenon as an attempt to damage the University. In this and other statements that followed, the Rector made a strong argument against any type of government intervention in university affairs in a climate of constant aggressions against public universities all over the country.[71]

Attempts to secure the reorganization of the student movement at UNAM after the recent liberation of the 1968 leaders were again destroyed by the criminal action of the government on June 10, 1971. On this day, *Politécnicos* and *Universitarios* demonstrated in favor of students who defended the autonomy of the *Universidad Autónoma de Nuevo León*. *Los halcones*, a paramilitary group controlled by the Mexico City government, backed up by riot police squads, attacked the demonstration with the horrible consequence of "more than 30 deaths, an unknown number of disappearances, and hundreds of injured" victims.[72]

The Rector, the directors, and other University officials issued a public statement condemning the attack and demanding punishment for government officials responsible for these events.[73]

The effects of this new aggression were severe for the student movement. Large numbers of students withdrew from the movement. Divisions between groups became exacerbated. This new repressive action by the government "confirmed" the most radical theses of the futility of mass movements and the need for extreme actions. The movement was again reduced to small "vanguards." The most extreme positions joined diverse revolutionary armed groups that were already operating after 1968. Others boasted of revolutionary tactics and roamed around campus, with no political program or purpose, becoming fertile grounds for external infiltration and provocation within the University.[74]

Uncertainty and violence seemed to grow during 1972. The presence of gangs increased and the so–called radicals committed criminal activities all over campus, frequently engaging the *porros* in gang–wars,[75] and attacking legitimate left–wing students organized around the 1968 leaders.[76] Conservatives within and outside the University had supplemented these provocations with a spectacular campaign in the media demanding the reversal of university reforms and the intervention of judicial authorities.[77] The Rector and the University Council denounced this situation as an orchestrated campaign by ultra–reactionary forces against public universities and UNAM in particular.[78]

This is the End...

In this era of exacerbated authoritarianism and renewed populism, the government was not about to let the University constitute itself into an agent for social transformation and move away from State control. Diverse government figures, including President Echeverría, tried to interfere repeatedly in University affairs in an attempt to shape policies and establish external control over the institution. They contributed to create an environment of political confusion, confrontation, and lack of stability, and exploited these circumstances in order to weaken the administration and the moral standing of the University among other sectors of the population.

The next section shows that most evaluations of the extent of UNAM's autonomy completely failed to recognize the multiplicity of forms and pressures that the Mexican government used in order to ensure the allegiance of University authorities, to its policies, and political designs. This section elucidates diverse instances of government intervention through blunt methods of provocation and sabotage. It shows how the President, the articulating voice of party and government political positions, played a sophisticated political game by combining a policy of silence and complicity with an alleged support for the University and its directives.

The decline of the González Casanova administration began when a small group of graduates from teacher education schools (*normalistas*) occupied the Rectory building on July 31, 1972. Miguel Castro Bustos, Mario Falcón, and other members of the law–school combat committee (*comité de lucha*), where the "radicals" were organized, led this group.[80] The occupation occurred in the midst of a confusing set of petitions ranging from access to the Law School for the *normalistas* to compensation for the families of two students run over by a bus.[80]

The Rectory building was occupied during 31 days (from July 31 to August 30, 1972). During this period, the University was systematically portrayed in the media as a chaotic institution, lacking organization and discipline.[81] González Casanova was consistent in his statements about this problem. According to him, the University was the object of externally organized provocations in an attempt to destroy political liberties within UNAM and at the national level. He distinguished between legitimate student dissent and actions committed by criminals against the University. He demanded respect for University autonomy but also that the government act against these criminals at the judicial level. The discourse seemed contradictory when he stated that the University did not have the means to exercise any action against these individuals, and at the same time demanded that police forces not act within University grounds.[82]

Students and faculty almost unanimously repudiated the occupation of the Rectory building. Faculty and university authorities supported the Rector's statements. Student assemblies and combat committees (with the exception of those articulated around the Law School committee) denounced Castro Bustos, Falcón, and other members of the law–school combat committee, as provocateurs, linked to the PRI. At the same time they were annoyed by González Casanova's ambiguous accusations, arguing that they could bring about a generalized repression against student organizations.[83]

Printed media editorials supported the Rector but also demanded that he denounce the external and local groups that tried to damage the University.[84] On August 5, 1972, University authorities finally "revealed" the names of the occupants of the Rectory building. They also complained that judicial authorities had not acted against these criminals in spite of UNAM's legal accusations and that these armed individuals wandered all over the city.[85] Many demanded more information from González Casanova. Who were the external groups that used the occupants of the Rectory to attack the University?[86] The Rector never responded. He used rhetorical formulations very much in tune with the style of Echeverría's government accusations against ultra–reactionary forces and even US imperialism.[87]

It is not until August 11, 1972 that a government authority made a statement about this problem. The new attorney general of Mexico's Federal District promised to act against the occupants of the Rectory. He claimed that nobody knew where Castro Bustos and Falcón were hiding.[88] This was obviously false since many people had identified the places and restaurants where they gathered outside of the University City. The attorney general also said that politically it was very delicate for them to intervene since the University was so sensitive about the autonomy issue.

The nature of University autonomy had once again become a major issue in the discussion. González Casanova's statements were unclear. He said that the University does not demand any special statute or extraterritorial condition but he also required respect for autonomy and no intervention within UNAM.[89] This position was criticized as inconsistent by some intellectuals and by members of law associations. Ojesto, director of the School of Law, and accused by students of being the protector and financial support of *porros*,[90] undermined González Casanova on several occasions by stating that the autonomy was not at stake and that the police should intervene immediately to remove these criminals from the University campus.[91]

On August 14, President Echeverría made his first public statement about this problem. He said that the government would not act beyond the limits of autonomy and that no arrests would be made within UNAM unless the Rector requested the police to intervene on campus.[92] It was the first expression of Presidential support for González Casanova, but this statement also put enormous pressure on the Rector who was made in some way responsible for these criminals' free roaming of the University campus. Ojesto attacked again stating, "since when do judicial authorities have to wait for the Rector's permission to carry out the law?" He continued by saying that University autonomy had been made into a myth and the current situation was the Rectorship's problem.[93] Two days later the President put pressure on González Casanova once again by stating that "autonomy is not extra–territoriality" and continued "the members of the university shall either oust the invaders themselves or tell us how to throw them out."[94]

González Casanova stood his ground. An official statement by the University declared, "UNAM does not have nor demand a special statute; but the use of public enforcement agencies on campus is inconvenient." A few days later, in a symbolic public appearance with President Echeverría, González Casanova declared, "UNAM will only use persuasion."[95] For anybody who knew the rules of the Mexican political system the message was clear. For the time being González Casanova had recovered the President's support.

Media attacks on the Rector immediately decreased. The occupants of the Rectory building split. Most of the *normalistas* left and those who remained in the building offered to open negotiations. While some members of the law school combat committee contacted university authorities, Castro Bustos and Falcón physically attacked some of the 1968 leaders who had long since denounced them as provocateurs and members of the PRI. A few days later they abandoned the Rectory building.

Surprisingly, the police never detained Castro Bustos and Falcón. For almost two more months, they attacked student assemblies that had repudiated them and committed diverse burglaries and aggressions on campus. They wandered in and out of the University grounds and talked to police agents, but they were not caught. Finally on October 25, 1972 Castro Bustos was securely transported, in a vehicle that belonged to Ruben Figueroa, the PRI senator from the state of Guerrero, into the Panamanian embassy, whose government had awarded him political asylum. In his trip to the embassy, during his stay in that residence, and when travelling from there to the airport, he was protected by the Senator's personal secretary and followed by the police who never intervened to stop Castro Bustos.[96]

When the problem was over, everybody believed that behind the occupation there were many political actors, as González Casanova had stated. Over time, the roles of some University authorities like Ojesto and Carvajal Moreno, who had dealings with violent groups, were put into question.[97] Ojesto, Dean of the Law School, and Carvajal, a long time member of the

PRI and a second level University official, were implicated by students as the promoters of *porros* who continuously hindered progressive students' attempts to rebuild the movement and its organizations.[98] Ojesto's continuing attacks on González Casanova prove that at least there was animosity against the Rector. Even Guillermo Soberón, who very soon became Rector, has been mentioned in relation to these events because of his old relation with the Figueroa family. It must be said that there is no evidence to prove these rumors.

Through all the conflict González Casanova maintained a consistent attitude in attempting to keep internal unity, reject repressive solutions, preserve autonomy, and protect legitimate student organizations. He walked a fine line in demanding respect for University autonomy while rejecting the notion of extraterritoriality and still refusing to accept the intervention of police forces within UNAM. This sophisticated political position was based on solid principles, which he maintained at a high cost, making him the object of pressures and attacks by government officials, the media, and by some members of the University.

His reluctance to provide information about the real directors of this attack upon the University baffled friends and foes. It also made him the object of severe critiques. Many thought that accusations about conservative and ultra–reactionary plots tried to conceal real internal causes of University problems like students' lack of discipline and the inability of González Casanova's administration to control UNAM due to the Rector's permissiveness. Students considered that González Casanova's use of the ambiguous accusation discourse utilized by the Echeverría government opened the way for repression against them and that it was an attempt to protect the real aggressors within the government.[99]

None of these seem to be the real causes for his decision. Most probably, González Casanova's initial reluctance to even provide the names of the occupants was based on two issues. First, in his belief that legitimate radicalized student activists might have mistakenly been involved with the provocateurs. Second in his concern about the response of other students groups who were not part of the occupation, to the Rector's direct accusations and a possible reaction in favor of "fellow students" who could be the object of repression. When most of the student groups expressed their opposition to Castro Bustos and Falcón, and the occupants of the Rectory were clearly isolated from the student movement, González Casanova was in a position to allow direct accusations. In this way, the possibility of indiscriminate repression against the student movement, or the danger of extended legitimation of the occupation through martyrdom, were avoided.

González Casanova's silence about the major actors in these conflicts is more difficult to explain and can be very revealing of University–government relations. I present here the following hypothesis. González Casanova knew that high government officials, and perhaps even the President himself, were the instigators of this attack against the University. Castro

Busto's personal history, his membership in the PRI, his involvement in Echeverría's presidential campaign, and the impunity he had enjoyed from judicial authorities for many years,[100] were at least proof of government complicity. Presidential lack of support for the Rector for almost fifteen days seems like a good confirmation of government involvement.

González Casanova's naming of high government officials or the President implied a direct confrontation between the University and the government. The Rector must have thought that there was very little to gain from the confrontation that such an accusation would produce. Ambiguous accusations of conservative sectors of the government involvement did not bring the University administration in a collision course with the Executive. It even could exercise a small amount of pressure on the government itself. At the very least government officials had to not make these accusations credible or the guilty parts too evident. At the same time, it allowed the President to change his attitude or to control his subordinates without producing a loss of face to his administration.

According to Luis Villoro, a member of the *Junta* at that time, Flores Olea, López Cámara, Villoro, and others of González Casanova's closest friends at that time had suggested a different course of action. They called on the Rector to become "an activist, an agitator," to go to the schools and inform the community, as well as public opinion, about who was in fact responsible for this attack upon the University. However, according to this account, González Casanova did not accept that strategy. He did not want to take the risk of driving UNAM to a direct clash against the government. He thought that there was a strong possibility of a terrible repression and he feared that once the truth was known students, would resort to violent actions against the government.[101]

In the short run, González Casanova seemed to have been proven right. The provocateurs were out, the University appeared almost intact, and the threat of repression had been avoided. However, the costs for the University as a whole, and for Gonzalez Casanova's Administration, are enormous when judged from the distance of time.

González Casanova's calls for the expansion of participation and democracy within the University were not effective to coalesce faculty and students in retreat.[102] He even called for the defense of public Universities in the light of the aggressions against the public universities of Puebla and Sinaloa by the governors of these states.[103] However, the essential actors of University life, students and faculty, had almost entirely abandoned the field. In the midst of confusion and hopelessness, a new actor, the staff and manual workers, stepped on to the complex political stage of the University catching everybody by surprise.

Administrativos on Strike

The University did not settle down when the occupation of the Rectory building ceased. The provocateurs "holed in" at the Law School and launched their attacks against student assemblies or University property from there. González Casanova tried to inject some spirit on to the University by putting forward the possibility of a reorganization of governance and participation. He was willing to go as far as changing the University Statute, but change had to take place within the limits established by the Organic Law.[104] Very few students or faculty engaged this project, and it failed to connect with local governance reforms in the schools of Medicine, Economics, and Architecture.

Expressions of dissatisfaction against González Casanova's policies appeared among groups of faculty. These came from traditionally conservative schools like Business Administration.[105] Progressive faculty groups from the schools of Sciences and Economics, as well as social and political sciences, on the other hand, were willing to take the challenge of participating in the democratization of UNAM. The latter denounced the aggressions that the provocateurs directed against progressive students and faculty who tried to reorganize their communities[106] and called for a general campaign against violence.[107] However, the University was essentially stunned and demobilized and would not react in order to stop violence and build a more favorable political environment.

In this context staff and manual workers, generically labeled *los administrativos* (administrative workers), threatened to go on strike starting October 25, 1972, if their union was not recognized and a contract established between the union and the University. These demands were not new. Unionization attempts by the *administrativos* had begun in 1929.[108] Demands for the establishment of a labor contract between the University and its workers were rejected several times until 1944 when the right to unionize was explicitly denied in the approval of the new Organic Law.[109] Workers' unions continued to exist without recognition from the government or the University until 1966. In that year, Rector Ignacio Chávez, following the guidelines established by the Organic Law, promoted the approval of a special statute for administrative personnel and consequently created ATAUNAM (see previous chapter).[110]

Historical struggle for unionization and collective bargaining. In the transition from the older union to ATAUNAM, a new leadership emerged. The most prominent new representatives were Evaristo Pérez Arreola and Nicolás Olivos Cuéllar. The association and its leaders had established a sound relation with Rector Chávez.[111] Perhaps this explains why ATAUNAM did not become involved in the student movement against Ignacio Chávez in 1966. In 1968, however, the student movement engulfed the Association, like it did with most of the University. ATAUNAM's leaders participated within the teachers' coalition, adhered to the students demands, and subscribed to most of the professors' public communications.[112]

Like other sectors of the University, the 1968 student movement and its tragic outcome radicalized the administrative workers. Surprisingly, ATAUNAM's leaders criticized the students after the government had massacred them again on June 10, 1971 and accused the recently liberated 1968 leaders of being "well known agitators."[113] This statement damaged the relations with the student movement and would partially explain their contradictory attitude towards the workers' movement.

According to Pérez Arreola, the shift toward the left in the base and the leadership of the Association strengthened the idea of becoming a union with a labor contract and the right to strike.[114] The worker and employees' union (STEUNAM) was founded in November of 1971. ATAUNAM split in two factions, its legally constituted leadership promoting STEUNAM and the older generation rejecting it. Immediately it requested recognition from the labor board. On January 14, 1972 the labor board rejected STEUNAM's request. After filing several legal suits, STEUNAM began a series of demonstrations in June of 1972. Eighteen days after the occupation of the Rectory building the dissident ATAUNAM supported González Casanova and condemned the action by Castro Bustos and Falcón.[115] Soon after Castro Bustos and Falcón left the Rectory, STEUNAM resumed its demonstrations demanding recognition.

Hard bargaining. The worker's strike began on October 25, 1972. In spite of divisions among administrative workers,[116] STEUNAM successfully paralyzed activities in most of UNAM. A few hours before the strike the University Council issued a statement:

> Administrative University employees too, must promote their organization in an authentically representative and democratic way, preventing it from being manipulated against its own interests and those of the institution. The University Council supports the workers in the defense of their rights, among these the right to organize themselves within the norms that guarantee university autonomy, and without pretending to confront workers against each other, against students, or against University authorities damaging the good pace of our house of studies.[117]

STEUNAM's demands were simply described by Peerez Arreola as the "essential aspects of any union: recognition, collective bargaining, and the right to strike."[118] The union leadership considered that the Labor Board had denied them official recognition because of the moral weight of the University whose authorities had historically rejected the union.[119] STEUNAM wanted de facto recognition by UNAM: "we exist because of the will of University workers," they claimed.[120] STEUNAM demanded rights that were established in the Constitution and had been unfairly denied to them in the name of autonomy. STEUNAM's workers considered that these arguments were unfounded,

> the exercise of our right to unionize and to demand a collective bargain, through the use of the strike, in no way violates university autonomy, moreover it helps to reinforce it, since autonomy and unionization rights stem from the same legal order.... We respect and defend university autonomy and in turn demand respect for union autonomy.[121]

González Casanova recognized the workers' right to organize but, like Chávez and Barros Sierra before him, he did not think that unionization was compatible with University autonomy. In the name of the University Council he supported "the workers in the defense of their rights, among them the right to unionize within the norms that guarantee university autonomy."[122]

González Casanova declared that the University did not have the legal basis to formally recognize STEUNAM (this matter was for the labor board to decide).[123] His attempts to solve the problem were driven by two basic concerns: ensuring the compatibility of autonomy with workers' rights; and guaranteeing the democratic nature of the University workers' organization.[124]

Along these lines, the administration's proposals focused on establishing a collective agreement (not a contract) with the union. The agreement would be sanctioned by the Council through the Administrative Personnel Statute and could be revised every two years. The union's right to strike would be limited. It would only be allowed in case of repeated violations of the agreement but never as a mechanism to obtain economic or other material gains. On the second issue, the University administration completely rejected the union's demand to control worker's access (exclusiveness clause) and stability in the job (exclusion clause). These two clauses were the foundation of PRI controlled corporatist and authoritarian unions in Mexico.

The administration argued this point in terms of the need for a democratic union that would not hinder political liberties in the University. But this position also responded to a major tactical consideration in an attempt to deal with different workers' organizations independently. The administration recurrently made the mistake of overestimating the strength and legitimacy of alternative workers' organizations that challenged STEUNAM. This attitude was also the product of the extended misgivings about the leadership of the union.

Students reacted cautiously towards the workers' strike. The union leadership provoked distrust among student organizations on the left. The recent statement about the June 10 massacre caused much of this feeling. Some student groups and intellectuals were concerned that the strike was part of the campaign against public universities.[125] There were different reactions within the faculty towards the workers' strike. Large numbers of them remained distant and perceived the conflict as a problem between University authorities and workers. Those that did assume a political stance *vis-à-vis* the workers' movement ranged from open disapproval to moderate support.[126]

In two direct negotiations with STEUNAM's leaders, González Casanova offered to reform the Administrative Personnel Statute and establish a provisional agreement while a broader piece of legislation, sanctioning the special condition of university workers, was promoted at the level of Congress. STEUNAM consistently rejected González Casanova's offers and insisted on establishing a contract with the University. The talks failed and the second meeting ended in turmoil when students and workers shouted at and threatened González Casanova.[127] Later that same day, González Casanova resigned the Rectorship stating that

> my efforts have been useless to achieve a policy in accordance with my own principles, ...I would incur in grave responsibility if I allow the siege against the University, its autonomy, and the democratic and independent organization of its workers to continue, I consider it necessary for the University and the democratic and progressive movement in Mexico, that I present my resignation to the post of Rector of the *Universidad Nacional Autónoma de México*....[128]

González Casanova's resignations. González Casanova's resignation had multiple effects. STEUNAM stated that "the Rector's resignation put an end to the authorities' intransigence towards workers" and declared that it would maintain the strike until the new Rector signed a contract.[129] A sector of the student movement agreed with the union's leaders and demanded the Governing Board to appoint a new Rector.[130] In contrast, dozens of statements by faculty and students were published demanding that the Board not accept González Casanova's resignation.[131] While some faculty organizations declared their "unconditional support to the Rector," others rejected the resignation but also strengthened their support of the workers' union. Very important among these was the Professors and Researchers Union Council (*Consejo Sindical*), the most important factor in faculty unionization in the years to come. Finally, a sector of faculty in the research institutes started to voice their opinion against the strike and its effects on academic activities. This sector carefully recognized the worker's right to unionize but rejected the strike and became increasingly critical of STEUNAM.[132]

On November 20, President Echeverría stated that UNAM's problems would be solved very soon.[133] One day later the Governing Board unanimously decided not to accept the Rector's resignation.[134] The next day,

González Casanova presented three necessary bases for withdrawing his resignation. These were:[135]

1. university workers have to stop the strike in the shortest possible time, and the professors have to clearly state that we will make no concessions in principal matters regarding unionization and autonomy;

2. directors of schools and faculties as well as professors have to agree to a project for a new University statute and the creation of general and local mixed councils that are representative of faculty, students and workers insuring their legal participation in a democratic arrangement, the most effective for University governance; and

3. the federal government has to expressly acknowledge its commitment to stop any criminal actions against UNAM through the use of the law in such a way that there will never exist any doubt of leniency, arbitrary action, or impunity for material or intellectual aggressors against the University.

With the distance of time, the "bases" seem desperate, clumsy, and discordant with the situation in the University. It is not clear what González Casanova attempted with this declaration. Demands upon workers and the government were practically impossible to produce immediate results. The call upon directors and faculty was blunt in addressing an issue that produced internal tensions. González Casanova voiced a commitment towards governance reform in a desperate and ineffective way, probably trying to positively channel local conflicts over governance like the one taking place in architecture.

Echeverría and other members of the government "responded" to González Casanova's demands. In a joint appearance with González Casanova, the President made an ambiguous offer to legislate university autonomy in order to protect the institution from external threats and regulate the relations between the University and its workers. Federal and city attorney generals declared their commitment to stop criminal activities against the University. Minister of the interior Moya Palencia stated his agreement with the Rector's call.[136]

The effect within the University was not that spectacular. STEUNAM responded, "we will not stop the strike."[137] Guillermo Soberón, Sciences Coordinator during González Casanova's administration and future Rector of UNAM, openly expressed his disagreement with the Rector's conditions.[138] The *Junta* accepted the "bases", declared its support for the Rector, and summoned the *universitarios* to find adequate ways to express their differences and find solutions to the University's problems.[139]

González Casanova then appointed a group of his representatives to establish negotiations with the leaders of STEUNAM. Flores Olea (director of the Social and Political Sciences School), Fix Zamudio (director of the Legal Research Institute), and García Cantú were the most important negotiators for the administration. For a few days it appeared as if they would reach an agreement with STEUNAM's leaders Pérez Arreola and Olivos Cuellar on the basis of 14 points presented by the administration on November 28. Among the most important propositions were:[140]

a) workers and employees would freely decide their organization in unions, b) unions will be democratic and independent, c) there would be no single union to which all workers will forcibly be affiliated, d) university unions will be free to unite with other similar organizations, e) a collective agreement will be established with the union holding the largest membership, f) neither contracts nor salaries will be interrupted in case of strike, g) no exclusion or exclusiveness clauses, h) political affiliation will always be individual and voluntary.

STEUNAM's leaders rejected the new proposal and the union confirmed that position officially on December 6. STEUNAM insisted on a contract instead of an agreement. The administration's attempt to recognize the existence of several unions; however, seemed to be the most important cause, and was regarded as an attempt to divide the workers and an intrusion in the union's internal affairs.[141]

That same day, González Casanova asked the Governing Board to accept his resignation.[142] A day later the *Junta* did so, and opened a consultation process for the appointment of a new Rector.[143] In such a way, in the midst of internal conflicts and external threats, the most far–reaching and progressive attempt to reform the *Universidad Nacional* in all its history abruptly ended.

SUMMARY: POST–1968 POLITICIZATION

In the theoretical discussion of the conceptual frame for this work, I argued that the conflictive nature of education had a different meaning in democratic and authoritarian regimes. Throughout the historical analysis of the National University I have provided historical evidence of the multiplicity of roles that higher education has been forced to assume in the modern development of Mexico.

In the political sphere, the absence of political and societal institutions that escape corporate control by the State apparatus, and the tradition of relative autonomy of UNAM, explain the high degree of politicization of University conflicts and the importance of government intervention in the life of this institution. The University constituted a relatively independent environment where resistance struggles by conservatives, and increasingly during the 1960s by the left, articulated broader societal opposition to the authoritarian regime. Let us recall the examples of Vasconcelos' presidential campaign in 1929 and the struggle against socialist education between 1933 and 1938.

On no previous occasion, however, did UNAM, and other higher education institutions, pose a political challenge to the authoritarian regime of the PRI, as the student movement did in 1968. The criminal response to the student movement in 1968 by the Mexican government highlights the magnitude of this challenge to the political structures and practices of the PRI regime. It also set up a special state of mind in the government's depiction of the University as a political adversary and a dangerous enemy. Only a characterization like this can explain the political "treatment" applied by government forces to democratization attempts at the University after 1968. If compliance could not be established through the attraction of populist policies over the progressive *Universitarios*, the traditional methods of the State's political machine had to be used to bring UNAM back into the presidential project. In the pursuit of this task, the government found powerful conservative allies within the University itself.

A Democratic Interregnum

There have been different attempts to characterize the Barros Sierra and González Casanova administrations. Some authors (Jiménez Mier y Terán 1987; Kent Serna 1990) have argued that they represented a rupture with their predecessors in that they led a process of democratization and reorientation of University life. Others (Domínguez 1986; González Casanova 1997; Pinto Mazal 1974) consider that they represented the continuity of the traditions and values that gave birth to the 1945 Organic Law. Both characterizations are right to some degree; although interpretations of rupture and continuity tend to be somewhat exaggerated.

Historical evidence shows that there was both continuity and rupture. The two Rectors rejected demands for the transformation of the Organic Law and the elimination of the Governing Board. In the name of autonomy and academic freedom, they rejected university staff and manual workers' unionization, sharing the tradition of every other Rector since 1929. On the other hand, their interpretation of traditional values, their understanding of the social role of the University, and their political practices differed from those of most of their predecessors.

The discourse on autonomy and politics. I have shown above that Barros Sierra and González Casanova went beyond the spiritualist humanist interpretation of University autonomy. They went beyond the ideas of self–determination to demand absolute respect for the University as a space of liberty and democratic rights. González Casanova went even further to recognize that the University was a site of ideological struggle and an agent for social change. For him the University was a privileged space of social freedom and political liberties. This position contradicted the idea of the University as a homogeneous community put forward by Alfonso Caso in 1944. However, González Casanova was not always consistent in this argument. Much of his reticence to accept and recognize the existence of a union within UNAM was based on an idealization of the University as a community where labor–employer conflicts did not exist.

Implicitly, Barros Sierra and González Casanova had put forward an idea of autonomy that implied a relative degree of extra–territoriality. Both demanded the right to solve administrative and political problems of the *Universitarios* without external interference. Both rectors explicitly rejected the intervention of the police and the military on campus even in the face of criminal activities. In this attitude, they understood the status of the University as a special jurisdiction following the tradition of the colonial university.

Expansion of political participation. I have mentioned that Barros Sierra and González Casanova did not agree on the transformation of the 1945 Organic Law and the governance structure that it sanctioned. However, historical evidence shows that both of them were convinced of the importance of broadening faculty and student participation. They emphasized the need for increased representativeness in the election of faculty and student, university as well as technical council members.

Barros Sierra and González Casanova promoted and supported the creation of independent faculty and student organizations. Barros Sierra provided student representatives with information and support in order to get rid of *porros* that hampered student organizations. At the end of his administration, Pablo González Casanova called directors, students, and faculty to establish mixed committees, with equal faculty and student representation.

The Governing Board. The expansion of political participation even reached the *Junta de Gobierno.* Barros Sierra criticized the lack of legality of the Governing Board during Chávez's Administration given that some of its members' terms had already expired. He also censured Board members' subordination to the Federal Government. During the Barros Sierra and González Casanova administrations, the Governing Board became more diversified in terms of disciplines. The table below shows the disciplinary composition of the *Junta.*

Governing Board members by academic discipline 1945–66 and 1967–73 (years in the governing board)

	1945–1966		1967–1973	
Unknown	5	1.52%	6	4.00%
Social Sciences	0	0.00%	7	4.67%
Business Administration	15	4.55%	10	6.67%
Architecture	21	6.36%	13	8.67%
Medical and Biological Sciences	73	22.12%	26	17.33%
Law	115	34.85%	14	9.33%
Economics	22	6.67%	10	6.67%
Exact Sciences	13	3.94%	20	13.33%
Humanities	25	7.58%	10	6.67%
Engineering and Chemistry	41	12.42%	34	22.67%
Total	330		150	

Source: University Biographies

The table above shows that in only six years the weight of traditional professional groups in the Governing Board (medicine and law) decreased notoriously. Engineering and chemistry increased their presence as well as the exact sciences. These groups were Barros Sierra's constituency. The social sciences established some presence in the Board for the first time while economics maintained its influence and the humanities were slightly reduced.

The ideological diversification of the Board was not nearly as spectacular as its disciplinary broadening. Barros Sierra included two *carrillistas* and a democratic socialist like López Cámara. In three other appointments, he had to accept physicians who were members of Chávez's group. González Casanova appointed two *carrillistas* and another socialist. In the next chapter I will show that while these appointments brought new ideological positions into the Board, the conservative reaction of many members of the University establishment, after González Casanova's ousting, reoriented most members of the Board around the traditional *elitist* group.

Access and Social Role of the University

While important transformations occurred during Barros Sierra administration before 1968, it was during González Casanova's Rectorship that UNAM became involved in a profound reform project. I have reviewed González Casanova's ambitious University program. Barros Sierra and González Casanova addressed the expansion of student enrollment as an academic challenge and not an administrative problem. In González Casanova's view, enrollment growth was part of an overall expansion in the social responsibilities and commitments of a University that tried to recover its national standing by addressing the problems of national development and marginalization and by reaching to all the regions of the country.

Barros Sierra explicitly rejected government pressures to increase tuition or substitute federal funding by government sponsored individual payments as proposed by Ortiz Mena, Minister of the Treasury, in 1966. Chávez had explored the possibility of increasing student fees but later dropped the issue in the face of student unrest. González Casanova was adamant in his project to expand the possibilities of access for marginalized sectors of society. Tuition amounts and regulations put in place since 1949 remained practically the same.[144]

Political Implications of González Casanova's Downfall

González Casanova's resignation, sparked by the unionization process, was the product of an intense campaign against a democratic modernization of the University. This project became uncomfortable for the government and a threat for conservative sectors within UNAM. In spite of González Casanova's reluctance to address the modification of the Organic

Law, traditional power arrangements were being transformed in favor of broader participation and democratic representation. González Casanova's reform was truncated and his resignation had important implications for the reorganization of UNAM.

González Casanova's abrupt departure and of the dynamics of confrontation that was promoted within the University after June 10, 1971 had significant effects. Building upon the already difficult situation of the student movement after the 1968 and 1971 massacres, the role of the "radical" provocateurs generated distrust and fear towards the students. In the light of the whole dynamics of violence and confrontations between "radicals" and *porros*, large sectors of students distanced themselves from the movement. Student politics were restricted to multiple semi–isolated groups on the left and a few on the right. Political differences between students widened and the prospect of building broad social representative organizations in this sector disappeared. On this sad note, the students abandoned the center of University politics for almost fifteen years.

The principle of University autonomy that had been strengthened and enhanced in significance as a consequence of the 1968 student movement was weakened when the dilemma of autonomy versus extraterritoriality was presented. Autonomy appeared as an obstacle for stability and order when the principle of no external intervention in University affairs had to be invoked in the light of criminal actions that were heavily loaded with political meaning. Diminishing the symbolical value of autonomy set the tone of the loss of effective independence of the University *vis-à-vis* the federal government.

The political standing of González Casanova was eroded within the University, at the level of public opinion, and among the sectors of the Echeverría administration, that had initially supported the Rector. The conflict debilitated the Rector's will to continue at the head of UNAM. González Casanova was convinced that the President wanted him out and had even thought of formally presenting his resignation to the Board, during the occupation of the Rectory building.[145]

The emergence of workers' unionization in this context contributed to the polarization of UNAM. Tied to a conservative understanding of the relation between the University and its workers González Casanova was unable to cope with this new phenomenon of University life. Following their logic of confrontation, STEUNAM workers were oblivious to the effects of their struggle within the political system. With this, they contributed to the termination of González Casanova's democratization attempt. A few months later, in the midst of the workers' strike González Casanova resigned definitively.

The progressive reform impulse that was generated by the González Casanova administration was almost brought to a complete halt. After these events, academic transformations were sporadic. Organizational change was limited to the primary stages of the CCH and the open-university system, and governance changes in representation and access to decision-making for faculty and students were cut at the root. Not only that, local transformation efforts, like the *Autogobierno* in Architecture, and the mixed committees in Medicine and Economics, were hindered by extreme polarization within the community in the different schools.

Finally, it set the emotional and political foundations for a conservative restoration within the National University. Changes within the faculty were especially relevant. I will identify a few of them here. Large sectors of faculty shifted their political attitudes towards more conservative positions. They tended to identify participatory arrangements as lacking stability and order. If reform objectives were not completely disregarded, they concentrated more on internal issues, as opposed to a broader vision of university reform, in its relationship with other sectors of society and other higher education institutions.

NOTES

[1] The role of the presidential figure is extremely significant in understanding this period of University and State relations. The reader must be reminded that in the Mexican version of authoritarianism, called *presidencialismo*, the presidential figure articulates and symbolizes party and government official politics.

[2] Aguilar Camín and Meyer (1993).

[3] For example see chronologies on staff and manual worker unionization at UNAM in Pulido (1981) and (1986) as well as Silva Guerrero (1979). On academic unionization see document compilation by Woldenberg (1988). On the 1977 union conflict see Molina Piñeiro (1980).

[4] Consejo Nacional de Poblacion (1983 p. 7).

[5] Cárdenas (1996).

[6] In Carmona (1970 pp. 50,51).

[7] Jorge Carrión provides a summary of these conflicts and a good description of government treatment of the opposition during the López Mateos and Díaz Ordaz administrations (in Carmona 1970).

[8] For more details on these movements see Guevara Niebla (1988 pp. 24–37), and Mabry (1982 pp. 234–236).

[9] Among the most notable testimonies are those provided in Poniatowska (1971), and González de Alba (1971). Ramón Ramírez (1969) presents an excellent compilation of documents. Guevara Niebla (1978), and Zermeño (1978) among others, offer some of the best descriptions and analyses of the 1968 student movement. Insights on the internal tensions within university authorities and

their relations with the student movement and the government can also be found in García Cantú's conversations with Barros Sierra (1972).

[10] This will be the basic reference for the 1968 student movement unless an alternative source is explicitly cited.

[11] On July 26, 1968, two student demonstrations coincided in the streets of Mexico City. The traditional celebration of the Cuban Revolution over Batista involved students from the Communist Party and a variety of radical groups that were known as the New Left. The other demonstration, led by the *Politécnico's* corporatist student organization, protested the violent aggressions of *granaderos* (riot police) against students from one *Vocacional* (IPN's vocational schools). These aggressions occurred when riot police intervened to stop a brawl between the latter and some private school students after a street soccer match. The leaders tried to end both demonstrations. However, some participants decided to march towards the *Zócalo* (main plaza in Mexico City) to protest the violence against students. They were brutally attacked by the police, but students resisted the attack. Many students were beaten and taken to jail. The confrontation extended all over the old university quarters where students burned buses and built barricades around their schools.

Students and the government responded politically while combat continued around University and *Politécnico* schools. A few hours after the first confrontation, most of the schools at the *Politécnico* were on strike. Coordination meetings with the *Universitarios* were not very successful given that only the "left wing" schools at UNAM had reacted to these events. The government put forward its traditional response by blaming the events on a foreign communist conspiracy against the Mexican State. In an attempt to give credence to this version the police ransacked the office of the Communist Party and put a few of its members in jail.

On July 29, the government decided to occupy the *Preparatorias* and *Vocacionales* in the university borough and deployed the army. Infantry soldiers were able to overcome resistance in most schools. Fleeing from the army, students from the *Politécnico* and the *Universidad* took refuge in the latter's old Preparatory School building. Soldiers blew the famous wood carved door of this historical building with a bazooka and penetrated the school to beat and arrest its occupants.

[12] The CNH took the direction of the movement from August 2. Composed by elected student representatives of schools on strike, the CNH combined an enormous legitimacy with a slow and difficult operation. It was not suited for fast political responses but its simple composition and operating rules eliminated some of the most dangerous features of previous student movements like sectarianism and opportunism. It also prevented the possibility of leadership corruption through shared direction and direct student control.

[13] These were: a) liberty for political prisoners; b) dismissal of Mexico City's police chiefs; c) abolition of *granaderos* (riot police corps); d) abolition of Articles 145

and 145 *bis* of the Penal Code; e) indemnification of families of dead and injured students since July 26; and f) indictment of public officials responsible for police, *granaderos*, and army repression against the students. These demands did not seem particularly radical if analyzed outside the political context in which they were developed. At the time they carried an enormous symbolic weight way beyond their particular content. CNH's six demands embodied a serious criticism of the Mexican authoritarian political system.

14   A long tradition of leadership cooptation or intimidation by the government had created distrust in political negotiations. The student movement tried to prevent these practices by demanding public negotiations between student leaders and public officials. This demand was unacceptable for the government. Student distrust and vigilance are stated in a public manifesto published on August 10, 1968 in (in Flores Zavala 1972 pp. 160–161 and 162–163).

15   See *Declaración Pública del Consejo Universitario* (in Flores Zavala 1972 pp. 164, 165), and *Acta del Consejo Universitario*, sesión del 15 de agosto de 1968 (Alarcón 1979).

16   CNH's successful demonstration was tarnished when the army attacked a small student camp on the *Zócalo* a few hours after the demonstration. The government tried to shift the momentum by calling bureaucrats to a demonstration in favor of the regime on the next day. It proved to be a big mistake when bureaucrats chanted anti-government slogans in an attempt to show that they had been forced to demonstrate for the government. They too had to be dispersed by the army.

17   From Díaz Ordaz's *Informe Presidencial* (state of the nation address) (in Flores Zavala 1972 p. 180).

18   From Díaz Ordaz's *Informe Presidencial* (state of the nation address) (in Flores Zavala 1972 p. 180).

19   From Díaz Ordaz's *Informe Presidencial* (state of the nation address) (in Flores Zavala 1972 p. 180).

20   Poniatowska (1971 p. 277).

21   Student brigade members were persecuted all over the city. Many of them were imprisoned. The huge "silent demonstration" on September 13 seemed to restore the students' preeminence in a new demonstration of unity and organizational capacity. But the lack of response to presidential authority and the increasing effects of the movement on other sectors of society were too much of a threat for the government and so they bet their hand on a repressive "solution." Gangs organized by the government vandalized the city in the name of the students. The media depicted the movement as a plot by organized criminals and communist agitators. Deprived of safe meeting places within IPN and UNAM's campuses, the CNH operated under clandestine conditions for several days. Surprisingly the student brigades increased their activities all over the city.

22 The first meeting between student and presidential envoys took place a day after the army abandoned the University City in what seemed to be a message of goodwill.

23 President Díaz Ordaz assumed full responsibility for all government decisions regarding the 1968 student movement (*Informe Presidencial Septiembre*, 1969). Thirty years later the official archives of 1968 have not been made public.

24 *Novedades*, October 3, 1968.

25 *The Guardian*, October 3, 1968. In a recent book Aguayo (1998) compiles different versions on the number of dead during the Tlatelolco assault.

26 González de Alba (1971).

27 See Chapter 5.

28 *La Autonomía Universitaria. Declaración a nombre del Consejo Universitario*, 1966 (in Pinto Mazal 1974 pp. 275).

29 Pinto Mazal (1974 p. 276).

30 Barros Sierra issued a few statements with these warnings against provocateurs (see Flores Zavala 1972 pp. 148, 149, and 152). At the beginning of the student movement Barros Sierra did not express a clear definition regarding students demands but he used all the power of the institution and the action of diverse members of his administration to protect students, and negotiate their release from prison.

31 *Declaración Pública del Consejo Universitario*, 17 de agosto de 1968 (in Flores Zavala 1972 pp. 164–165).

32 González de Alba (1971)

33 See the letter that four of the most important student leaders of the CNH sent to Barros Sierra while they were still in jail (Barros Sierra 1972 p. 205). See also Zermeño (1978 p. 19).

34 See Barros Sierra (1972 pp. 102, 103), and Silva Herzog (1974).

35 (emphasis by the author). In his state of the nation address, Díaz Ordaz stated "I must add that I consider, and prominent lawyers agree with this criterion, that if recent events are examined with dispassionate objectivity and technical rigor, that legally there was no violation of university autonomy." A few paragraphs later, he added "the Mexican State has to keep watch over university autonomy and not only respect it..." (in Flores Zavala 1972 p. 177).

36 Barros Sierra (1972 p. 115).

37 *Excélsior*, México DF, April 25, 1970, p. 1–A.

38 See Appendix 2.

39 See Appendix 3.

40 See Appendix 4.

[41] At the time of the election of Barros Sierra's successor in 1970, the Board included 2 engineers, 1 accountant, 1 chemical engineer, 2 economists, 1 architect, 1 historian, 2 mathematicians, 1 sociologist, and 1 lawyer.

[42] Each of the factions had at least one third of the Board.

[43] The relation of forces within the University Council is probably expressed in the vote to select Barajas, a notable *carrillista* like Barros Sierra, to the Governing Board with 37 votes in favor and 20 against. Acta del Consejo Universitario del 24 de abril de 1970 (Alarcón 1979).

[44] Henrique González Casanova, the former Rector's brother, related that the two families were very close. According to his testimony Antonio Caso was an important father-like figure for them. When the elder González Casanova died, the two brothers spent a few days at Antonio Caso's home (González Casanova 1997).

[45] The latter three were members of the Editorial Board of the only opposition journal of that time *Política*. For some time, they had also been members of the *Movimiento de Liberación Nacional* (National Liberation Movement) a broad left–wing coalition originally led by former president Lázaro Cárdenas. In the early sixties, Flores Olea, González Pedrero, and López Cámara publicly stated that they were Marxists. At one time or another during the 1970s and 1980s they would all become government officials and even members of the PRI.

[46] University Biographies database.

[47] *Excélsior*, México DF, April 29, 1970, p. 1–A.

[48] Antonio Carrillo Flores and Jesús Reyes Heroles resigned before April 25, 1970. *Excélsior*, México DF, April 25, 1970, p. 1–A. Agustín Yáñez resigned on April 25, 1970. *Excelsior*, México DF, April 26, 1970, p. 1–A.

[49] *Excélsior*, México DF, May 2, 1970, p. 1–A.

[50] *Excélsior*, México DF, April 22, 1970, p. 13–A. The reader should be reminded that 8 votes are required to designate a director of faculty, school or institute while 10 is the established minimum for the selection of Rector.

[51] *Excélsior*, México DF, April 26, 1970, p. 13–A, and *Excelsior*, México DF, April 29, 1970, p. 1–A.

[52] In a recent interview with the author, Villoro stated, "Pablo [González Casanova] told me that the election was very difficult" (Villoro 1999).

[53] Villoro (1999).

[54] Ibidem.

[55] See *Excélsior*, México DF, from the beginning of April until mid May of 1970.

[56] For a full description of the student movement during these years see Guevara Niebla (1988 pp. 52–63). Guevara describes how in the midst of a repressive climate, where students were continuously harassed by the army and the police as well as by an increase of *porros* (gangs used against them), students resisted within the University in creative ways. But the sequel of the student massacre in

1968 initiated a process of sectarianism and vanguardism that characterized the student movement for many years after 1968. Some groups of students left the University to become involved in other social struggles and even in the creation of guerrilla organizations. Others focused their efforts on the transformation of their schools and the University as a whole.

[57] Domínguez 1986; Ramírez and Domínguez (1993; Universidad Nacional Autónoma de México (1985b).

[58] Ordorika (1996)

[59] See Appendix 5.

[60] See Pablo González Casanova's statements regarding the presence of gangs and violence at UNAM (González Casanova and Pinto Mazal 1983) and about the attacks upon the *Universidad Autónoma de Nuevo León* (pp. 144–147).

[61] Pablo González Casanova, *Discurso de protesta como Rector*, May 15, 1970 (Universidad Nacional Autónoma de México 1985b).

[62] See Pablo González Casanova's statement during the occupation of the Rectory building (in Pinto Mazal 1974 pp. 277–284).

[63] Universidad Nacional Autónoma de México (1985b).

[64] Ibidem.

[65] Ibidem.

[66] González Casanova and Pinto Mazal (1983).

[67] From *La Universidad y el Sistema Nacional de Enseñanza* (González Casanova and Pinto Mazal 1983).

[68] Aguilar Camín and Meyer (1993).

[69] In one of his first actions as a Rector, announced during his inauguration speech, González Casanova presented the University Council with an initiative demanding immediate amnesty for the professors and students imprisoned since 1968. The University Council approved the Rector's initiative and it was publicly addressed to the government. This attitude never changed even in the presence of student conflict. To González Casanova's credit, he never exercised a traditional authoritarian response against opposing students. More than that, he frequently assumed a protective role in favor of student organizations and explicitly rejected repressive "solutions" to conflicts within UNAM.

[70] *Declaración de Pablo González Casanova*, September 2, 1970 (González Casanova and Pinto Mazal 1983).

[71] *Declaración de Pablo González Casanova en defensa de la autonomía de la Universidad Autónoma de Nuevo León*, May 31, 1971 (González Casanova and Pinto Mazal 1983).

[72] (Comité Estudiantil de Solidaridad Obrero Campesina 1981). For a full description of these events see also Comité Coordinador de Comités de Lucha del IPN y la UNAM (1971); Comité Estudiantil de Solidaridad Obrero Campesina

(1981); *Revista Punto Crítico,* No. 1, January 1, 1972, México DF; and Guevara Niebla (1988).

[73] *Protesta contra la violencia y la represión* (González Casanova and Pinto Mazal 1983).

[74] Extremist groups with a radical discourse and lacking any coherent revolutionary program assumed fictitious armed struggle strategies within several universities. They called themselves *los enfermos* (the sick ones). In some cases they viewed universities as factories where teachers and authorities were considered the owners of the means of production and students the workers. They directed their discourse against the capitalist State and their actions against *reformists* (those groups on the left that attempted to produce university reforms) killing left-wing students and faculty and destroying student organizations (Comité Coordinador de Comités de Lucha del IPN y la UNAM 1971; Guevara Niebla 1988). At UNAM the former combat committee in the school of law organized this group. They threatened the 1968 student leaders and engaged in criminal activities all over campus.

[75] On June 13, 1972 radicals from the *comités de lucha* of Engineering and Law had a gunfight, with *porros* from the Francisco Villa group, in the midst of a student assembly in the School of Engineering. Two *porros* were killed, allegedly by their own friends. One of the most probable killers, Raúl León de la Selva a "radical" from Engineering and a friend of Castro Bustos and Falcón, was never prosecuted. Judicial authorities accepted his version of these events as true in spite of alternative versions by several witnesses and participants. *Excélsior,* June 14 and 15, 1972.

[76] Martínez Della Rocca (1997).

[77] A group of faculty from UNAM met with President Echeverría on December 12, 1971 depicting the University as "a gutter" and demanding the government's intervention against criminals on campus. González Casanova walked a fine line and rejected this intervention while accepting that UNAM did not claim any special privilege or an extra-territorial condition (González Casanova and Pinto Mazal 1983). From June of 1971 to December of 1972, newspapers *Excélsior* and *El Universal,* were full of police reports about the National University; statements by conservative faculty, businessmen, and public officials demanding an end to this "chaotic situation;" the attorney general and the chief of police offering to intervene; and paid political statements by different factions commenting on these events.

[78] *Excélsior,* June 14 , 1972 p. 1–A and June 16, 1972 p. 1–A.

[79] Romo Medrano (1997) compiled a long sheet on Miguel Castro Bustos. According to the information she presents, Castro Bustos had been a registered student in the School of Law since 1956. He had been part of a group that split the opposition to Chávez's first election to the Rectorship, in 1961, and ended up supporting the new Rector. He became a council member of the FUSA, the student federation created with Chávez's support, but later broke up with this

organization when he led a group of applicants that had been rejected by UNAM. After insulting Chavez he was expelled from the University for six months. Between 1961 and 1966 Castro Bustos was involved in all sorts of protests and scandals, put in jail for failing to pay his bill in a bar, and later inexplicably liberated. After an incursion against the Rectory building in 1964 Castro Bustos was expelled definitively from the University. Detention orders were issued against him and others, but the police never detained them. Castro Bustos was identified in 1965 as a member of the youth organization for the PRI, and a member of that party since 1957. He supported Luis Echeverría's presidential campaign in Nayarit and Sinaloa in 1969 (*Excélsior* December 19, 1969). Mario Falcón was never registered as a student at UNAM.

[80] *Excélsior*, August 1, 1972, p. 17–2A, and August 2, 1972, p. 24–2A.

[81] It is possible to perceive the existence of this campaign on the media when reviewing Mexico City newspapers like *Novedades*, *El Universal*, *Excélsior*, and others following the June 10, 1971 aggression against the students. A study by the University Center for Cinematography Studies (CUEC) revealed how the electronic media presented biased in an attempt to portrait the University as a disorganized and unstable institution (*Excélsior*, August 12, 1972).

[82] See González Casanova's statements along the conflict in *Excélsior*, June 14, June 16, June 20, August 3, August 18, and August 19, 1972.

[83] See *Excelsior* August 4, 5, 8, and 9, 1972. The organization of progressive student expression against the occupation was centered on the combat committees of Psychology, Sciences, Economics, and Philosophy. Castro Bustos and Falcón attacked the leaders of these committees, imprisoned in 1968, who had been recently released from jail. One of the most noticeable is the attack on Salvador Martinez Della Rocca during a student assembly in the Sciences faculty on August 25 (*Excélsior*, August 26, 1972).

[84] Since the assassination of two students in the School of Engineering, op-ed writers, and editorials in *Excelsior* demanded more information from Rector González Casanova. A few examples are the articles by Gringoire (*Excélsior*, June 17, 1972); Trueba Urbina (*Excélsior*, June 20, 1972); Gringoire (*Excélsior*, August 5, 1972); *Excélsior*'s editorial piece (*Excélsior*, August 7, 1972); and more.

[85] *Excélsior*, August 6, 1972.

[86] See footnote # 79, *supra*. Also Leñero (*Excélsior*, August 8, 1972), statement by the PAN (the Conservative Party) (*Excélsior*, August 8, 1972), and Cosío Villegas (*Excélsior*, August 12, 1972 and September 9, 1972).

[87] *Excélsior*, September 5, 1972 and October 21, 1972.

[88] *Excélsior*, August 11, 1972.

[89] González Casanova in *Excélsior*, August 3, 1972.

⁹⁰ On several occasions, student leaders and assemblies that later rejected the Rectorship occupation had pointed at Ojesto as the person who organized and financed the *porros* of the Francisco Villa group (*Excélsior*, June 15, 1972).

⁹¹ Ojesto demanded police intervention on campus to detain Castro Bustos and Falcón (*Excélsior*, August 7, 1972). One week later Ojesto and Alfonso Noriega, former member of the Board, argued that police forces should have free access to the University in order to prosecute criminals. They say that autonomy had become a myth (*Excélsior*, August 14, 1972).

⁹² Echeverría declared: "Nothing beyond the autonomy; no arrests will be made within UNAM; only if the Rector makes the request" (*Excélsior*, August 15, 1972).

⁹³ See footnote # 88, *supra*.

⁹⁴ Statement by President Luis Echeverría (*Excélsior*, August 17, 1972).

⁹⁵ See González Casanova's statement in *Excélsior*, August 19, 1972.

⁹⁶ Senator Rubén Figueroa's intervention to protect Castro Bustos is clearly established by the use of his car and the presence of his secretary Primo Reyes (*Excélsior*, October 25, 1972, p. 20–A). Figueroa later became governor of the state of Guerrero and one of the most polemic political figures during the Echeverría and López Portillo administrations. He was famous for his use of violence and terror as political methods.

⁹⁷ Villoro considers that Ojesto and Carvajal Moreno operated directly against González Casanova (Villoro 1999).

⁹⁸ See diverse statements by student leaders in *Excélsior*, June 15 and 17, 1972.

⁹⁹ See resolutions of student assemblies (*Excélsior*, June 15, 1972).

¹⁰⁰ For information on Castro Busto's political trajectory see footnote # 76, *supra*.

¹⁰¹ Villoro (1999).

¹⁰² González Casanova made different statements after the Rectory building was abandoned by the provocateurs. He called for decentralization of authority and for the establishment of a political plan against violence (*Excélsior*, September 20, 1972). He also called the community to assume more governance responsibilities (*Excélsior*, September 22, 1972).

¹⁰³ See González Casanova's statement (*Excélsior*, October 21, 1972).

¹⁰⁴ *Excelsior*, September 20, 1972.

¹⁰⁵ In a meeting with Business School professors, the faculty representative demanded an end to "weaknesses and ambiguities in regard to the necessary State function of exercising penal action within campus" (*Excélsior*, September 22, 1972).

¹⁰⁶ Paid advertisement in *Excélsior*, September 30, 1972.

¹⁰⁷ Paid political advertisement in *Excélsior*, October 20, 1972.

¹⁰⁸ The first employee union at UNAM (UEUNMA) was founded on September 26, 1929. Rector García Téllez presided over the foundation ceremony. But peace-

ful relations with the administration would not last. The first conflict occurred in 1931 over the reduction of employee salaries approved by the University Council. A first contract was drafted and approved but later rejected by the University Council. Stemming from one branch of the UEUNMA, a few years later, in the wake of the 1933 Organic Law, the labor relations board registered the first employee and workers union for the University (SEOUAM). But the new union was not recognized within the University. Rector Gómez Morín stated that there could be no compatibility between the University and a union. SEOUNAM virtually disappeared by 1935. The other branch of UEUNMA revived this organization in 1935. In 1938 Rector Chico Goerne refused to recognize the union (that tried to become SEOUNAM once again) and rejected the notion, presented by the employees, that the University was their boss. The confrontation increased when the Rector tried to create a parallel union controlled by the administration until the leaders of SEUNAM were expelled from the University. The workers of the university press created another union (STIU) in 1938 but no linkages were established between the two unions (Pulido 1986).

[109] The only aspect of the proposal sent by the Constitutive University Council that was debated by Congress was the proposal, by congressmen who were also union representatives, to establish union rights for University workers. It was finally rejected (Pulido 1981).

[110] SEOUNAM lost its registration in 1949 and a new union, STUNAM, is created in its place. In spite of not being officially recognized, STUNAM leaders met with different rectors and obtained some benefits for its workers. It changed its denomination to SEOUNAM again in 1963. In 1966 it disappeared when ATAUNAM was created (Pulido 1981).

[111] Evaristo Pérez Arreola, the most important leader in the history of workers' unions within UNAM, explains that Chávez was patronizing but trustworthy. The leaders admired Chávez and were thankful for the workers' statute and the recognition of the association in spite of its severe limitations. The relationship with Barros Sierra was not as good. Barros Sierra had brought a modern management team from his government office, and the administrative workers at UNAM did not accept this situation easily. According to Perez Arreola, the new administrators earned much higher wages and displaced many workers (Pérez Arreola 1998).

[112] Pulido (1981 pp. 54–63).

[113] *La ATAUNAM ante los acontecimientos sucedidos el día 10 de junio...* (in Pulido 1981 pp. 68, 69).

[114] Pérez Arreola (1998).

[115] *Excélsior*, August 18, 1972.

[116] The media and Pulido's account of this struggle record at least two additional workers' factions. One of these was the old generation of ATAUNAM directives who established an alternative executive committee to that of Olivos Cuellar and Perez Arreola and rejected the union and the strike. The second faction consti-

tuted an independent strike council and created a parallel union called SITU-NAM (Pulido 1981).

[117] Declaración del Consejo Universitario in *Excélsior*, August 26, 1972.

[118] Pérez Arreola (1998).

[119] Pérez Arreola said that he did not believe that González Casanova had requested the government to make this decision but that the Labor Board, which included many former *universitarios*, had tried to comply with this anti-union tradition (Pérez Arreola 1998).

[120] Pérez Arreola (1998).

[121] *El Dia*, October 23, 1972.

[122] *Excélsior*, October 26, 1972.

[123] *Excélsior*, October 28, 1972.

[124] *Excélsior*, October 28, 1972.

[125] *Punto Crítico*, # 11, November, 1972.

[126] (Woldenberg 1988 p. 50).

[127] A faction of the student movement led by members of the communist party youth now voiced the support for the union and its leadership (Woldenberg 1988 p. 52). In this meeting they challenged González Casanova in harsh terms (*Excélsior*, November 17, 1972). Perhaps this change in some students' attitudes was the product of Pérez Arreola's and Olivos Cuéllar's recent entry to that same party (Pérez Arreola 1998).

[128] *Excélsior*, November 18, 1972.

[129] *Excélsior*, November 18, 1972.

[130] Once again it was the leaders of the communist youth that argued that González Casanova's resignation was a demonstration of the administration's lack of capacity to solve the current problems of the University (*Excélsior*, November, 18, 1972).

[131] See letters to the editor, editorials, and op-ed pieces, and paid political advertisements in *Excélsior*, November 18 to 22, 1972.

[132] For a detailed description of faculty attitudes towards STEUNAM and González Casanova's resignation see Woldenberg (1988).

[133] *Excélsior*, November 21, 1972.

[134] *Excélsior*, November 22, 1972.

[135] *Excélsior*, November 23, 1972.

[136] *Excélsior*, November 24, 1972.

[137] Statement by leader Nicolás Olivos Cuéllar (in *Excélsior*, November 24, 1972).

[138] Guillermo Soberón explained that González Casanova privately presented a set of conditions that were unacceptable to the Board. These were then modified

into the "bases" that appeared publicly. Soberón did not like these either but thought that the first set was even worse (Soberón Acevedo 1994).

[139] *Excélsior*, November 24, 1972.

[140] *Excélsior*, November 29, 1972.

[141] *Excélsior*, December 3 and 6, 1972.

[142] *Excélsior*, December 7, 1972.

[143] *Excélsior*, December 8, 1972.

[144] Universidad Nacional Autónoma de México. Comisión Técnica de Estudios y Proyectos Legislativos (1977).

[145] Luis Villoro says that González Casanova had talked to members of the Board about resigning and was talked out of this position. Villoro is still convinced that it was Echeverría himself who wanted the Rector out (Villoro 1999).

A Conservative Restoration
The University in the Crisis of Authoritarianism (Part II)

> No hay nostalgia peor que añorar lo que nunca jamás sucedió.
>
> Joaquín Sabina. *Con la frente marchita*

This chapter deals with a period of intense political confrontation within UNAM. The purpose of addressing these historical events is to show specific facets of the political arrangement of the University and the relations between this institution and the State in the light of internal political conflict. The historical events that are analyzed in this chapter highlight the way dominant groups of the University coalesced in response to perceived external political threats by University actors, outside the legitimate political apparatus. They also shed light on how the dominant political faction interpreted University traditions to define itself and its political adversaries in the face of political confrontation. Finally, they draw the attention to the objects of political dispute and the way in which the groups that control the University agenda defined them in this moment of conflict.

This chapter completes the task of revealing the political nature of the University in its internal workings and in the dispute over the institution. It also provides additional elements for the analysis of the relationship between the University and the State and the assessment of autonomy. This chapter provides evidence of additional processes that were not considered in Levy's study of autonomy at UNAM. In the introduction to this work, I have noted that Daniel Levy explicitly established a distinction between University and State. He argued that intra–university power distribution, while important, should not be confused with autonomy. Evidence provided in this chapter will show that by assuming this stance Levy missed important aspects that have a profound effect on University autonomy.

In failing to focus on internal conflict and by not recognizing that the University is simultaneously an arena and an object of political dispute, Levy failed to understand the fact that the government played a significant role in these confrontations. Historical evidence highlights two relevant factors in relation to autonomy. On the one hand, the government interfered through different mechanisms and in varying degrees in the handling of these conflicts including definition of political strategies, conducting negotiations, etc. in direct violation of the right to solve internal conflicts without external intervention. On the other hand, government support for the University administration was provided in exchange for political loyalty and subordination to government designs, with consequent negative effects on autonomy.

Levy also failed to understand that internal political arrangements in the face of conflict constrained and shaped University autonomy. I show how in the confrontation against the unions and democratization attempts, dominant groups within UNAM relied heavily on the expansion of the bureaucratic apparatus that would enhance their operational capacity and broaden their constituency. This body developed political interests and expectations of political careers in the government apparatus. The pursuit of these expectations provoked an internal renunciation of the autonomous capacity to administer the University.

Longing for the "Golden Years"

The confusion and lack of political stability that prevailed in Mexico and consequently in the University during the mid–1970s was used to legitimize a conservative restoration. This occurred when the regime and traditionalist sectors within UNAM coincided in their objective to stop González Casanova's project. In this context, dominant groups of the University longed for an idealized version of UNAM of 1945 to 1966 with profound nostalgia. This nostalgia and the polarization of the University opened the possibility for a reorganization of alliances within the political system. The discourse about the University changed radically. University traditions of autonomy and academic freedom were now used to discredit democratization attempts. Instead of political liberties and critical attitudes, autonomy and academic freedom came to symbolize an aspiration for order and stability.

With the appointment of Rector Soberón, the role of the University was redefined. The new administration renounced any project of national scope, any social responsibility, or any commitment for change. In fact, the goals of the University were reduced when one of its activities and sectors, the research subsystem, was the ultimate object of attention and promotion by the administration.

The political environment was narrowed. Political opportunities within the governing structures were non–existent for those who opposed the dominant group. Participation outside the legitimate structures was condemned and systematically attacked. Collegial bodies were subordinated to executive authorities in their practices and functions. The spaces for student and faculty representation were controlled or destroyed. University regulations and traditions were used constantly to confront those who struggled for alternative university projects.

During this period, the authoritarian political system of the University also presented its harshest features. The downfall of the opposition, symbolized by the defeat of academic unionization, opened the way for a long period of exacerbated authoritarianism and the consolidation and expansion of an expanding University bureaucracy that played a significant role within the new dominant coalition.

THE JUNTA APPOINTS A NEW RECTOR

During González Casanova's Administration (from 1970 to 1972), four changes were produced within the Governing Board. The *Junta* appointed lawyer Ricardo García Villalobos, one of the leaders of the 1929 movement, to substitute for lawyer José Castro Estrada. The University Council elected philosopher Luis Villoro, physicist Alba Andrade, and engineer Emilio Rosenblueth. Villoro has been the most progressive member of the Board. He was private secretary to Chávez during his first Rectorship and was now part of González Casanova's closest circle. Rosenblueth had been Barros Sierra's friend and collaborator. He was one of the most important constituents of the populist scientists. Alba Andrade was also related to this group in the physics research institute.

The political orientation of the Governing Board had shifted by December of 1972. If we analyze the political composition of this body, by considering the old alliance between the populist scientists and the liberal left, we would show a clear majority of this group *vis-à-vis* the elitist scientists or *chavistas*. However, the political events of 1971 and 1972 had a profound effect in the relation of forces within the Board. The alliance split when the populist scientists and liberal leftists presented two different candidates: Graef Fernández and Flores Olea respectively. The elitist scientists presented Guillermo Soberón.

Dr. Graef Fernández had directed the Physics Institute and the School of Sciences at UNAM. He was an internationally recognized physicist who had pioneered the development of nuclear energy in Mexico. Graef had been director of higher education and scientific research in the Ministry of Education several times since 1927. He was notable among the populist scientists with Sandoval Vallarta, Barros Sierra, Rosenblueth, and Alberto Barajas (the last two members of the Governing Board at the time).

Lawyer Flores Olea was director of the Social and Political Sciences School. Flores Olea was a well-known Marxist. He had been founder of opposition journal *Política* with Carlos Fuentes, González Pedrero, and López Cámara (a member of the *Junta*). Flores Olea had been a leader of the *Movimiento de Liberación Nacional* (National Liberation Movement), a broad leftwing coalition founded by former president Lázaro Cárdenas.

Flores Olea was one of González Casanova's strongest supporters as well as a close friend and political ally.

Dr. Guillermo Soberón was a biochemist, former director of the Biomedical Research Institute of UNAM, and sciences coordinator under González Casanova. Soberón was the candidate of the elitist scientists and the medical professionals. At the time of the election, he was perceived as a prestigious scientist, with no political definition.[1] He was very close to Zubirán, his mentor, and to Chávez who was Soberon wife's uncle. Chávez explicitly conveyed his full support for Soberón to several members of the Board.[2]

According to Luis Villoro, then a member of the Board, the selection was very difficult and it took many rounds to chose the new Rector. Villoro explains that initially the proportion of votes was "40% for Flores Olea, approximately 35% for Soberón, and more or less 25% for Graef."[3] He continues: "the Board leaned towards Soberón because the minority that supported Graef switched to Soberón and gave him the majority."[4]

This move was loaded with symbolism. A historical alliance between populist scientists and the liberal left was broken in the process. The new arrangement of forces did not take place only within the Governing Board. This arrangement was the expression of a conservative reaction that had reached broad sectors of the faculty at UNAM that had been profoundly shaken by internal violence, external threats, and the emergence of administrative unions. Certain members of the *Junta* believed that the election of Flores Olea would be a continuation of González Casanova's policies and they considered these dangerous for the University.[5] At that time, Soberón did not look like the right–wing candidate, "he appeared as ideologically neutral in the face of populism that was attributed to Pablo [González Casanova]."[6]

The Governing Board had allegedly carried out a consultation with the community starting on December 12, 1972. This "consultation" took place while the strike was going on and during the Christmas break. When the Board met, at the beginning of January, Guillermo Soberón was appointed Rector by "a majority vote" on January 3, 1973.[7] There is no evidence of presidential intervention in this process. Villoro stated: "I can not provide evidence of external intervention by the President but I am pretty certain there was."[8]

RECTOR SOBERON'S FORCIBLE ENTRY

Soberón assumed the Rectorship in January 8, 1973. From the very beginning of his administration he projected a heavy–handed image that contrasted with González Casanova's emphasis on dialogue and negotiation. Soberon's inauguration was symbolic of this attitude. He entered the School of Medicine, headquarters of the workers' strike, pretending to hold the inaugural ceremony in that place. Surrounded by some faculty and students, others claim that also by *porros* and security guards, he had to make a hurried pledge in the parking lot and run away in the midst of projectiles and insults by groups of students and workers.[9]

Soberón inherited a massive and continuously expanding University. Student enrollment had grown above 130 thousand students, a 40% increase since 1968.[10] Part–time teachers, numbering 11 thousand, constituted the main faculty body next to around 600 and 280 fulltime professors in the institutes and schools respectively.[11] Faculty as a whole had grown almost 20% with a significant expansion of fulltime professors. The administrative body had reached approximately 10,200 workers, 12% more than in 1970. Since 1970, the University had experienced a considerable increase of the University budget (80% in real terms) thanks to a sustained growth in the federal subsidy.[12]

The End of the Strike

When González Casanova resigned, negotiations between STEUNAM and the administration had almost broken down. On January 2, 1973, Fix Zamudio and Flores Olea, published the terms of a possible agreement with STEUNAM with a unique disagreement over the exclusion and exclusiveness clauses, remaining in the agenda.[13] Solution had been very near, but it did not happen until the new Rector was appointed. The strike continued while the remaining members of the González Casanova administration promoted rival organizations to STEUNAM and established a "collective agreement" with SITUNAM that managed to end the strike in a few schools.[14] But STEUNAM had been able to maintain a high degree of internal cohesion by the time it entered this new stage of negotiations with the new administration. As soon as he was appointed Soberón put together a new negotiating committee with Fiz Zamudio and Casillas, director of the School of Engineering. On January 11, 1972, UNAM's authorities and STEUNAM reached an agreement. The agreement was based on the 12 points published by Fix Zamudio and Flores Olea and included a qualified admissions clause (that subtituted for exclusiveness) and no exclusion article.

The issues that prevented STEUNAM from reaching an understanding with González Casanova had been qualified or dropped. STEUNAM settled on having a collective agreement and not a contract. In the end, the main difference between the new agreement and the last proposal of the González Casanova administration was the unchallenged recognition of STEUNAM as the sole representative of UNAM's *administrativos*. The terms of the accord that ended the strike are evidence themselves of how González Casanova's administration mishandled the situation by trying to interfere in the union's internal practices. They also show, however, that STEUNAM was more willing to reach an agreement after having provoked the fall of the previous Rector.

SOBERON'S UNIVERSITY PROJECT

According to Guillermo Soberón, when the members of the Governing Board interviewed him, before they decided who was to be the new Rector, he enunciated the issues that would comprise his program. These can be summarized as limiting student enrollment, stopping political activism within the University, separating the National Preparatory School and the recently created CCH from UNAM, and charging higher fees to students.[15] Two of these concerns became the core of Soberon's program for UNAM: political stabilization and enrollment contention (Kent Serna 1990 p. 17).

Soberon's project ran almost in the opposite direction to that of González Casanova. Soberón openly disagreed with the former Rector's ideas in several aspects. Regarding access, Soberón established limits to student enrollment at the baccalaureate and undergraduate levels. He was convinced that the CCH project should have been developed outside UNAM.[16] In his inauguration speech Soberón declared:

> The constant growth of the number of students in the University creates serious difficulties for the efficient performance of our functions. When the high number of those who will soon knock at our doors are considered, we must conclude that it is impossible to totally satisfy that demand, **running the risk of having that plethora annihilate us.**[17]

The content and style of this statement is a continuation of the one made by Chávez in his own inauguration twelve years earlier: "the human torrent of sixty thousand young people that pours upon the University, compromises everything, drowns everything."[18]

Regarding the social role of the University, the positions were also contradictory. While González Casanova was convinced that UNAM could play a major role in transforming social and political relations at the national level, Soberón emphasized the academic nature of the institution in its most traditional forms.[19] As we saw above, González Casanova was concerned with expanding the interaction of the University to other spheres like production, healthcare, and the family. This drive to assume a broader social role was expressly rejected by Soberón:

> In the social division of labor, the University's role is to teach. The exercise of politics, the organization of business, and the practice of religion, for example, are some of the tasks that do not concern the University; they correspond to areas of competency that are different from those of the University.[20]

Gonzalez Casanova had expressly tried to integrate University activities (teaching, research, and outreach) and levels (baccalaureate, undergraduate, and graduate). The CCH project had been created with the double purpose of articulating activities and levels, as well as extending the reach of the National University to other sectors and regions. Soberón viewed the University as a system and reorganized it in separate subsystems splitting functions and levels apart. The University was reorganized into the following subsystems under distinct administrative branches:[21]

a. Teaching, was organized in schools and faculties, under the administration of the secretary general;

b. Scientific research, organized in the institutes and centers, under the administration of the sciences and humanities coordinators;

c. Outreach in specific entities outside the schools and institutes, under the administration of the outreach coordinator;

d. Communication, under the secretary of the Rectorship;

e. Administration and financial issues under the control of the general administrative secretary; and

f. Judicial and legal matters under the attorney general of the University.

Each of these subsystems was supposed to be hierarchically equivalent. This situation in itself would be enough to show that the University was viewed more of as a political and administrative problem than as a cultural challenge.[22] However, the subsystems were not equally relevant for the new administration. For Soberón, the core of academic activities and the essence of the University were concentrated in research.

> Research is a primordial function of universities. It is an essential component of higher education; it signifies an element of constant renovation of knowledge and, for graduate studies, it constitutes an indispensable platform. The best teachers are those that search for knowledge. Research is in this way the means through which education institutions can affect national and regional problems.[23]

But in his organization, research did not play a connecting role for the rest of University activities. This subsystem became the spoiled sector of the University. Soberón viewed this subsystem as a fundamental constituency that had preserved, and would allow, the continuation of University traditions.

Research has been able to develop in an amazing way at UNAM in spite of immeasurable institutional growth at the end of the sixties and beginning of the seventies, and in spite of the conflicts that have afflicted it [the University]....

...the number of students and conflictive situations affected the places where teaching occurs –schools and faculties– in a primordial way and the institutes and centers very little. ...

This particular condition has thus preserved, institutes and centers in a certain way, and has affected faculties that have developed research divisions less. We are fully convinced that the thrust provided to scientific research in the last few years, was a very favorable factor for successfully resisting the attacks, mainly of union type, that were made upon the institution.[24]

A vast amount of resources and attention was directed into this area of the University to the detriment of schools and faculties. While the baccalaureate component of the CCH was academically and financially neglected and subjected to intense political control, its graduate component was used to strip graduate programs away from schools and faculties and into the research institutes.[25]

DISPUTE OVER THE UNIVERSITY

The years from 1973 to 1977 were marked by political disputes over the nature and organization of the university. Soberón clearly understood that the possibility of establishing his project would be subject to a vast political confrontation between left and right.[26] In this perspective, the administrative, judicial, and communication subsystems became extremely relevant as basic tools in the political conflict. This situation explains the relevance of these subsystems in the organizational arrangement of UNAM during the Soberón Administration.

Soberón tried to define the terms of this political confrontation as a battle against massification, violence, anarchy, and unionization.[27] In this way he attempted to characterize the disputes over governance and democratization; unionization of faculty and administrative workers; demands for access to higher education; as well as what he called "criminal and revolutionary violence."[28] In his discourse, all of these were depicted as different components of an articulated attempt to use the University as a political device for revolutionary purposes. These would be accomplished through an intentional misrepresentation of autonomy as extraterritoriality, an attack on academic freedom, and the subversion of the technical nature of the institution established in the 1945 Organic Law.

Massification

In Soberón's view massification was the most severe problem of the University and one of the most important causes of University violence and anarchy. It merited a significant reference during his inauguration address (see above). The expansion of student enrollment had concentrated the attention of every University administration since the Rectorship of Nabor Carrillo. The attitudes of these administrations had been divergent. While Chávez attempted to establish a selection mechanism to contain student growth, Barros Sierra and González Casanova (especially the second) had concentrated their efforts on expanding University options for students who demanded access. Barros Sierra established the automatic transition from University preparatory schools to undergraduate education in opposition to Chávez's selection exam. González Casanova created a new baccalaureate option, the CCH, established the open–university system, and committed the University to the creation of five more campuses.

Soberón had to live with the CCH (but he stopped the creation of another five CCH schools as planned in the original project) and continued the expansion of the decentralized campuses. The ENEP project was hurriedly designed between 1973 and 1974. The first ENEP in Cuautitlán was founded that same year. The five ENEP schools were completed by 1976.[29]

At the beginning of the Soberón administration, student enrollment had reached 198 thousand students. The new administration was keen on stopping enrollment expansion. Admissions policies were set outside the University Council, by the Rector and directors. It established entry limits at the baccalaureate and undergraduate levels in general, and particular limits for 24 of 56 professional programs. An entry limit of 40 thousand students was established for the baccalaureate in 1975. A significant part of admits was diverted to the new campuses.[30]

Autonomy and Extraterritoriality (Violence)

In his inauguration speech, Soberón stated "we will not try to define the concept of autonomy; it has already been done by other renown teachers. We believe that it is in the essence of the University itself. We will exercise it and not turn it into a myth." A few paragraphs later he said, that it was "the State's and the society's responsibility to protect it from external attacks."[31] This statement coincided exactly with Díaz Ordaz's definition of the role of the State as guarantor of University autonomy.[32]

This was not a minor thing for Soberón. He was fully aware that the repercussions of the provocations and violence that had followed the 1968 events until González Casanova's resignation a few weeks earlier were a mater of grave concern for large sectors of University faculty. He purposely conflated the acts of criminal violence and provocations, with the local struggles for the democratization of school governance. He called this a situation of anarchy and violence of different origin. According to Soberón, there was violence exercised by the union, there was "revolutionary" violence practiced by a mosaic of ideological groups that stemmed from the 1968 movement, and there was also criminal violence. Without establishing a clear distinction, Soberón called the attorney general demanding the entry of police forces onto campus in August of 1973.

By design or chance, the situation had become ripe for a decision like this. The media reported true and false crimes committed on campus almost everyday.[33] According to a statement by UNAM's office of information Soberón himself had almost been abducted by members of the law–school combat committee.[34] Simultaneously, the media had carried out an ongoing campaign depicting University cafeterias, run by local student organizations, as hideouts for criminals and drug trafficking centers.[35]

In this context, the attorney general of Mexico City made a public statement saying that he would exercise judicial action on campus if the Rector made a formal request. According to Soberón's version, he did not want to be in the same situation that González Casanova had faced. A situation in which the Rector did not want to call the police and the police did not want to take the initiative to act, walking the fine line of autonomy *versus* extraterritoriality. Moreover, he claims that, against the opinion of the President and the Minister of the Interior, he publicly called for the police to intervene on campus and arrest the criminals.[36] The police entered campus on the night of August 9, 1973.

Police forces captured well-known professors who had attended a faculty meeting to discuss unionization, nineteen fishermen visiting from another state, and a few University workers among the 39 persons detained that night.[37] None of the criminals denounced by University authorities was captured. Almost everybody was liberated the next day.[38]

The community was profoundly divided by the Rector's decision. The administration inaugurated, however, a communication strategy that would prevail for many years. Central authorities promoted and financed dozens of paid advertisements by faculty and alumni organizations congratulating the Rector. Numerous support statements by politicians and former Rectors were requested.[39] Obviously, expressions by faculty and student groups criticizing the decision did not receive financial support for their publication. Consequently they were barely heard.[40] In one daring stroke, the Rector had settled the debate over autonomy and established new rules of political engagement. He would soon call the police again, in this case to settle a political dispute.

A few days later, when the students were out on break, the administration closed all the University cafeterias and reconverted them into classrooms. This is a clear example of how Soberón framed a political conflict as a criminal situation. His real motivation was clearly expressed many years later. The cafeterias "were used by certain groups to make proselytism and organize their combat strength, and I used to say we are crazy, we are, making payments to our enemy, because we provided students with food scholarships."[41]

Local Democratization Struggles (Anarchy)

The action against criminals on campus and the closure of the cafeterias set the political tone for every subsequent political conflict on campus. In 1973, there were ongoing democratization processes in the schools of Medicine, Economics, Architecture, CCH *Oriente* (one of the five CCH campuses), and Sciences. The first two had established *cogobiernos*, mixed committees of faculty and students, after a long route of consensus building. Particularly noticeable was the process at the School of Medicine where even some current members of the Soberón administration had a relevant participation in the design and unanimous approval of a general mixed committee.[42] The mixed committee in the school of economics organized a broad academic discussion in 1974 and established a new curriculum in which political economy (instead of economic theory) constituted the backbone of economic studies.[43]

The *autogobiernos* (self–governance) in Architecture and CCH *Oriente* were more confrontational. The first case featured an ambitious and innovative reorganization of the curricula in order to organize the learning process around service architecture activities in favor of marginal groups in Mexico City. Almost everybody within and even beyond the school agreed that the academic program was innovative and masterfully designed.[44] The internal division came when the proponents, a large group of faculty and students, rejected traditional governance forms (disavowing the director and the technical council), and established an elected body of faculty and students to administer the school in April of 1972.[45] The majority of students were with the *autogobierno* but the faculty was split almost in half. CCH *Oriente* also established an ephemeral self–government based on equal student and faculty representation.

The school of sciences established a different modality of shared governance in 1973. It was founded on a whole alternative structure of department councils and a central coordination, all of them based on equal representation of faculty and students. Embedded in these new democratic structures were the legal governance bodies established by the Organic Law.[46]

Soberón labeled these and other local attempts for curricular reform and democratization of governance as examples of the prevailing anarchic situation. The projects were constantly harassed. Its promoters were labeled enemies of the University, external provocateurs, or political agents. In no case did the administration encourage or engage in a creative discussion to produce a consensual transformation of academic programs and a reorganization of University governance.

The outcome of these projects was diverse. The democratic structure in the school of sciences continued to exist as originally designed until 1981. During the Soberón era, this school was in constant conflict with the central administration over the appointment of authorities and the recognition of decisions made by the department council. The mixed committee in the school of economics developed into an expanded technical council with equal student and faculty representation. As in the case of the school of sciences, the school of economics was hampered by conflicts over the designation of directors. These democratization projects were able to survive because of the large consensus that existed among the faculty. Isolated from the rest of the University and constantly harassed by external authorities, the democratic projects lived in a ghettoized political atmosphere plagued by internecine conflicts within the left.

After reaching a political compromise in 1974, the school of architecture was divided in two sections. One section was organized in accordance with the structures and rules set by the 1945 Organic Law. The other section, *Autogobierno*, was organized through equal representation and appointed its own executive authorities. *Autogobierno* followed its own curricula. The program had survived the division within faculty and the pressures from architects' professional organizations and central authorities thanks to the strength of student participation. Overtime, *Autogobierno* was constantly eroded by a decrease in student political participation, the partiality of central authorities in the allocation of resources, constant obstacles to student enrollment, and internal conflicts between groups. Many years later (in the early 90s) the two sections were unified into a conventional structure but important parts of the academic philosophy of *Autogobierno* permeated the new curricula.

The democratization projects in the School of Medicine and in CCH *Oriente* were completely annihilated. The creation of the mixed committee of students and faculty reached a high degree of consensus. In spite of this, the joint action of local and central university authorities and the pressures of medical professional associations worked systematically to end the shared–governance project. The case of the CCH was even worse; not withstanding the vast internal consensus in favor of self–governance among faculty and students, the central administration used open repression procedures to defeat this project. The locally elected director, as well as student and faculty activists were put in jail. The police constantly surrounded the school.[47] This recently created school, located outside the main University campus, did not have the tradition and moral stance of the older professional schools. The *ceceacheros* (members of the CCH) were more radical, better organized, and they were able to generate more participation. However, they were also less protected geographically and symbolically.

It is not clear why the CCH received so much of the concentrated wrath of University and government authorities. Perhaps it was the *ceceaheros* unlimited political dynamism and their capacity to extend their solidarity to a diversity of social and political movements in one of the most marginal regions of Mexico City. Perhaps because *Oriente* symbolized the democratic activist tradition of 1968 embedded, through large numbers of young professors from that generation, in all the CCH schools. But in spite of this defeat, *Oriente* and the other CCH schools established a long tradition of student and faculty organization and political mobilization that stands to our day.

This dispute between the University left and the administration was in no way an organized external conspiracy as UNAM's authorities frequently argued. It was the expression, even within each of the democratization projects, of multiple perspectives about the University.[48] Coordination between these attempts was almost none existent except for a few particular instances.[49] The aspirations of thousands of *universitarios* involved in these disputes on the progressive side were synthesized in the slogan *"por una universidad democrática, crítica, científica y popular"* that everyone interpreted in a different way. The University should be run in a more democratic way. It should maintain a critical stance *vis-à-vis* the Mexican State and unequal societal relations; and that this critical stance should be based on the scientific understanding of society and nature. The University should be popular in its composition by opening the doors of higher education to young students from the countryside, the *barrio*, or the workplace. It should be popular in its orientation, by focusing on the problems of the vast impoverished majorities of their country. What did each of these declarations really mean? If such a project existed, how could it come to place? Each faculty or student group had a different idea.

On very few occasions had the University been closer to the working classes and the urban poor than when the architects of *autogobierno* learned their trade building popular housing projects. Or when the medicine students set up free medical clinics in poor neighborhoods. When the *ceceacheros* and other student activists supported workers' strikes and provided organizational and even legal advice. Much of this mobilization was expressed in radical outreach programs, but a significant part was also linked to the discussion of University reform and the transformation of the contents and orientation of higher education.

The traditional University, enclosed in itself and unwilling to face external challenges and demands, was horrified. The lack of a unified reform project, the absence of a cohesive student organization, and the mistakes of radicalized student activists, allowed the University authorities to purposefully confuse these movements with criminal activities and provocations against the University. However, a large sector of UNAM was willing to accept these versions. The Rector recognized this fact and used it against his adversaries. In many situations the opposition reacted to the cautious or even conservative sector of the University by becoming more sectarian and isolated as radicalized self–proclaimed vanguards.

Unionization

The fourth problem, according to Soberón's depiction of the state of the University, was the emergence of staff and faculty unions. This problem would receive most of the attention of the Soberón Administration from 1973 to 1979. Soberón and his collaborators defined this problem as a battle against attempts to control the University by external actors and parties who attempted to do away with University autonomy and limit academic freedom.[50] This "battle" will occupy the next section of this chapter.

THE BATTLE FOR UNIONIZATION

In this context, the emergence of faculty unionization became an option for the unification of atomized reform struggles. For the promoters of the faculty union, the *Consejo Sindical* (Union Council), this project went far beyond the organization of labor and economic interests of faculty. It was an attempt to "deal with the University as an object of transformation."[51] They described themselves as

> a group of University professors and researchers...[whose purpose] is to freely discuss and make concrete decisions with respect to the future of the universities in the country, the relations that should be maintained between the members of the university community, the role that that post–secondary institutions can and should play in Mexico, and, fundamentally, the best way to organize them to accomplish these goals.[52]

Antecedents

The *Consejo Sindical* was founded in 1972. It recognized the critical situation of the University and tried to offer a political alternative in the midst of student atomization, and the growing confusion that events like the occupation of the Rectory building had produced. According to Del Valle, a member of the *Consejo Sindical* and one of the main leaders of the faculty union, academic "unionization was a defensive reaction, it was not a traditional response by the left, it was the most basic form of organization."[53] It therefore combined the features of a labor as well as a political organization, committed to the defense of faculty interests, concerned with substantive matters of academic production,[54] and attempted to produce a profound University reform that would enhance the role of this institution in a socialist transformation of Mexico.[55]

The *Consejo Sindical* had walked a fine line in the light of violence and provocations late in 1972. It condemned the occupation of the Rectory and tried to clarify the difference between the student movement and the presence of extreme radicalism, provocations, and government promoted violence.[56] During STEUNAM's strike the *Consejo Sindical* supported the *administrativos* right to unionize and expressed the need for a similar organization process for faculty[57] but maintained a certain distance from the leaders of STEUNAM.[58] Later they rejected González Casanova's resignation while still maintaining their support for the workers' organization.[59]

There had been a few previous experiences of faculty unionization. None of them had established a formal relation with UNAM. With a few exceptions, the administration unilaterally defined labor issues until that point. Most notable among these had been the *Sindicato de Profesores de la UNAM* (professors' union of UNAM–SPUNAM). This union operated in the Preparatory School since 1964,[60] and had struck against Barros Sierra in 1968, demanding salary increases.[61] The treatment that SPUNAM received from the Barros Sierra administration was very similar to the one González Casanova had given STEUNAM. According to these two Rectors, UNAM was a community, there was no antagonism between teachers and the administration, and unionization was not compatible with University autonomy.[62] The *administrativos'* strike had both a positive and a negative effect on faculty unionization. On the one hand, it became an example for many academics that unionization was possible.[63] On the other, it had produced fear and polarization among many faculty members.[64]

The Foundation of SPAUNAM

In spite of this, the process of faculty unionization made headway among important sectors of academics. The faculty union, *Sindicato del Personal Académico de la UNAM* (Union of Academic Personnel of UNAM–SPAUNAM) was founded in July 13, 1974. At the time of its creation the new union had 1,891 members, 541 were from schools and faculties, 179 from the Preparatory School, 1,038, from the CCH and 103 from the research institutes and centers.[65] SPAUNAM immediately demanded recognition from the University administration and the establishment of a collective agreement like that of STEUNAM. But Soberón's administration was not willing to concede any of these points.

The confrontation between the faculty union and the administration over these issues lasted until 1977. During this period, University authorities and the union used their traditional mechanisms of struggle. While the union organized meetings, demonstrations, and strikes, the Rectory countered by mounting media campaigns, applying sanctions, promoting alternative faculty organizations, and eventually, by using the repressive forces of the State against the unions. For most of this period, the fight was sordid and continuous but the largest definitions were produced in three intense confrontations: SPAUNAM's strike in 1975, Soberón's legislative proposal in 1976, and the unified unions' strike in 1977.

Division between Academic and Labor Issues

Conservatives countered the foundation of SPAUNAM with a Federation of Academic Personnel Associations (FAPA) established by an agreement between the leaders of 5 faculty colleges.[66] The administration and FAPA criticized SPAUNAM's demands for bilateral negotiations of academics' labor conditions by stating that this was beyond the scope of the Organic Law.

After a one–day strike for salary increases, SPAUNAM demanded that the University Council legislate for the possibility of a collective agreement. The Council rejected this proposal on June 10, 1975 but opened the possibility for negotiations over a faculty statute. SPAUNAM went on strike six days later demanding a collective agreement including a new proposal for the selection, promotion, and tenure for academics. It was based on the establishment of collegial bodies of faculty and evaluating committees elected by those bodies. These would be independent from the administration and the union, both of whom would only supervise that adequate procedures were followed by the independent faculty bodies. This proposition would become the center of the attacks by the administration and conservative faculty organizations that accused SPAUNAM of attempting to control faculty hiring, promotions, and tenure.[67]

SPAUNAM's strike started on June 16, 1975. It lasted nine days. The Rectory opened negotiations with SPAUNAM at the beginning of the strike. They tried to include multiple faculty representations in the same negotiation table but SPAUNAM refused. The administration maintained the farce by establishing parallel negotiations with other organizations. Very soon, the demands were divided into two areas: labor issues and academic issues. University authorities refused to negotiate over academic issues dealing with the creation of faculty representative bodies as proposed by SPAUNAM. SPAUNAM accepted the division between labor and academic issues and a few days later the two sides agreed on the establishment of a Labor Conditions Chapter in the Faculty Statute.[68] The administration recognized SPAUNAM as a faculty union (in addition to other faculty representations). University authorities and the faculty organization that held the larger membership would bilaterally agree upon labor conditions. This chapter would be revised every two years and salary agreements would be revised every year.[69]

SPAUNAM had obtained a partial victory. University authorities, however, had been able to organize a counterpart of collegial organizations to dispute the majority and therefore the right to negotiate these agreements. In the long run, this strategy would be favored by the lack of cohesion among faculty and by the fact that SPAUNAM never asked for recognition as the unique representation of all academics.[70] The campaign against SPAUNAM in the media lasted until the end of the strike. Local and central authorities promoted public statements by collegial organizations against SPAUNAM. The center of attacks was an alleged attempt by the union to take control over academic processes.[71]

The First Labor Conditions Chapter and the Apartado C

While faculty representations gathered individual affiliations to establish their membership, local authorities constantly harassed SPAUNAM's chapters. Union members were expelled in the Business School and the University attorney general tried to establish a statute of responsibilities to constrain political and civil rights within UNAM.[72]

Twenty nine organizations, including SPAUNAM, presented their individual affiliations to a mixed accrediting board. SPAUNAM was by far the largest of these with 3720 members more than the other 28 associations put together. This gave the union the right to bargain and sign the first agreement. On February 1, 1976, SPAUNAM went on strike for a few hours, before reaching an agreement over salaries and the content of the Labor Conditions Chapter.[73]

The faculty union had concentrated most of its efforts in the labor negotiations with the administration. The negotiations over the academic issues proposed by SPAUNAM did not make any progress. The attempt to create faculty bodies to decide on academic issues was blocked by the authorities. In August of 1976, SPAUNAM made a major attempt to define a program for reform and organized a university forum with student representations, faculty and staff unions, as well as the Rectors of some state universities.[74]

Even this national gathering would be altered by Rector Soberón's proposal to Congress to legislate a special chapter for University workers in the national labor laws. Soberón's proposal, called the *apartado* C (section C), limited unionization rights for university faculty and staff by restricting the legitimate causes to strike and by denying the possibility of unified unions.[75]

Faculty and staff unions all over the country reacted against this proposal. On the other side, a cataract of paid advertisements by faculty associations sponsored by the administration flooded the newspapers.[76] Echeverría opened public hearings to debate the *apartado* C. Faculty and staff unions, associations, colleges, and individuals participated against and in favor of the *apartado* in these hearings.[77] However, the reaction against it had been very strong and Soberon's proposal was gradually diminished and discreetly retired from the political arena.

The Defeat of Independent Academic Unionization

The confrontation between the administration and SPAUNAM continued in the University. Among other issues, it was renewed in a sordid battle over membership accreditation. Soberón had promoted all sorts of anti–union faculty organizations. In spite of this, SPAUNAM, who withdrew from the accreditation process, was still the largest of all but now slightly smaller than the sum of the others' memberships.[78] Some time later the rest of the organizations were brought together into the *Asociaciones Autónomas del Personal Académico de la UNAM* (Autonomous Associations of Academic Personnel–AAPAUNAM) and they were recognized as the majority by the administration.

Since the end of the 1975 strike, SPAUNAM had provided support to workers' struggles and social movements all over the country. It also became a protective umbrella for local student and democratization movements at UNAM's schools. Participation by students in support of the faculty union had produced a limited reorganization of the student movement but this sector continued to be a secondary actor in these struggles.

While the administration reached an agreement with the rest of the organizations, SPAUNAM and STEUNAM united into a single union and demanded a collective agreement for faculty and workers. The two organizations dissolved into the new *Sindicato de Trabajadores de la UNAM* (Workers' Union of UNAM–STUNAM) in March of 1977. A few months later, on June 22, 1977, STUNAM went on strike demanding a unified collective agreement to regulate faculty and staff labor relations with the University.

The strike lasted 20 days. During this period, STUNAM was the center of a large solidarity movement involving industrial and university workers' unions, peasant and urban social organizations, opposition parties, and massive student representations. Huge demonstrations took place all over Mexico City. University unions in the states called for solidarity strikes.

The Rectorship also received enormous support. The University authorities promoted hundreds of public statements.[79] The printed and electronic media criticized "this attempt by manual workers to control the academic process in the university, destroying academic freedom and eliminating University autonomy" and transmitted University courses over the TV.[80] Private schools provided their buildings for "out of campus classes."[81] The government controlled labor board declared that the strike was illegal.[82]

University authorities fired the whole executive committee of STUNAM. After 200,000 people demonstrated in support of the union, faculty members of STUNAM's leadership were captured and beaten by the police on July 6, 1977. The next morning at Soberon's request, 12,000 policemen entered the buildings to "recover" the University for the administration.

But the strike did not come to an end. A few days later, Reyes Heroles, the Minister of the Interior called University authorities and the remaining union leaders to a secret negotiation. Pérez Arreola, Secretary General of STUNAM, and Jimenez Espriú, Secretary General of the University, narrate how Soberón and Pérez Arreola "were forced" to negotiate when the Rector thought that he had already beaten the union.[83]

STUNAM survived, the leaders were liberated and reinstalled, and a collective agreement was signed between the union and the administration. The strike ended on July 10, 1977. The agreement was based on the Rector's original proposal. Faculty–labor issues were not part of the agreement.

In his report on the state of the University at the end of 1977, Soberón summarized the conflict in the

clear contrast between two opposing trends that have become known in the Institution during the last years:

On one hand, the urge to project the University to its highest academic levels in order to make it more capable of fulfilling its primary functions....

On the other, the continuous attack against University interests. The obstinate pretension to distort its nature to convert it into a political battering ram, the closing of buildings through violent means, in sum, the periodical agitation with the pretext of labor claims (Universidad Nacional Autónoma de México 1977).

Soberón had successfully been able to depict the confrontation in the University and the actors involved in this struggle in such a way. The unions were unable to portray the conflict as the confrontation between alternative ideas about the University. The political struggle had been defined at the level of discourse and the relation of forces, and independent faculty unionization had been defeated.

After the *Academicos'* Defeat

Rector Soberón was re–appointed for a second period in December of 1976. During his first period, the University Council had chosen 8 members of the Governing Board.[84] The professional groups of law, chemistry and engineering, business administration, and medicine regained control over 50% of the Board. The rest of this body included one sociologist, two historians, one philosopher, one physicist, and one mathematician. With the exceptions of López Cámara and Villoro, the Board had become relatively homogeneous on the conservative side. Soberón's reelection in December of 1976 went smoothly. A large list of candidates was proposed while Soberón repeatedly declared he would not accept a second period. Finally he "changed his mind" when the Board asked him to occupy that post for a second time.[85] Soberón received immediate support from new President López Portillo. The Rector had performed an unprecedented act when he and other Rectors visited López Portillo, recently appointed presidential candidate by the PRI, and expressed his "approval and support" for López Portillo's candidacy.[86] Having been able to orchestrate a consensus among internal "electors," and counting on unfettered government support Soberón had no real contenders.

López Portillo had proven his support for Soberón during the STUNAM strike. After the 1976 devaluation of the Mexican peso and in the midst of the discovery of new oil fields, López Portillo increased UNAM's budget to unprecedented levels. The University budget had a total growth of 105% in real terms since 1973, in the beginning of Soberón's first period. In spite of notorious budgetary growth, Soberón followed government adjustment guidelines regarding staff and faculty salaries. The latter sector's wages had reached an all time high in 1975 and steadily decreased in real terms since that time.

Full time faculty suffered salary reductions ranging from 10% in the lower categories to almost 20% in the highest. On average, part–time and

Full time faculty salaries (1975–1980) by categories
(constant prices base=1976)

CATEGORY/YEAR	1975	1976	1977	1978	1979	1980
INVEST./PROF. ASOC. A	11116	11500	11557	11002	10519	9993
% respect to 1975		3.46%	3.97%	-1.02%	-5.37%	-10.10%
INVEST./PROF. ASOC. B	12853	13000	13070	12442	11896	11302
% respect to 1975		1.15%	1.69%	-3.19%	-7.45%	-12.07%
INVEST./PROF. ASOC. C	14011	14000	14074	13399	12810	12171
% respect to 1975		-0.08%	0.46%	-4.36%	-8.57%	-13.13%
INVEST./PROF. TIT. A	15747	15500	15579	14832	14179	13471
% respect to 1975		-1.57%	-1.07%	-5.82%	-9.96%	-14.45%
INVEST./PROF. TIT. B	18063	17600	16966	16152	15441	14670
% respect to 1975		-2.56%	-6.07%	-10.58%	-14.51%	-18.78%
INVEST./PROF. TIT. C	20379	19700	18985	18073	17278	16416
% respect to 1975		-3.33%	-6.84%	-11.31%	-15.21%	-19.45%

Source: Martínez Della Rocca and Ordorika Sacristán (1993)

full–time salaries for academics were reduced by 10% for that same period. This trend would continue until the early 1990s reaching total loss of 69% in 1991 for average salaries with greater reductions for full–time faculty.[87]

University unionization expanded outside of UNAM. Faculty and staff unions emerged in higher education institutions all over the country. In 1979, López Portillo responded to this phenomenon, and to the attempt to build a unified national union of academic and administrative university workers, spearheaded by STUNAM, with a new piece of legislation. The new legislation (addition to Article 3 of the Constitution) defined the terms of university autonomy,[88]

> Universities and other higher education institutions which have been granted autonomy by the law, will have the power and responsibility to govern themselves; they will carry out their goals to educate, research, and

spread culture in accordance with the principles established by this article, respecting academic freedom and the free examination and discussion of ideas; they will determine their own curricula and programs; they will determine the terms of entry, promotion, and permanence of their academic personnel; and they will administer their patrimony.

The new addition to Article 3, curtailed any attempt by faculty unions to intervene in the selection, promotion, and tenure processes. The new legislation however, unquestionably established the right of faculty and administrative workers to unionize, jointly or independently in each institution, to establish a contract with the university, and to strike following the terms of Mexican legislation. With the exception of the right to organize a national union, explicitly forbidden by the new law, university workers labor rights were fully recognized.[89]

The two unions at UNAM, STUNAM, for administrative workers, and AAPAUNAM, for academics, were automatically granted recognition, contracts, and the right to strike. Nobody in the University questioned this decision by López Portillo. The administration's corporatist control over the faculty union had appeased any of the conservatives' previous fears.

In 1979, Soberón attempted to institutionalize his reforms with the approval of a new University Statute. The student movement in a brief return to the political scenario, stopped him. However, this was the only incident that would blemish the conclusion of his administration. Putting this minor defeat aside Soberón organized a lavish celebration of the 50 anniversary of University autonomy. Paradoxically this celebration of autonomy symbolized a victory over internal attempts to democratize the University and closed an eye to government intervention in UNAM's internal affairs.

These new rules of political engagement were solidly in place until 1986. In the next two processes for the designation of rectors, competitors within the Governing Board would all be part of the Soberón conservative coalition. The effects of the political confrontation during the two Soberón administrations on the disruption of the social fabric of students and academics, the bureaucratization of University life, and the isolation of authorities from the community continue until this day.

BUREAUCRATIC AUTHORITARIANISM

Without any doubt, during the Soberón administration the University political system entered a distinct phase that I have labeled as bureaucratic authoritarianism. This phase entails a redefinition of the relationship between University authorities and the State; the reduction of the political arrangement and confluence of previous political alternatives into a unique conservative coalition within the legitimate power structure. Soberón and his team had the capacity to put together a large hegemonic block with a conservative discourse based on the reinterpretation of selected university traditions.

The new relation of forces was institutionalized through a re–composition of the Governing Board. The administration extended its control over collegial bodies, and disrupted the practices and existence of faculty collegial and representative organizations. The conservative coalition stregthened its operating capacity and its control over the University through the consolidation of a political bureaucracy and the expansion of a political constituency in newly created directive offices and with administrative appointments. Overall, this refurbished version of University governance set the stage for many years of control over the political system by a relatively cohesive conservative political expression, stressing the authoritarian features of University governance.

The Soberón Administration and the Federal Government

There is no doubt that Echeverría's concerns about the National University coincided with Soberon's project. The new administration of UNAM constituted a "modernizing" team, whose objective was efficiency, a group that accentuated the need for control, and was willing to dispute each and every space of the University."[90] Soberón and the members of his administration agree that the relation between the government and UNAM during his administration was respectful and supportive.[91] Former Secretary General Jiménez Espriú explains,

> Dr. Soberón had great support from president Echeverría, a great support. We later suffered some attacks because of that obviously, but it was unconditional support, it was never subjected to any type of negotiations.[92]

He describes that President Echeverría gave Soberón the authority to call upon any government secretary whenever he needed. Echeverría created a big problem when he decided to inaugurate the 1975 courses at UNAM. Jiménez Espriú and Minister of the Interior Moya Palencia tried to make him change his mind but it was impossible.[93] Echeverría went to the University with Soberón in March of 1975. There, he was rejected by students who did not let him talk and finally made him retreat under a rain of projectiles one of which hit him on the forehead.[94] However, the acquiescence of the Soberón Administration to hold this presentation symbolized a fracture with the *universitarios* who loathed the government, and particularly Echeverría, for the 1968 and 1971 student massacres. Unlike Barros Sierra and González Casanova, Soberón was willing to "forget," and in this way reduce the distance between the University administration and the government.

The new relationship did not imply that the government would cease to intervene in University affairs. Perez Arreola describes that high government officials always intervened in the University when there was conflict. He states,

> It was evident that they intervened with the disgust of the two positions, University and union... None of us liked it, I can tell you that non of the Rectors liked to go, or that they called us in to discuss about salaries... We did not like it, but in the end we ended up negotiating with the intervention of government authorities especially in problems of economic nature.[95]

In the case of political problems, the negotiations always took place with the *Secretaría de Gobernación* (Ministery of the Interior). Jiménez Espriú recalls several instances in which University authorities' negotiation strategies with the unions had to be discussed and approved by President Echeverría himself or with the members of his administration.[96]

The largest confrontation between the Soberón Administration and the union SPAUNAM occurred at the beginning of López Portillo's presidency. Again, the government supported the Rector, even using public force when 12,000 policemen entered the University City in July of 1977.

After the police intervention López Portillo's Minister of the Interior, Reyes Heroles, participaed directly in negotiations between Pérez Arreola and Soberón. Reyes Heroles compelled Soberón to establish an agreement with Pérez Arreola. Soberón threatened to resign if he was forced to make an agreement with STUNAM. According to Jiménez Espriu's version, Reyes Heroles said to Soberón "its OK, we don't want to sacrifice the Rector," and a few seconds later he added "but there is going to be another Tlatelolco and this time the dead are all going to be yours."[97] Soberón accepted the government guideline and the administration reached an agreement with STUNAM that would put an end to the 1977 strike.

The Emergence of a Conservative Coalition

University politics suffered profound changes after 1972. Paradoxically none of the formal structures and legal foundations of the University were deeply altered. The Organic Law remained untouched. It was the political environment that changed, drastically allowing for transformations in the political operation of the administration.

The already limited political dispute within the legal structures that had been present since the establishment of the Organic Law in 1945 became even narrower. The election of González Casanova constituted the most radical political option the *Junta* had adopted since its foundation. It responded to a radicalization of the University after 1968 and to the emergence of a populist regime at the national level. González Casanova tried to expand political participation for faculty and students within the limits of prevailing structures and regulations.

He tried to reduce the influence of the medical and law professions and their organizations in University governance. This was a continuation of Barros Sierra's policy and is easily observable in the disciplinary composition of the Governing Board. González Casanova strengthened the position of liberal leftists and populist scientists in this body.

But the political contraction within the University, after the Falcón and Castro Bustos episode and in the face of unionization, reversed González Casanova's intended democratization. This historical account shows that in spite of major differences in other areas, Chávez, Barros Sierra, González Casanova, and later Soberón shared a similar view about unions as a threat to University autonomy and academic freedom. This view was deeply embedded in the conscience of many *Universitarios*. And they reacted accordingly, uniting around the strongest position in the presence of an external threat. Inside the political structure it was Soberón, representative of the elitist scientists, who united their former populist adversaries and even many members of the liberal left, once its most radical elements, Pablo González Casanova and Flores Olea, were defeated.

Outside the legitimate political structures, the University was polarized. For the first time in history, the left, in its diverse expressions, disputed the institution. In the absence of a unified student organization, students and faculty engaged in local democratization attempts, like the ones mentioned above. In spite of the importance of local democratization processes, none of these was able to dispute the University as a whole. The unions appeared as a threat to the administration and the emerging dominant coalition.

In an environment plagued by despair and uncertainty after González Casanova's resignation, local democratization attempts, radical outreach activities, and union struggles were combated but also utilized by the Soberón Administration to broaden and solidify its own constituency. A conservative political trend, that had rightly feared the extinction of their ideal of the University, was able to put together a relatively cohesive discourse. Based on this discourse they built a broad alliance with moderate and conservative sectors of the faculty and even the student bodies.

The Political Discourse of the Administration

The 1945 Organic Law provided the basic ideological foundation for the conservative coalition in opposition to those who demanded a democratic transformation of the university. The essence of the Law was the differentiation between political and academic issues within the institution. This discourse served the conservative groups perfectly. The emerging political formation argued that politics had no place in an academic institution.

Politics were condemned as a negative and anti–university practice. In a particularly revealing passage Soberón wrote:

> It must be understood that even when the cause of a university conflict can be evident, it can never be fully established if there are perverse intentions of political nature or of clear anti–university character behind statements that originally can be judged of a purely academic or administrative nature. On other hand, these polluting factors are attached at the first chance, because everybody wants to 'bring water to his mill.' Do not forget that UNAM has played and will continue to play a relevant role in the development of Mexico and it constitutes an agent of social mobility; therefore, in every conflict it is said that, ... national or extra national interests opposed to the development of the institution can come into play.[98]

This perspective constituted the basic discursive guideline in the struggle with the unions. Faculty colleges, university authorities, and students on the conservative side constantly repeated that SPAUNAM and later STUNAM were trying to get hold of the University and destroy autonomy and academic freedom. The official political discourse portrayed the union struggle as a "conflict with evident political goals"[99] and the leaders' motivations as "political and anti–university."[100]

Faculty union leaders recognize that they lost the ideological dispute. One leader noted: "we lost an intellectual debate,"[101] According to Del Valle,

> they succeeded because they won the hegemony, they sold their discourse, they did not only win in the exercise of power, they won the discourse, that is what you have to do...

> the fact that we had to debate if faculty were workers at all, the fact that many professors argued that they were not workers illustrates that that we lost the debate. ... It was the worse terrain in which we had to debate [workers or not workers], because the academic union was not a labor project, it was a University transformation project. Once the dispute was set in terms of workers yes or no, we were going to lose any count [of affiliations]."[102]

Soberón argued in a similar fashion: "once I was able to establish a distinction between academic and labor issues, the solution was set."[103]

The University Council and the Collegial Bodies

Soberón agrees that the dynamics of the University Council changed with respect to the Rectorships of González Casanova and Barros Sierra.

The administration reached a high degree of consensus, "the proportion between us and the opposition was more or less 75% against 25%."[104] He recognized the absence of free debate within the University Council. He said,

> it is not that I feel, let's say happy, satisfied that there was the need to have a block that really always voted in one direction, perhaps it is not good for free debate, the thing is that in the circumstances of reorganization after such a conflictive situation, well it happened in this way.[105]

According to Pérez Correa, one of Soberon's most important collaborators, the University Council was perceived as a scenario in which conflict could be expressed. He said,

> our University Council was a piece of political engineering. It was constructed vote by vote. We talked to everybody, we twisted their arms, we squeezed them, we heard them, we offered. **Everything was in sum a great consensual project.**"[106]

Many faculty members recall how the *Colegios de Profesores* (faculty collegial bodies) were controlled or permanently harassed by local school or institute administrations.[107] Martuscelli, a member of Soberón's team, remembers that the control over collegial bodies did not only take place at the University Council. He describes the situation in these bodies very dramatically,

> I do believe that academic directors, whenever they can, try to prevent faculty from organizing collegially. The discourse that was used then [to justify that] it was because of the union movements, that is, we needed to keep close ranks in a terrible *mayoriteo* [imposition by a majority at any cost]. It was not even *mayoriteo*, it was *carro completo* [it is said when an overwhelming majority is forced], votes of 90 to 10 or 95 to 5. The 5 evil characters in this movie always sat together. They had to defend themselves, it is so clear. This is what happened to me as a director, ... I wondered if Soberón was right, perhaps these guys [the evil ones] received instructions from somebody...The fear that was generated was like a kind of terrorism. I remember a few occasions in which somebody was distracted and did not vote as he should or as it was expected that he should have voted, and this caused a terrible scandal.[108]

Not only were collegial bodies subjected to intense control. For all purposes, they were also stripped of many of their functions and decision realms. Soberón governed with the college of academic directors (formed by academic directors of schools and institutes and, on occasion even administrative directors), a de-facto body that is not sanctioned as a university authority by the Organic Law. It was established in 1971 in an amendment to the University Statute. (Universidad Nacional Autónoma de México. Comisión Técnica de Estudios y Proyectos Legislativos 1977). During the Soberón Administration, the importance of *Colegio de Directores* grew. It became the body through which the administrations decisions were implemented or filtered to the University Council.

The Bureaucratization of UNAM

The subordination of collegial bodies to personal authorities and the dilution of faculty representative organizations into a quasi–labor corporate organization to confront the emergence of faculty unionization increased the unbalance, already embedded in the governance structure, between bureaucratic and academic governing structures. This process was compounded by a notable expansion of bureaucratic appointments and the particular conditions in which this phenomenon developed.

During the González Casanova Rectorship, administrative personnel grew in 12% (from 1970 to 1973). This period included the establishment of five *Colegios de Ciencias y Humanidades*. During the 1973 to 1980 period, corresponding to Soberón's Rectorships, administrative workers grew from 10,230 to 23,716, that is, by 132%. The Soberón Administration in some way continued González Casanova's project for the establishment of decentralized campuses. Five of them were established during the Soberón Administration.

A comparison of faculty, student, and administrative worker growth renders surprising data:

The expansion of administrative workers is much larger than the growth in the number of students, during the Soberón period. The increase of staff directly dependent on executive authorities, called *de confianza*, was enor-

UNAM: hired personnel and students, 1970, 1973, and 1980

	Research			Teaching			Administrative			Students
	total	Fulltime	%	total	Fulltime	%	Total	*confianza*	%	Total
1970	525	210	40%	8,885	210	2%	9,126	248	3%	106,718
1973	611	418	68%	11,040	458	4%	10,230	513	5%	198,294
%	16%	99%		24%	118%	·	12%	107%		86%
1980	1,911	1,700*	89%	27,515	2,000*	7%	23,716	4,808	20%	294,542
%	213%	307%		149%	337%		132%	837%		49%

* Estimates
Source: *Anuarios Estadísticos, UNAM*, 1970, 1973, and 1980.

mous (837%) between 1973 and 1980. It is estimated that at least 50% of these 4,808 employees were appointed University officials of different levels including directors, academic secretaries, division and department chiefs, coordinators, technical secretaries, and advisors.[109]

If the growth of academic services or the increasing complexity of the University can explain the first number, the second one can only be understood in terms of a political decision by the Soberón administration. Soberón, Jiménez Espriú, and Martuscelli agree that the explanation for this expansion of the University bureaucracy is the confrontation against the unions.[110] Soberón said that the expansion of bureaucracy

> was a defense that we had and that everybody requested. Because those were times of terrible mutual distrust... the directors and everybody else said 'I need to have somebody I can trust for this function,' in its fulfillment and in dealing with it, because it was a continuous confrontation.[111]

The expansion of the bureaucracy provided the Rector and his administration with an increased operational capacity at every level of University life. This growing bureaucratic corpus also constituted a loyal constituency for the upper echelons of the administration and the power structure of UNAM.[112] The bureaucracy extended to every area of the University and substituted the eroded fabric of academic organization, replacing academic discussion with a bureaucratic rationale.[113] The bureaucratic apparatus constituted the only connection between academic units and the central administration.[114] In the long run, this situation evolved into a costly process for the University. In his detailed study on the process of bureaucratization at UNAM, Kent (1990) summarizes this cost as a profound distortion of University life:

> the organizational identity of academic workers is still mediated by organisms that are extraneous to them. This prolonged condition of lack of professionalization and subordination of the professor appears in strong contrast –but in intimate and perverse coherence– with the professionalization and political autonomy of officialdom. The successful policy oriented towards university stabilization and union contention had, as a requisite and as an outcome, the dispersion of academic functions and the consolidation of bureaucratic functions (p. 127).

From the University to the State: the Limits of Autonomy

Smith (1979), Ai Camp (1995b) and Centeno (1994) have extensively shown that UNAM has been one of the most important recruitment centers for the Mexican political system. Until the 1970s the most important recruitment processes occurring at UNAM were the incorporation of faculty who had been student peers of high–ranking public officials (especially the president), and the enrollment of students by party intellectuals–professors who would integrate their disciples into the government party and/or public office.

On a few occasions before 1973 University officials had moved into the State apparatus. Solana (Secretary General at UNAM during the Barros Sierra Administration) and González Pedrero (director of the Social and Political Sciences School during that same period) were among the most notable recent cases.[115] But the Soberón administration widened the path from the University administration to public office. At least 35 members of the Soberón administration were integrated to the ministries of health, interior, education, and communications by 1982.[116]

Kent has carefully examined the effects of this process as a basic foundation of the internal cohesion of the Soberonian bureaucracy. In addition to the ideological component that identified the unions as a common enemy, "the strength and internal cohesion of the new profession of [university] official received, as a consequence of the opening of new circuits towards the State apparatus, a considerable encouragement" (Kent Serna 1990 p. 130).

In addition to this, it is important to emphasize the fact that the future of political careers in an authoritarian political system depends on personal loyalty and allegiance to the groups in power. Soberón and his group within UNAM had established linkages with diverse groups within the State apparatus and these allegiances had to be preserved through the subordination of University officials to their counterparts in the Mexican government. The net effect of this articulation was the subordination of University autonomy to external political actors through an informal mechanism based on the political expectations of University bureaucrats.

By the time of their transition to government positions at the end of the Soberón administration, this group had put in place an effective political arrangement for the containment and political administration of the National University. It was precisely at the time that the legitimacy of the Mexican political system entered a critical phase and initiated a progressive decline that UNAM entered one of the longest periods of political control and bureaucratic authoritarianism. At the national level Echeverría's political aperture was followed by López Portillo's political reform, there was a progressive opening of the media, and increasing societal demands for democratic participation. The political system at UNAM however has remained closed and unchanged since the last restoration produced by Soberón more than twenty years ago.

NOTES

[1] (Villoro 1999). See also Froylán López Narvaez in *Excélsior*, January 4, 1973, p. 7-A.

[2] Villoro recalls that several members of the Governing Board visited Chávez "before the decision was made and he [Chávez] was **excessively favorable** to Soberón. Chávez undoubtedly exercised a strong influence in this decision." (Villoro 1999, emphasis added by author).

[3] Villoro (1999).

[4] Ibidem.

[5] Ibidem.

[6] Ibidem.

[7] *Excélsior*, January 4, 1973. This situation contrasted with previous occasions where the Board, once a decision was reached, voted unanimously for the candidate that had obtained the required 10 votes in an attempt to disguise internal discrepancies.

[8] Ibidem.

[9] *Excélsior*, January 4, 1972. See also (Pulido 1981 p. 90).

[10] Source *Anuario Estadístico de la UNAM 1972–73*.

[11] Source *Anuario Estadístico de la UNAM 1972–73*.

[12] See Appendix 5.

[13] Paid advertisement of UNAM administration signed by Fix Zamudio and Flores Olea in *Excélsior*, January 2, 1973, 24–A.

[14] *Excélsior*, December 23, 1972.

[15] Soberón Acevedo (1994).

[16] Soberón Acevedo (1997).

[17] Universidad Nacional Autónoma de México (1985b).

[18] Ibidem.

[19] Soberón Acevedo, Valdés Olmedo, and Knochenhauer (1983).

[20] Ibidem p. 112.

[21] Universidad Nacional Autónoma de México (1980).

[22] Kent provides a very good analysis of the reorganization of UNAM by Soberón and the significance of each of these subsystems. See Kent Serna (1990 pp. 21 and 66).

[23] Soberón Acevedo, Valdés Olmedo, and Knochenhauer (1983).

[24] Ibidem.

[25] An typical example of this is provided by Soberón's explanation of why he developed the graduate program in biomedical research away from the sciences faculty, in Soberón Acevedo (1997).

[26] Del Valle (1997); Soberón Acevedo (1997).

[27] Universidad Nacional Autónoma de México (1980).

[28] Soberón Acevedo (1997).

[29] Kent Serna (1990).

[30] Soberón Acevedo (1997).

[31] Universidad Nacional Autónoma de México (1985b).

[32] See reference to Díaz Ordaz's ideas about autonomy in the first section of this chapter.

[33] See *Excélsior* from January to August 1973. For a more trustworthy account see Gastón García Cantú in *Excélsior*, August 3, 1973, p. 6A.

[34] *Excélsior*, July 28 1973.

[35] *Excélsior*, August 1, 1973.

[36] Soberón Acevedo (1997).

[37] *Excélsior*, August 10, 1973.

[38] *Excélsior*, August 11, 1973.

[39] *Excélsior*, August 11, 1973.

[40] *Excélsior*, August 11 and 12, 1973.

[41] Soberón Acevedo 1997).

[42] See paid advertisements by the mixed committee in *Excélsior* on August 8, 1972, September 14, 1972, October 17, 1972, and November 29, 1972. Valentín Molina Piñeiro, one of the most important representatives to the mixed committee was appointed secretary of the Rectorship by Soberón.

[43] Comité Estudiantil de Solidaridad Obrero Campesina (1982).

[44] A group of very prestigious architects were supporters of the *autogobierno*, most notable among these were Benyure, Carral, and Augusto Álvarez (Aguirre Cárdenas 1997).

[45] The confrontation was extremely hard. The traditional sector was thrown out of the school and they organized their classes in another building outside of the University City (Aguirre Cárdenas 1997).

[46] Colegio de Profesores de la Facultad de Ciencias (1973).

[47] Del Valle (1997). Del Valle describes the confrontations between the *ceceacheros* and the police and how the director general of CCH, Perez Correa, maintained a permanent face–to–face battle against faculty and students in these schools.

[48] Huacuja Rountree and Woldenberg (1976 p. 107).

[49] Del Valle (1997); Imaz Gispert (1997).

[50] Jiménez Espriú (1997); Martuscelli (1997); Soberón Acevedo (1994); Soberón Acevedo (1997).

[51] Del Valle (1997).

[52] *Documento del Consejo Sindical de Profesores e Investigadores Universitarios* (in Woldenberg 1988 p. 26).

[53] (Del Valle 1997).

[54] *Manifiesto del Consejo Sindical de Profesores e Investigadores de Enseñanza Media y Superior*, May, 2, 1973 (in Woldenberg 1988).

[55] *Desplegado del Consejo Sindical, Excélsior*, June, 10, 1973. In this document the *Consejo Sindical* expressed the following goals: a) participate in the revolutionary transformation of society fundamentally through teaching, research, and outreach activities; b) to transform and defend post-secondary institutions as centers of independent critique and as promoters of social change; and c) to participate in revolutionary struggles for social, political, and economic democracy and for socialism in Mexico.

[56] Woldenberg (1988 pp.26,27).

[57] *Consejo Sindical* leaflet (in Woldenberg 1988 p. 52).

[58] In another communication by the *Consejo Sindical*, this group demanded from STEUNAM a clarification of their demands (in Woldenberg 1988 p. 53).

[59] *Consejo Sindical*, leaflet (in Woldenberg 1988 pp. 59,60).

[60] Pulido 91981 p. 47).

[61] Domínguez (1986).

[62] Domínguez (1986).

[63] Woldenberg (1988 p. 63).

[64] Del Valle (1997).

[65] Woldenberg (1988 p. 147).

[66] Perez Rocha (1974).

[67] One of FAPA's constituent colleges reproduced a statement by Alfonso Noriega, former member of the Governing Board, criticizing SPAUNAM for demanding an outrageous privilege in faculty hiring and tenure. This statement was published in three national papers *Excélsior*, *El Heraldo*, and *El Día* on October 21, 1974.

[68] This chapter would define salaries and benefits, academic workdays, scholarships, and working conditions among other issues.

[69] Woldenberg (1988 pp. 352–356).

[70] Del Valle (1997).

[71] See *Excélsior*, *El Día*, *El Universal*, and others during the month of June, 1975.

[72] Woldenberg (1988 pp. 423).

[73] *Excélsior*, February 2, 1976.

[74] *Excélsior*, August 10, 1976.

[75] *Propuesta de adición al artículo 123 de la Constitución Política de los Estados Unidos Mexicanos* (in Woldenberg 1988).

[76] For a compilation of these see Woldenberg (1988 pp. 624–648).

[77] See Woldenberg (1988 pp. 627–648).

[78] *Excélsior*, December 22, 1976.

[79] According to the weekly magazine *Proceso*, University authorities financed a total of 788 paid political advertisements in support of the administration and against STUNAM. The total cost of these publications for UNAM was 13.9 million pesos. STUNAM published 20 of these advertisements for a total cost of 691 thousand pesos. Other non-University institutions had 20 publications for a total cost of 1.5 million pesos. *Proceso*, September 5, 1977, No. 44, México, DF, p. 11.

[80] Molina Piñeiro and Sánchez Vázquez (1980).

[81] Ibidem.

[82] Pulido (1981).

[83] See Jiménez Espriú (1997) and Pérez Arreola (1998).

[84] Two of them had been part of Chávez's administration (Velasco Ibarra and Mantilla Molina). Zierold had been appointed director of the veterinary school under Chávez. The three of them and Soberón had resigned together when Chávez was ousted in 1966 (Romo Medrano 1997). León Portilla and Díaz y de Ovando were historians and among the most conservative sectors of the humanities. The other three were Alatorre Padilla, Barrón y Paz from the Business School, and Mateos Gómez from Chemistry.

[85] See *Excélsior*, December 1 to 16, 1976.

[86] *Excélsior*, September 26, 1975. Soberón was strongly criticized by many sectors for this action. Even some of his allies like Mario de la Cueva wrote articles to express their discontent with Soberon's endorsement of the PRI candidate. See Mario de la Cueva in *Excélsior*, October 3, 1975.

[87] Calculations based on data from Martínez Della Rocca and Ordorika Sacristán (1993).

[88] *Constitución Política de los Estados Unidos Mexicanos,* Artículo 3o. Fracción VII.

[89] *Ley Federal del Trabajo.* Título VI. Capítulo XVII.

[90] Del Valle (1997).

[91] Jiménez Espriú (1997); Soberón Acevedo (1994); Soberón Acevedo (1997).

[92] Jiménez Espriú (1997).

[93] Jiménez Espriú (1997).

[94] *Excélsior*, March 15, 1975.

[95] Pérez Arreola (1998).

[96] Jiménez Espriú (1997).

[97] Ibidem.

[98] Soberón Acevedo, Valdés Olmedo, and Knochenhauer (1983).

[99] Soberón in *Excélsior*, July 4, 1977.

[100] Soberón in *Excélsior*, July 8, 1977.

[101] Martínez Della Rocca (1997).

[102] Del Valle (1997).

[103] Soberón Acevedo (1997).

[104] Ibidem.

[105] Ibidem.

[106] Pérez Correa (1997).

[107] For examples of these opinions see De la Peña (1997), Peimbert Sierra (1997), and Martínez Della Rocca (1997).

[108] Martuscelli (1997).

[109] Kent Serna (1990 p. 100).

[110] Jimenez Espriú (1997); Martuscelli (1997); Soberón Acevedo (1997).

[111] Soberón Acevedo (1997).

[112] Kent Serna (1990 p. 109); Ordorika 1996).

[113] De la Peña (1997); Imaz Gispert (1997); Kent Serna (1990 pp. 109, and 131,132).

[114] Kent Serna (1990 p. 98).

[115] University Biographies database.

[116] University Biographies database and *Diccionario Biográfico del Gobierno Mexicano*, 1984.

CHAPTER 7

Conclusions

> Why worry?
> There should be laughter after pain.
> There should be sunshine after rain.
> These things have always been the same.
> So why worry now? Why worry now?
>
> Dire Straits. *Why Worry?*

This conclusions chapter ties together the political history of UNAM into four analytic sections. In the first section, I show that UNAM is a hegemonic apparatus of the State and consequently the site and object of political confrontation. This section establishes the distinction between internal and external levels of conflict and describes the institutionalization of the new relation of forces in the 1945 Organic Law.

A second section deals with the distribution of power and the political arrangement at the University. The purpose of this section is to provide a thorough analysis of the political nature of university governance. It looks at the authoritarian political structure, describes the ideological components of the discourse of domination, and analyzes the two levels of confrontation within UNAM. The last part of the section focuses on the nature of dominant groups at UNAM. It shows how the group that I have labeled the elitist scientists, originally led by Chávez, have controlled the *Junta* until this day. Finally, it provides a characterization of the distinctive traits of the University elite and the bureaucracy.

The third section synthesizes an essential objective of this work: assessing the real limits of University autonomy. It provides an evaluation of the extent of autonomy in three components: political autonomy, academic and campus autonomy, and financial autonomy. At the end of the section these findings are brought together in order to show the structural factors that determine the degree of University autonomy, the mechanisms of State intervention, and the limited nature of autonomy.

The fourth and final section addresses the relationship between politics and change at UNAM. It argues that conflict is the most significant factor in explaining transformations in the National University and describes four types of change processes produced by political conflict.

THE UNIVERSITY AND THE STATE: AUTONOMY AND CONFLICT

Throughout its history, the *Universidad Nacional* has played a significant role in reproducing the elites and in preparing the professionals and technicians required by the Mexican State. Even during the periods in which politicians and government leaders were extensively recruited from among the ranks of the revolutionary armies, and throughout the years in which the State relied on other higher education institutions, there was significant institutional presence through notable *Universitarios* who participated in the government. I have shown that this presence increased after 1940 and that the National University thrived as the most important producer of professionals during the process of industrialization and urbanization of the *milagro mexicano*.

In addition to this reproductive role, the University has constituted a vehicle for social mobility. This condition became especially relevant since the 1940s, and more particularly during the 1950s and 1960s. Up until today, the University is still perceived as a mechanism to create social opportunities with a strong influence on the possibility of upward social advance.[1] In accomplishing these tasks, the University has become a source of legitimacy for the Mexican State. At the same time, historical evidence provided in the previous chapters shows that it has constituted a space in which the ideology, structure, and practice of the State has been both challenged and reproduced. It is in this sense that I argue that the *Universidad Nacional Autónoma de México* has historically been a State institution, a hegemonic apparatus of the State.[2]

Historical evidence establishes without any doubt that the University is a hegemonic apparatus, a space of society in which and from which State hegemony is disputed. This process was very evident from 1920 to 1944 when urban intellectuals used the University as a protected environment to resist against State policies. In some cases, like those of the Vasconcelos movement in 1929, the campaign against socialist education from 1933 to 1938, and the 1968 student movement, the University became a political vehicle in attempts to produce societal change.

The relationship between the University and the State has been extremely dynamic. Changes in government policies like the *viraje de los años 40* had a profound effect upon the organization of the University and on the attitudes of important sectors of faculty and students towards the Mexican State. In the early 1940s the schism between the University and the government, openly expressed in the granting of autonomy in 1929 and in the confrontations over socialist education between 1933 and 1938, was closed. A new era of cooperation and interdependence came about when the government reoriented its policies in favor of urban expansion and industrialization and when a liberal education program for *national unity* replaced the radical instruction project of the *cardenismo*.

This study has documented effects in the opposite direction as well. That is, occasions in which processes within the University have produced transformations at the broader State level. This is the case with the 1968 student movement. The student revolt has had a long–term impact on the Mexican political system. The consolidation of the authoritarian regime and the redirection of economic policies in the early 1940s strongly shaped the organization of the University and its political processes. In contrast with this, the student rebellion in 1968 closed the cycle of political stability and inaugurated the long decline of the authoritarian regime. In this sense, the student movement of 1968 was a precursor of social mobilizations for the democratization of the political system.

The conflicted relationship between the University and the Mexican State has been regulated, since 1929, by the legal formulation of institutional autonomy. I have shown that the legal foundations and the real limits or degrees of autonomy of the National University have varied historically. A new relationship between UNAM and the State was institutionalized in the 1945 Organic Law. While the law retained a relatively high degree of formal autonomy, the linkages between dominant groups at the University and the Mexican government ensured compliance and full cooperation with State policies. These connections also opened the way for presidential intervention in the appointment of rectors and the definition of University policies.

The history of University and State relations shows that the government eventually accepted this arrangement because urban intellectuals demanded an independent arrangement *vis-à-vis* the Mexican State. University autonomy developed into an essential component of the pact between liberal intellectuals and the Mexican State. By 1945, that historical conquest by liberal intellectuals had become one of the foundational myths, an ideological component of the National University.

An essential concept in understanding the relationship between the University and the State is to evaluate how relative this "relative autonomy" really is. The evaluation of the limits of autonomy at UNAM has been one of the objectives of this work, and will be the focus of further analysis in the following sections. Contrary to what Levy states in his work on Mexican universities, I contend that the evaluation of the extent and limits of institutional autonomy for UNAM greatly depends on recognizing the nature of this institution as a site of conflict. Consequently, it is essential to understand the levels and dynamics of confrontation, and to identify the political actors and their connections with the State apparatus.

The University as a Site of Confrontation

In previous chapters, I have shown that the University, as a hegemonic institution of the State, has been the site and object of political disputes. University conflicts occur at least at three different levels: the permanent tensions between the University and the State political apparatus, confrontations that take place within the University, and conflicts within other State institutions that are reflected within the University. These levels are difficult to differentiate on many occasions. In some situations, conflict between the State and the University became manifest as political battles within UNAM. This is the case of the struggle against Rector Medellín and Lombardo Toledano in 1933 or the provocations against González Casanova in 1972. In situations like these, opposing internal actors express the contest between University and State apparatus. In other occasions, the struggle between the University and the government is more clearly defined as a clash between institutions. This is the case of the open opposition stance of Rectors Ocaranza and Gómez Morín *vis-à-vis* the Cárdenas Administration, or the confrontation between UNAM and the Díaz Ordaz government in 1968.

Conflicts within the University have often been permeated by State intervention or the interference of government officials. These become political actors of the internal struggles in their own right. The historical review of University politics that was presented in the previous chapters shows that confrontations within this institution have been relevant for society in general and the government in particular. Consequently, these confrontations have usually involved internal and external actors, including the political apparatus of the State itself. Student conflicts against Rectors Fernández MacGregor and Zubirán in the late forties and the struggles over unionization in the 1970s are instances of this type of external intervention.

The high degree of interrelation between internal and external political processes and corresponding political actors can only be explained by the enormous centrality and the political weight of the University in the Mexican political system. This situation is due to the historical development of the University, as a relatively independent political space within an authoritarian political regime. In the absence of alternative political institutions that would allow for a limited degree of participation, the University was loaded with political tasks and responsibilities that go well beyond the formally defined goals of a higher education institution.

The history of political confrontations at the National University shows that in 1929, 1933, and 1944, domination crises developed because of profound changes in the relation of forces within the University and with the broader State. In these occasions, political disputes were institutionalized into new political arrangements. The processes of institutionalization were grounded on new legislation approved by the Federal Congress. These include the law of autonomy in 1929, the granting of full autonomy in 1933, and the Organic Law of 1945. In these three moments the State took legal action in order to formalize new governance structures and legal arrangements that sanctioned the relations between political forces and those between the University and the State. The last instance of State legislation in 1979 was the product of internal conflicts over unionization.

State intervention in these institutionalization processes has varied according to different political circumstances. In 1929 and 1933, the State alone defined the new relationship with the University and established the new basis for the organization of the University as well as the regulations for its operation. In 1944–45, the State did not have to directly intervene after the President provided a mediation mechanism. The alliance with a new dominant group within the University was very strong and the government was satisfied with the new political arrangement that the *Universitarios* provided. The President and Congress sanctioned the legislation produced by the University Council.

In 1979, the State intervened again to regulate the relationship between the University administration and the unions that had created a large number of conflicts in UNAM and other public universities. On this occasion, the State intervened as a mediator. It granted some of the administration's demands, separation between academic and labor issues, and constraints to unionization at the national level, and granted unions' demands for recognition, bilateral contract negotiations, and the right to strike.

UNAM: POWER AND POLITICS

The legislative process of 1944–45 established the structure and legal frame that rules UNAM until today. I have shown how in 1944, liberal intellectuals coalesced around its most notable members and established the new dominant formation at UNAM. Alfonso Caso brought together a long University tradition and symbolized the linkage of University intellectuals and the State through his participation in the Ávila Camacho government. Under Caso's leadership, the emerging dominant coalition was able to establish a restrictive political arrangement that mirrored the essential characteristics of the Mexican authoritarian political system.

The Political System after 1945

The political organization at UNAM after 1945 has been extensively described in Chapter 3 and its evolution in Chapters 4, 5, and 6. The basic elements of the governing structure are the Rector, the directors of schools and research institutes, the *Junta de Gobierno*, the *Patronato*, the University Council, and the *Consejos Técnicos*. These elements are linked together in a complex arrangement that establishes the subordination of collegial bodies to executive authorities, limits political competition, and reduces the possibilities for participation.

Personalized power. Individual authorities are preeminent over collegial bodies. The Rector and directors preside over the University and technical councils respectively. The Rector holds enormous control over the appointment of directors given his attribute to put together the threesomes from which the Governing Board makes the designation. Directors preside over their technical councils. In turn, they constituted 50% of the University Council and exercise control over the election of student and faculty representatives to this body.

Additional elements explain the subordination of collegial bodies to executive authorities. In 1974, Pérez Correa, coordinator of the CCH and secretary general during the Soberón Administration, stated that

> in practical terms, power has concentrated in the Rectorship and the directors for several reasons. The mere existence of a university bureaucracy, with all that it entails in terms of information, skills, specialization, control of processes, and budget design, places executive [authorities] in an advantageous situation in the face of collegial bodies...[3]

Limited political competition. The capacity to influence appointments to the Governing Board, the Rectorship or directorships has been limited to the dominant groups that stem from those who originally held control over the *Junta.* I have shown that the groups that originally established their control over the Governing Board have influenced the appointment of Rectors and directors. In this way, through the University Council and by direct recruitment, they have shaped the composition of the Board. The system is geared towards the reproduction of power relations and the preservation of these dominant groups.

Limited participation. Faculty and student organizations have no influence or representation in governing bodies. During the period of this study, faculty and student representatives to the University Council were elected through indirect processes overseen and influenced by local as well as central authorities.

The fourth characteristic of authoritarian political arrangements is the ambiguous nature of official ideology. University ideology assumes the form of a collection of dominant traditions that can also be characterized as vague and ill defined. However, this does not imply that the dominant discourse is unimportant. The political system at UNAM is founded and legitimized by these traditions articulated into a discourse of power.

The Discourse of Power

The concepts of autonomy and academic freedom are the essence of the University and symbolize the struggle of the *Universitarios* to establish their own identity *vis-à-vis* the State. I have shown how these traditions developed in the confrontation between the University and the State. These traditions are vaguely defined and are constantly reinterpreted in the process of confrontation with internal and external actors. The emergence of a new dominant formation in 1945 was founded on a selective interpretation of the history of the University. Embedded in these traditional values, a new ideological understanding of the relations between the *Universitarios* provided the foundation for the new political system established in the 1945 Organic Law. The four basic concepts of this emerging tradition are the following:

• Since 1945, the University has been characterized as a technical institution. According to this perspective, its only objective is the discovery and transmission of knowledge. This is the common purpose and unique legitimate interest of all the *Universitarios*.

• The University is a community. Since there is a unique goal and objective for all the members of the University, there can be no conflicting interests within the University.

• The University is an apolitical institution. Since there are no conflicting legitimate interests within the University, politics must be eradicated. The presence of politics symbolizes the fact that extra–university interests are attempting to use the University for some purpose other than its unique goal.

• University governance is a meritocracy. Those that lead the institution at the local and central levels do so because they have special qualities that place them above the rest of the *Universitarios*. These merits are allegedly based on academic prestige but are not explicitly defined.

In previous chapters I have shown that these concepts are loosely defined and have been interpreted in contradictory ways by different University administrations. I have also shown that, with the exception of Barros Sierra's and González Casanova's administrations, this ideological ensemble has provided the fundamental arguments for the dominating group in times of overt political conflict against student movements and union struggles.

The Dynamics of Political Contest

In spite of ideological claims that gave birth to the 1945 Organic Law, political contest has existed at two levels: restricted political competition within the legitimate political arrangement, and the open confrontation by those excluded from the University political system.

Contest within the dominant coalition. From 1930 to 1938, University resistance to the populist State was led by a conservative coalition with a strong influence from militant Catholic groups. The political evolution of the Mexican State in the early forties had strong effects inside the University and this coalition was broken. A new alliance of moderate liberals and Catholics emerged and has become the dominant political trend even through the present. In spite of these changes, there was always an element of ideological and political continuity around Antonio Caso's moderate conservatism and his views on autonomy and academic freedom.

The dominant coalition shared these traditional values but it was not a completely homogeneous alliance. Within the dominant groups, there has been political competition involving two mutually accepted trends. Political differentiation within the dominant group became manifest during the administration of Rector Nabor Carrillo and practically disappeared during the Soberón Administration. One of the trends, labeled here as that of the populist scientists, brought together scientists from the physical sciences, mathematics, and professionals from engineering. This group controlled the coordination of scientific research from 1947 to 1961 and from 1966 to 1970.[4] This group was able to establish an alliance with the liberal left represented essentially by academics from the humanities, social sciences, and a few members of the School of Law. This latter group included Pablo González Casanova, Villoro, López Cámara, Flores Olea, and González Pedrero among others.

The other trend, labeled here as the elitist scientists, was grounded on the medical sciences and the medical profession.[5] This group was able to attract a sector of moderate Catholics with a strong influence in the School of Law and other areas of the University. Over time, this trend has increased its dominance of the governing Board and seems to have increased political strength and external connections with the government.

However, after 1973, these competing trends within the University elite closed ranks in the face of unionization and democratization demands. Elitist scientists led by Soberón coalesced different political expressions of the elites into a broad coalition. Zermeño (1987) provides a picture of the "dominant UNAM" in the late 1980s. In his view, there are two branches of the dominant group in the University. The first branch is

> the highly professionally oriented technical–scientific establishment: institutes and faculties in the areas of mathematics and physics, chemistry and biology, or engineering... that manifest in different condensations,

towards the right or towards the center and more or less politicized or professionally oriented, that go from the *Academia de la Investigación Científica* to the professional associations and whose project is the linkage between business and university (p. 3).

The second branch is that of the

liberal humanist UNAM; UNAM that opposed the revolutionary cast and *cardenismo* in the name of private property and individual liberty, the one that reached the rarest anti–state alliances when it joined Marxism in the sixties... and that in many occasions, after repeatedly going against the State, ended up within the State. At the right or the left, they share a common feature: the cultural heritage associated with their family names... (p.4).

The 1945 Organic Law narrowed the limits of political competition. The members of the dominant coalition controlled the legitimate political scenario and competed among themselves for the control of governing structures and University resources. This competition took place in the University Council, over the appointment of Governing Board members, and finally over the designation of Rectors. The *Junta* became an essential element in this restricted political competition.

Los olvidados del campus[6]

The majority of students and faculty are completely alienated from the dominant political arrangement. There is an absence of faculty collegial life and influence on the decisions of their academic centers. When these sectors have the need to voice a proposal or disagreement with University policies, the lack of participation channels immediately produces political conflicts of varying magnitudes.

Before 1945, it was more difficult to identify the differences between confrontations among the University elite and confrontations involving other participants. The political arrangement allowed for a somewhat broader political participation. It was standard practice for the elites to articulate extended coalitions in the confrontation for control over the University. Since 1945, this practice by the elites has become more concealed. It still happens in a masked way, but connections between overt conflict and actors within the elite, are strongly denied. There are two clear examples of these hidden practices. The first one is Del Pozo's concealed support for the student movement against Chávez, when the latter was designated Rector for the first time. The second are the conservative attacks against González Casanova during the occupation of the Rectory building in 1972.

Demands from those outside the University political system for participation and other issues existed during the "golden years." However, after
1968 these demands increased in number and in magnitude until they constituted a true dispute over the University. After the provocations of 1972
and in the face of challenges by staff and faculty unions, the University elite
reacted in a unified way against "external" threats to their dominance over
the institution. The appointment of Rector Soberón was the product of this
reorganization of the University elite around the conservative pole. The
alternative position within the political system, represented in its most progressive version by Pablo González Casanova, Flores Olea, and others, van-
ished as a political alternative for any practical purpose.

Since 1929, and more strongly after 1945, challenges against the
University political system by internal actors, have been labeled as external
threats to University autonomy and academic freedom in what has become
a recurrent mechanism for political disqualification. The ambiguity of these
ideological constructs has been useful for the dominant groups who decide
in which cases these concepts must be invoked against these "threats."
Almost every administration has shared this practice, and in most occasions,
this has been the discourse of University elites against student movements.
This ambiguous discourse has been used in varying historical conditions and
with different political intentions. In 1972, González Casanova vaguely
denounced the actions of government–sponsored provocateurs as aggressions against the University. In diverse occasions Soberón, used a similar
discourse against students, faculty, and staff who pursued alternative transformation projects. The two Rectors used these same concepts in reference
to different actors but pursuing a similar purpose of rallying internal forces
against "the enemy."

I have shown that the student movement also underwent a political transition from the right–wing positions that were characteristic in the 1930s
and 1940s. During the 1950s and early sixties it was profoundly influenced
by the traditional practices of cooptation, opportunism, and corruption
fostered by the authoritarian PRI regime. A strong progressive tradition
emerged in 1966 and consolidated in 1968. The consequences of the 1968
massacre were deeply embedded in the student movement during the 1970s
when the massive nature of the movement decreased giving way to sectarian and isolated political "vanguards" and a multiplicity of student projects. The University left, however, extended its influence in the University
and became the most significant contender in the transformation of
UNAM.

The student movement suffered an additional type of political evolution.
Since 1923 and until 1944, students were the central political actors in the
University. The 1929 movement accomplished the autonomy that previous
petitions by faculty and University directives could not gain. Conservative
resistance against socialist education in 1933 and 1934 was also grounded

on student mobilization. Students organized and suffered the consequences of the resistance against right–wing Rector Brito Foucher in 1944, opening the way for a reorganization of the University. However, in 1945, the emergent dominant group had no further use for students and made them the scapegoat in their de–politicization project. Students were marginalized from University governance but remained a relevant political entity, gaining weight and notoriety in 1968. The outcome of that movement diminished the political centrality of students who become subordinated to newly emergent political actors, the staff and faculty unions, during the seventies and early eighties.

Historical Composition of the Board (1945–1997)

Political contest within the dominant group at UNAM has centered over the appointment of Rectors and members of the Governing Board. A study of the political dynamics of the *Junta* provides evidence of the composition of internal groups. The Constitutive Council elected the first governing board of UNAM on January 29, 1945. Each member of the Council was able to vote for eight of the fifteen members in an attempt to give some representation to minorities. Over time, the results do not seem quite diverse in terms of disciplines, university groups, ideologies, or gender.

Professions and disciplines. From January of 1945 to January of 1998 the Governing Board had 111 members. A study of the composition of this body since 1945 shows three groups have dominated the Board over time.[7] These groups have been medicine with 22.68%, law with 19.16%, and engineering and chemical engineering with 14.99%. The rest of the membership has been divided between the humanities with 10.48%, the exact sciences with 9.61%, architecture with 6.03%, business administration with 5.76%, the social sciences with 4.74%, and economics with 4.27%.[8]

Governing Board members by academic discipline 1945–1997
(years in the governing board)

	1945–1966		1966–1973		1973–1997	
Unknown	5	1.52%	6	4.00%	6	1.90%
Social Sciences	0	0.00%	7	4.67%	30	9.52%
Business Administration	15	4.55%	10	6.67%	21	6.67%
Architecture	21	6.36%	13	8.67%	14	4.44%
Medical and Biological Sciences	73	22.12%	26	17.33%	75	23.81%
Law	115	34.85%	14	9.33%	25	7.94%
Economics	22	6.67%	10	6.67%	1	0.32%
Exact Sciences	13	3.94%	20	13.33%	45	14.29%
Humanities	25	7.58%	10	6.67%	50	15.87%
Engineering and Chemistry	41	12.42%	34	22.67%	48	15.24%
Total	330		150		315	

Source: University Biographies

The professional groups within the board have carried a much larger weight than the academic disciplines.

More significant perhaps is the evolution of the board composition during three periods: from 1945 to 1966, from 1966 to 1973, and from 1973 to 1997. Each of these corresponds to a distinct phase in the history of UNAM.

I have previously stated that lawyers and physicians dominated the Governing Board during the first period (1945–1966). During the Barros Sierra and González Casanova administrations (1966–1973), the Board became more diverse, the representation of the exact sciences increased, and the engineering profession gained preeminence. Since the Soberón Administration (starting in 1973) the medical profession once again gained influence over this elective body.

Board membership and government appointments. From 1945 to 1997, 29 members of the board (27%)[9] had previously been high–level government officials. Nine members (8.5%) occupied a government post (from director general to minister) at the same time that they were part of the *Junta*. At least 7 members of the Board (6.5%) occupied a position in the federal government after leaving this body. Eight board members held the post of government ministers, two of which did so while serving their term in the *Junta*.

Professional groups have traditionally been linked to the Federal Government. All of the economists and 77% of the lawyers have occupied public postings at the levels of secretary, under–secretary, director general, judge, or supreme–court justice. Thirty–two percent of the members from the medical profession have held postings in the Secretary of Health (secretaries and under–secretaries). They have exercised enormous influence on the leadership of major public hospitals, particularly the *Instituto Nacional de Cardiología* (Cardiology Institute) and the *Instituto Nacional de Nutrición* (Nutrition Institute). Two members of the Board (Chávez and Zubirán) founded these institutions.

It is frequently argued that ICA (Associated Civil Engineers) one of the largest private corporations in Mexico, has exercised a large influence on the Board through the representation of the engineering profession. While completing the University Biographies on which part of this research is grounded, I only found information about membership in ICA for two Governing Board members (out of 10 engineers).[10] Seven of them (70%), have also been public officials (*i.e.* secretary or under–secretary in the ministries of Public Works, Communications and Transportation, or Energy).

Chávez, Baz and Zubirán: the doctores dominate UNAM. The representation of the professional groups has been relatively homogeneous. Throughout this work, I have shown that while the representation of lawyers has been more heterogeneous, political homogeneity is most salient among the physicians group. Gustavo Baz and Ignacio Chávez were at some point directors of the School of Medicine. Baz, Chávez, and Zubirán eventually became rectors and they were counted among the most powerful members of the Board. I have shown that this group formed a closely–knit political cadre in University and government politics since the early 1930s. Baz, Chávez, and Zubirán were personal physicians to different Mexican presidents and had multiple connections to high–level PRI politicians.

In previous chapters, I have shown the political influence of Ignacio Chávez over the most important political body at UNAM. Let us recapitulate. Ignacio Chávez is the only case in which a Board member resigned from that body (in 1959) in order to become Rector (in 1961).[11] Seven members of the *Junta* had been direct Chávez subordinates in *Cardiología*, the medical society, or the School of Medicine. Several others had been disciples and friends. This group was also closely related to a number of lawyers and representatives of other professional groups and disciplines by friendship, family ties, and political bonds.[12]

Six former University officials appointed by Rector Chávez between 1961 and 1966 came to be part of the Governing Board. Additionally, eight directors of schools and institutes, designated (by the *Junta* from sets of three proposed by the Rector) during the time when Chávez was at the head of UNAM, later became members of this body. One more, Dr. Guillermo Soberón, would become Rector seven years later.[13]

Constituent councilors and the Board. Seven Rectors became part of the Governing Board.[14] Four of them had been part of the Group of former Rectors that gave birth to the 1945 Organic Law. *Cardenista* Rectors García Téllez and Chico Goerne, who had been members of this provisional body, were never elected to the *Junta*. Alfonso Caso was appointed in 1946.

Eight former directors of schools and institutes appointed by Caso in 1944, and eight faculty representatives who were also part of the Constitutive Council in the same year, eventually became part of the Governing board. None of the former student representatives or other disagreeing voices like that of Dr. Lucio Mendieta y Núñez (director of the Social Research Institute), ever became part of this body.[15]

Ideological composition. Most members of the Governing Board never openly state any political affiliation. According to the information that I have compiled in the University Biographies, 11 members of the *Junta* are identified as members of the PRI through explicit party membership, participation in this party's advisory board (IEPES), or having held an elected position in Congress or the Senate as PRI representatives.[16] A few others have not been officially recorded as members of the PRI although they have participated in this party's internal political processes. This is the case of Board member García Ramirez and Rector Soberón himself, who contended for the PRI presidential candidacy in 1987.

Given the authoritarian characteristics of the Mexican political regime, it is safe to assume that upper–level government officials accept and generally coincide with the dictates of the president who in turn is the leader of the official party. This relationship of loyalty and subordination is not usually broken after the termination of the political appointment. Participation in the high levels of public office implied, at least until 1982, ideological conformity with the president and the government party. At least 45 members of the Board have been appointed government officials under PRI administrations, reflecting a clear political and ideological orientation of the *Junta de Gobierno*.

Alternative political perspectives have had a much more limited presence on the *Junta*. Four members of this body were founders of the right–wing party *Acción Nacional*.[17] It is possible that there have been more adherents to that political position, a moderate Catholic conservatism, that have participated on the Board but there is no available information to confirm this.[18]

On the other hand, progressive trends at the University have been barely represented within the Governing Board. Some argue that only two members (Villoro and López Cámara),[19] appointed by Rector González Casanova after the 1968 student movement, could be considered as representatives of the university left. At least four well know and highly regarded scholars, proposed by the left, were rejected by the University Council in 1975, 1981, 1985, and 1993.[20]

Rector Barnés (1997–1999) agreed that the *Junta* is a conservative body and explains that the absence of progressives in this body is due to the fact that

> proposals made by the Rector carry a larger weight than those that emerge [from other actors] for many reasons. The Rector's proposal is usually more conservative than any of the other proposals, I absolutely agree. There is inertia in this process that although it provides the system with great stability, it also implies a slightly slower transformation in this collegial body's vision...[21]

At this point, it seems convenient to recall Villoro's appreciation of the composition of the *Junta de Gobierno* between 1972 and 1984.[22] These years encompass two distinct political epochs: the González Casanova and the Soberón administrations. According to his description, during this period the Board had three types of members. The first group was "the scientists." The components of this group were

> generally from the area of natural and exact sciences. They had a critical scientist formation and a liberal stance, in the American sense. Usually they had very limited background and paid little attention to political and

social issues. In most occasions, they considered that there was nothing political about their decisions. They represented between 40% and 50% of the Board.

Villoro called the second group *los obedientes al poder* (obedient to power). These are the ones that,

> received political directives from external, the federal government, or internal sources. They had to be very careful in the way they filtered these directives. Among these, those that really have political contacts are relatively few. They are usually two or three. The rest of the obedient group follows.

Villoro states that during his time on the Board, there was a very marginal group on the left. According to his own description, only himself and López Cámara could be considered part of this group.

An analysis of the members of the Board during the period that has been described shows the following disciplinary composition. Engineering and chemistry share 21.6% of this body. Medicine, veterinary and biomedical sciences represent 16.2%. The physical and mathematical sciences reached 16.2%. The humanities held 13.5% and law 10.8% of the *Junta*. Finally, the Business School had 8.1% and architecture 5.4% of this body. Only nine individuals can be clearly identified as natural and exact scientists. Villoro might have considered some engineers, chemists, and physicians as part of the scientists' group.

According to the information I compiled in the University Biographies, thirty percent of the members of the *Junta* during those years had been part of the federal government. Two can be clearly identified as members of the PRI. In my view, Villoro downplays these connections between the Governing Board and the Federal Government. His diagnosis seems closer to the composition of the *Junta* at the end of the González Casanova Administration, and fits the political behavior pattern that Villoro described in the election of Rector Soberón.[23] Villoro recognizes that "in González Casanova's time, the *Junta* was obviously more independent, and in some cases more oriented towards the left, than in latter [University] governments, like Soberón's, where the situation started to change."[24]

Gender composition. The final aspect that I want to address in this section is the gender composition of the Governing Board at UNAM. Female student population fluctuated between 15 to 20% of total enrollment from 1945 to 1960.[25] It increased to almost 35% in 1976[26] and to about 50% in 1979. In spite of this, in 53 years, the Governing Board has only included four women (two representatives of the humanities, one of the social sciences and one of the exact sciences). The first woman to become part of the board was appointed in 1976.

Summary. The Governing Board at UNAM has been the object of political competition among rival factions of the University elite. Over time,
members of the medical profession under the leadership of Ignacio Chávez
dominated the Board. It is not an exaggeration to state that Chávez has
been the most powerful and influential member of this body. The Board is
a relatively homogeneous representation of University liberals (in the old
tradition of the Caso brothers). Over time, it shows a high level of interrelation with the government through the presence of former and current
funcionarios, members of PRI–led administrations. A relatively high number of Board Members are recognized as obedient to power and openly
willing to carry political "suggestions" from the president or high–ranking
government officials. The presence of progressive representatives has been
extremely reduced and was concentrated during the Barros Sierra and
González Casanova administrations. After that, the University Council
always rejected progressive candidates.[27]

The Power Elite and the Bureaucracy

In the study of the dominant political groups at UNAM I followed a
two–pronged method discussed in the methodology section in Chapter 1.
In the interviews I conducted, key informants were asked to name the most
politically influential *Universitarios* they could recall. In every case, respon-
dents mentioned that the Governing Board and the rectors included the
vast majority of prominent political actors. In addition to these, respon-
dents provided 88 other names. These included 42 members of the
Governing Board; 9 rectors; 9 sciences and 5 humanities research coordinators; 6 secretary–generals; and 46 directors of schools and research institutes. Only seven of the names correspond to individuals that have held no
administrative positions.

The results of the reputational study in this case can only be indicative
of general patterns, but are not enough to identify the elite group with a
relative degree of accuracy. This is due to the size of the interviewee pool.[28]
However, the results of the reputational study show conclusively that the
Governing Board and the upper echelons of the administration constitute
the majority of members of the University elite. Therefore, I focused the
attention of this research in a positional analysis of the distribution of
power at UNAM. The historical study in the preceding chapters and the
positional analysis show that the group that exercises control over decision-making at UNAM has two essential components: power-holders—
following C. Wright Mills I will call them the *power elite*—and opera-
tives—I will label them *university bureaucracy*. The two groups are not
necessarily exclusive.

The university elite. The university elite is composed of individuals who
are or have been part of the University and play a major role in decision-making in this institution at the central or local level. This analysis

shows that their capacity to influence outcomes in the University stems from a combination of family heritage, political linkages, or academic prestige. Members of the university elite do not necessarily hold an official appointment at the university but this reputational study has shown that this elite has concentrated in the highest instances of UNAM's power structure. This study shows that the members of the power elite combine three different traits:

University aristocracy. Reflects family tradition and belonging to select University groups. This family tradition is usually associated to ancestors' academic prestige or with relevance in the foundational struggles of the University. These include the foundation of the University in 1910, the struggle for autonomy, the combat against socialist education and for academic freedom, and more recently the confrontation against unions and democratization attempts.

Political strength or centrality. Reflects the external and internal political connections and supports. Political alliances outside the University are important but not sufficient. Usually political strength is based on both of these components. In many occasions, political strength is the product of the temporary occupation of University posts.

Academic prestige. Actors gain political power and moral authority because of their academic recognition. During the "golden years" it was represented by a group of faculty that had gone beyond teaching activities and had received recognition for establishing the first steps of research in a variety of academic disciplines.

In order to maintain the legitimacy of the governance structure and its most important bodies, it is possible to identify a certain socialization of academic prestige especially for the benefit of the outsiders. Differences within the University elites are well recognized among their members. However, in their façade towards the rest of the University all of the members of the power elite and even some of the operators have received a coating of academic recognition. This can explain the vicious circle of membership to governing bodies, academic associations, and academic awards that constitutes a very interesting topic for research in its own right.

Political competition within the elite takes place in several instances. One of these is the contest over the composition of the *Junta*, and therefore over the appointment of executive authorities such as the Rector and the directors. The dynamics of this political competition have already been discussed above and in previous chapters.

University bureaucracy. The Governing Board defines the political balance of the University but it is the Rector, directors, and other elements of the bureaucratic organization of UNAM that manage the operations of the institution. Most rectors and some directors of schools and research institutes can be identified as part of the University elite, as shown by the positional study that I described in previous sections. They are also part of the bureaucracy. Consequently I have identified the university bureaucracy as the set of university officials appointed by either the Governing Board (Rector and directors of schools and faculties), the University Council (Governing Board and Board of Trustees), or by other appointed officials. This sector is comprised of several layers including the Rector, general and administrative secretaries, sciences and humanities coordinators, directors of schools and research institutes, administrative general directors, and other top–level administrative personnel at the central and local levels among others. It also includes the body of mid–level managerial and administrative that I identified as *personal de confianza* in the previous chapter.

I have shown in Chapter 6 that this bureaucracy constitutes both the operational base for the University elite and a significant part of its political constituency. I also provided evidence of the notable process of bureaucratic expansion, especially since 1973. This bureaucratic expansion involves the growth in the number of appointed officials and the creation of new appointed positions.

Bureaucratization can be explained in part by institutional growth and by increasing organizational complexity. These explanations can be valid for bureaucratic growth until 1973. However, during the intense confrontations against the unions and democratization attempts, bureaucratization became a mechanism to increase the operational capacity by the elite, and to expand its loyal constituency or social base.

In this research, I have focused on the data for administrative and bureaucratic expansion as a whole, and on the study of political trajectories for the upper rank of the bureaucratic apparatus (Rectors and secretaries). This data shows that UNAM officials at different levels have created their own labor markets and career paths towards upper echelons of the University administration and the Federal Government.[29] Hegemony of the elite over the bureaucracy was established through the creation of identity, *vis-à-vis* the adversary, and through an implicit offer of access to superior levels of the administration or the Federal Government.

This expectation of access to the Federal Government has created loyalties to external political groups. It establishes a self–imposed subordination of University authorities in order to increase possibilities of transit to the government. University bureaucrats respond favorably to government initiatives and, in practice, autonomy is diminished.

THE LIMITS OF UNIVERSITY AUTONOMY

In the first chapter of this work, I reviewed Levy's definition of university autonomy and it components: appointive, academic, and financial autonomy. The first category includes the hiring, promotion, and dismissal of faculty; the selection and dismissal of rectors, directors, and administrative personnel; and the definition of terms of employment. The second category includes access, career selection, curriculum and academic programs, degree requirements, and academic freedom. The third category includes the determination of who pays, funding levels, funding criteria, allocation

Analytical components of autonomy		
Political	**Academic/Campus**	**Financial**
• Appointment and dismissal of Rectors, directors, and administrative personnel	• Student access	• Funding
	• Faculty hiring	• Allocation of resources
	• Curriculum and academic programs	• Accountability
• Internal conflict resolution	• Degree requirements	• Tuition
	• Academic freedom	
	• Free speech	

of resources, and accountability. These categories include a comprehensive set of fundamental decision–making aspects for university life.

As stated in the first chapter of this work, I have shared Levy's operational definition of autonomy as the power to make decisions within the University. However, I consider that Levy's organization of three categories mixes some distinct decision–making realms. In an attempt to clarify these processes, I propose the following components for the evaluation of university autonomy:

Political autonomy. **Appointment of University authorities.** The appointment process for Rector and academic directors is concentrated in the Governing Board. University authorities and dominant groups reject the notion that these appointments take place essentially through a political process. The characterization of the Governing Board is one of the most contested political debates about UNAM.

Participant observation and several of the interviews showed that ample sectors of the University community consider that appointment procedures are undemocratic and favor a small group that has control over the Institution.[30] It is also widely believed that the Governing Board has no autonomy *vis-à-vis* the government. Former rectors and members of the Board Mario De la Cueva and Manuel Gómez Morín stated that the *Junta* has annulled the autonomy of the University. They also argued that it had excluded faculty and students from decision-making and opened the way for government intervention in all aspects of university life.[31] Former Rector García Téllez criticized the Organic Law of 1944 because "it followed a trend that limited university co–governance by creating bodies like the Governing Board in which students and faculty have no participation."[32] He argued that the University was governed by "a system that is oligarchic, centralized, and separated from the throbbing problems of students and faculty, [the situation is] worsened by projections of auto–perpetuation."[33] García Téllez concluded that this part of the Organic Law was "a fraud for autonomy."

Traditionally, University officials and members of the bureaucracy have argued publicly that the Board is independent and that it constitutes the most important element in guaranteeing institutional autonomy.

> I give you my word. I never felt any external influence in an appointment by the Governing Board. I do not tell you that there never was any, no. I can not give you my word. But I can give you my word that I never felt it or lived anything like it.
>
> And the discussions in the Governing Board, I always felt that they were very free. Very free, that is we discussed and we were convinced that the appointments were always for the best person. I never, never felt that there was any external attempt to influence my decisions, remember that I gave you my word, especially when we appointed a Rector.[34]

Historical evidence shows that the appointment process is complex and varies in time and for each designation.[35] Since 1945 there have been systematic instances in which presidents have exercised influence over members of the Board. I have provided evidence of this type of intervention in the designation and re–appointment of Luis Garrido, in 1948 and 1952; in the appointment of Nabor Carrillo in 1953; and in the designation of Ignacio Chávez in 1961. In previous chapters, I also described the importance of government connections in the appointment of González Casanova. It is not clear that Echeverría intervened in favor of the appointment of Soberón in 1973.[36]

Current Board member Jiménez Espriú explains that government intervention in the appointment of authorities follows no rules. Government intervention "depends a lot on the circumstances and depends also on the President."[37] Jiménez Espriú, a former secretary general and former director of the School of Engineering at UNAM, related how he lost the Rectorship in 1981. According to his testimony, on the day when the Governing Board appointed Rivero Serrano, one of its members (identified later by Villoro as an active part of the "obedient group") met with President López Portillo.[38] Jiménez Espriú argues that the President did not like the former secretary general as UNAM's Rector. In spite of being considered the strongest candidate, Jiménez Espriú lost.[39] He suspected that the Board had voted in agreement with the President's wishes.[40] Former sciences coordinator Martuscelli confirms this version.[41]

Soberón described attempts by government officials to influence the appointment of a Rector in 1985. According to his version, President De la

Madrid did not want to intervene. The Board appointed Carpizo, a close collaborator of then Rector Soberón, against the expectations of the secretaries of Education and the Interior. Soberón describes this event as evidence of independence of the *Junta*. However, he fails to recognize the fact that he was also a government minister, and could potentially exercise enormous influence on the *Junta's* decision.

Madrazo, Humanities and Social Sciences coordinator during Carpizo's Rectorship, agrees with this description of the Board's performance in this election. However, in reference to previous designation processes, he stated that

> I knew, for example, that in some cases there was a direct, more or less direct, intervention by the executive in the designation of Rector. In a subtle way, the executive let know who could be a good Rector, and he let the members of the Governing Board feel this.[42]

Villoro's accounts of the internal workings of the Governing Board from 1972 to 1984 provide insights into the level of autonomy of this body. In a general description of the internal workings of the Board, he said that

> the President was very careful not to give any appearance of intervention [in the Board's decisions]. Messages to the Board were indirect, always allowing the possibility of presidential denial. Intervention took place through some of the Board's members. Only a few of them played this role. In my time [as a member of the Board] it was only done through some members.[43]

But he warns against simplistic assessments that argue, "that the Governing Board is not independent and depends from the public voices" or those who maintain that "the Governing Board is totally independent and impartial."[44]

Bringing the evidence together it is possible to draw some conclusions about the political autonomy of the Governing Board. There is ample historical evidence showing that presidential intervention in the appointment of Rectors was an open and recurrent process before 1968. Given the delicate nature of the relationship between University and government after the student massacre, the forms of intervention evolved into more subtle mechanisms. At the same time, however, the government's political interest in UNAM also increased. The combined effect of these two dynamics provided some space for the interaction of internal and external influences within the Board.

Even the most ardent defenders of the independence of the Board agree that this body cannot appoint a Rector against the President's will. This statement has two implications. On the one hand, it shows that the President enjoys an unwritten right to veto. On the other, it shows that the relationship between internal and external influences depends precisely on the extent of the President's will. The President's interest on the designation of Rector is determined by historical circumstances. It increases in times of conflict or any other condition that enhances the centrality of the University. In a lesser way, it can also be spurred by personal commitments or political alliances. It is then possible to state that the independence of Board decisions is heavily determined by the President's willingness to intervene in the process.

However, subtlety and deniability are required in order to maintain the appearance of autonomy. This puts a relative constraint on the president's commitment with one candidate or another. The president's candidate requires a certain amount of legitimacy among the University elite. The candidate has to fit the image of a legitimate academic and a committed *Universitario*. He has to be able to garner a significant amount of support among the dominant groups. Given these conditions, the President can define the designation if he is willing to do so.

Presidential participation aligns the voices of other government officials. In his absence, government secretaries and other members of the administration try to intervene in the process in different directions and with varying weight. This is also what happens in the case of director appointments for a few schools or institutes. In this situation, however, the internal relation of forces within the Board carries more weight in the final decision.

Regarding the appointive autonomy of the University, Levy stated that

> while the government probably involves itself more in this university appointment than in any other, its power is quite limited compared to UNAM's power and *compared to government power in other nations* (Levy 1980).

The findings of this work are quite different. In summary, I argue that the appointment of Rector concentrates a high degree of attention from the Mexican government. When exercised with full commitment, external influences by the president and other major political actors outweigh the internal dynamics and relation of forces on the Governing Board. The presence of external influences in the appointive process depends on the political will of the executive as shaped by historical circumstances and political considerations. Finally, the President can exercise his political will under certain constraints, requiring a relative degree of academic and internal political legitimacy for the President's candidate.

Intervention in internal conflicts. The removal of University Rectors is part of a different political realm. This is one, among many situations of political conflict, in which the government has intervened in the University.

External interference in University affairs increases in the presence of political conflict. These interventions can be welcomed by University authorities or against their will. Again, it is the magnitude and political implications of these conflicts that condition the forms and the extent of government interference.

There is historical evidence of three types of government intervention in University conflicts. A first form of intervention has taken place by providing or denying support for the University administration in the presence of political actions by students; as in the cases of Rector Fernández McGregor, and Zubirán. This is also the case of the 1977 union struggle during the Soberón Administration. I have argued in chapter 4 that the government has played a balancing role in favor of University authorities in the presence of social movements that threaten the stability of the administration.

On other occasions, there have been instances of direct intervention in University conflicts. These include police and military repression against student movements in 1929, 1948, 1968, and 1971; or the occupation of the University by public security forces in 1968, 1972, and 1977.

Finally, the government has intervened by tolerating or promoting the actions of other external actors in order to produce political changes within the University. This occurred in the cases of Rector Chávez's ousting in 1966 and the occupation of the Rectory building against González Casanova in 1972.

Academic and campus autonomy. It is in this area that UNAM enjoys a larger degree of formal and real autonomy. There is barely any example of government intervention in the hiring of faculty. That is, beyond the case of government politicians in disgrace that are hired as professors and for whom formal requisites are waived. In the case of academic programs, curricular issues, or degree requirements, in general these matters are of little interest to government officials. The commonality of purpose between the dominant coalition that emerged in 1945 and the Mexican government ensured compliance with State demands for higher education. The University projects of Rectors Chávez and Barros Sierra followed government requirements and expectations about UNAM.[45]

Student access and University policy. Student access and broader issues of University policy have always attracted the attention and intervention of government officials. Soberón and Martuscelli argue that Chávez's reluctance to expand student enrollments at UNAM was the cause of his confrontation with President Díaz Ordaz.[46] González Casanova's attempt to democratize UNAM and expand its national perspective as an agent for the transformation of society was met by Echeverría's decision to control the political opposition within the University.[47] The interests of conservative *Universitarios* represented by Soberón matched the government demands for political control and stability.[48]

Academic freedom. Levy draws a useful distinction between *libertad de cátedra*, and academic freedom. According to his definition, *libertad de cátedra* is the right of every university professor to decide what to teach, or research. Academic freedom entails the right to voice any ideological or political position within campus. Because of the historical evolution of the concept *libertad de cátedra* has been equated with academic freedom since the Caso–Lombardo debate in 1933. Therefore, I reformulate the distinction posed by Levy as academic freedom, understood as *libertad de cátedra*, and free speech, as the expression of the right to hold political or ideological views.

I have shown that academic freedom is an entrenched value at UNAM and a constitutive element of the dominant discourse. This tradition also reflects the virtually unfettered practice of University professors to establish the contents and orientation of their courses and research projects. There have been few attempts to standardize contents and teaching practices. Some of them have been successful at the local level. Attempts to establish standardized tests as a general practice have generated wide repulse from students and faculty. This was the case of Carpizo's departmental exams established in 1986 and repealed a few months later in the midst of student and faculty protests.[49]

Research practices, on the other hand, have been increasingly affected by internal and external performance–based salary programs and research funding guidelines. Professors are still able to choose their research topics, theoretical frames, and methodologies independently, however, access to funds is determined by the established priorities and guidelines of funding sources. The government science and technology agency CONACYT,[50] and its compensatory salaries program SNI (*Sistema Nacional de Investigadores*)[51] constitute the principal elements through which the State attempts to direct research practices, selection of topics, and graduate programs in all higher education institutions. UNAM authorities have complacently accepted these external guidelines and mirrored them into their own performance–based salary initiatives and research funding programs. The effects and unintended outcomes of these externally driven policies on research practices are currently the object of intense discussions.[52]

Free speech. There is no doubt that UNAM has historically enjoyed considerable political liberties compared to other institutions within the authoritarian Mexican State. Political opposition and criticism against the government have been tolerated as long as they develop within campus. The government's violent reaction against the 1968 and 1971 student movements remind us of the limits of free speech *vis-à-vis* the State. The siege against González Casanova is another example of government intolerance towards real or perceived attempts to produce social transformations.

Given the political centrality of UNAM, this institution merits constant attention by government officials.[53] Government intelligence agencies monitor opposition groups as well as student, faculty, and staff organizations. In general, the government has entrusted the University administration with the task of political containment. However, the linkages between elite University groups and government counterparts make it difficult to distinguish the origin of political containment policies and actions. For many years, organized student gangs called *porros* have been promoted and employed by internal and external politicians in order to confront opposition groups within the University.[54]

Political opposition against University authorities or participation in conflicts is not always tolerated by the administration. Rector Fernández MacGregor sanctioned student leaders and organizers of different political orientation in 1945.[55] Since the first day of Chávez's Rectorship in 1961, opposing students were systematically sanctioned, expelled, or the object of legal prosecution promoted by the University administration.[56] During the Soberón Rectorship, union organizers as well as student and faculty adversaries of the administration were the object of repression.[57]

In summary, the National University in Mexico exercises full control over academic activities such as faculty hiring, design of curricula and academic programs, and definition of academic requirements. The government is not at all concerned over these areas. There is an implicit understanding that these issues are entirely the responsibility of University authorities. From 1968 to 1976, the government was essentially concerned with establishing political control over the University. Since then, the Federal Government has tried increasingly to orient and shape University policies towards the assumption of efficiency measures, the establishment of University–business partnerships, and increased competition.[58] Given the political characteristics of the University administration that have been analyzed extensively in this chapter, UNAM's authorities are in most cases compliant with government designs for higher education. At the same time, high–level authorities at UNAM carry much weight in defining and negotiating government policies towards this sector. There have been situations, however, in which UNAM has rejected government directives.[59] On some of these occasions, the government has forced UNAM to adapt to these directives through political or financial intervention. The next section will show how financial measures have been increasingly used to shape and orient University policies.

Finally, to some extent UNAM constitutes a relatively safe political sanctuary in which critical attitudes toward the State are tolerated. That is as long as these critiques are circumscribed to the University. When political opposition expanded outside the campus, the State responded with violence and repression. The University administration traditionally tried to contain political conflict. Internal dissent is marginalized and the opposition has been the object of isolation or repression from the administration.

Financial autonomy. Historically UNAM has relied heavily on federal subsidy. In 1954, federal appropriations constituted 80% of the total budget. Since 1970, they have represented more than 90% of the University budget.[60] It has been argued that such a degree of financial dependence constitutes the most important threat to autonomy. However, there is no evidence that the government used University funding to control the institution before 1982.

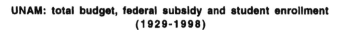

**UNAM: total budget, federal subsidy and student enrollment
(1929-1998)**

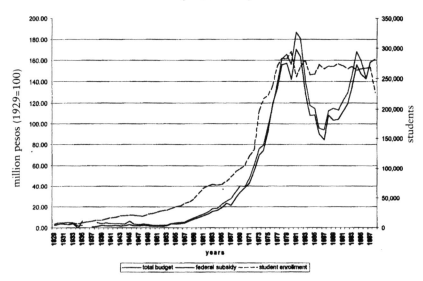

During the "golden years," from 1945 to 1968, government subsidy increased 774% (percentile subsidy gains in this section are calculated in constant prices 1929=100), while student enrollment grew 342.8%.[61] The graph shows that subsidy increased every year, except for 1967. The average annual rate was 15.5%. From 1968 to 1973, subsidies increased 142.78% while enrollment grew 107.45%. Federal funding grew at an average annual rate of 19.41%. The growth in student enrollments and public subsidy responds to the State's attempt to recover legitimacy among urban middle classes and intellectuals and overcome the trauma of 1968.

This policy continued until 1981, a year after the second Soberón Administration. From 1973 to 1981, federal appropriations grew 141.5% at an average annual growth of 11.65%. During that period student enrollment grew 27%. It reached an all–time–high in 1980. Federal subsidies had slowed in 1978 and decreased in 1979 due to the economic crisis of 1976. The "oil boom," however, allowed for a notable expansion from 1979 to 1981 when the subsidy for UNAM reached an all–time high.

Subsequently, the economic crisis and structural adjustment policies agreed with the IMF shaped the government's expenditure policies towards education and particularly UNAM. From 1981 to 1987 federal subsidies decreased 50.43%. University authorities were forced by the government to establish strict efficiency measures including enrollment reductions. The government also forced salary caps on faculty and staff in 1976. Faculty salaries decreased steadily until 1987. The highest salary for a full professor was reduced in 72.8% (salary gains are calculated in 1975 pesos) while the lowest associate professor lost 70.4%. While federal subsidies grew by 84.4% from 1987 to 1994, adjustment policies forced upon the University only allowed salaries to grow 5.7% for the lowest associate professor and 25.4% for the highest full professor.

In the mid–1980s the government applied pressure on UNAM administrators to diversify the University's financial sources. The most obvious source was student tuition. The government demanded fee increases, in a decision that broke one of the constitutive elements of the social pact between urban middle class students and the Mexican State since the forties. University authorities were happy to comply with this directive. In 1986, they tried to amend tuition regulations that had been in place since 1947. This initiative was part of a package of reforms that followed government directives to reduce costs and improve the efficiency of higher education. After being approved by the University Council, the reform package was repealed due to the enormous student protests that it had generated.

Autonomy and accountability. While institutional autonomy and public accountability are clearly two distinct processes, the nature of the pact between the State and University elites has blurred this distinction. Historically, the Mexican State has allowed absolute independence to University administrations in handling financial resources. In this way, the absence of public scrutiny over University finances has been equated with institutional autonomy and any "external" claim to exercise control over University budgets and expenditures is considered by many *Universitarios* as a violation of autonomy.

Students, faculty, and staff have all been the target of efficiency-oriented policies since 1982. The administration of the University, however, has not been threatened by accountability measures that were applied to other institutions of the State. In this area, the political pact between the University elites and the State has not been touched. University authorities are only accountable to the University Council and the trustees who are part of the internal circle of power. Internal demands for financial accountability have been neglected even in the face of corruption scandals.

Government officials have supported University administrators against faculty and students' demands for accountability. Autonomy was formally preserved and political dependency on the government increased.

In sum, federal subsidy trends show that the federal government did not exercise financial restrictions as a control device until the 1980s, in the midst of an intense financial crisis. Based on financial efficiency considerations, the government finally agreed with University elites and bureaucrats on the need to reduce student enrollment. At the same time, the government intervened in the allocation of resources within UNAM by establishing salary controls for faculty and staff. Salary data shows that University authorities have complied with this guideline. University authorities also embraced Government policies demanding tuition increases. Student movements, however, were able to stop increases in 1986 and 1992. The debate and conflict around tuition continues on to this day. It is possible to conclude that for many years UNAM enjoyed substantial autonomy in financial matters. However, since 1982, the autonomy of UNAM in financial matters has been greatly reduced and government interference in the internal allocation of resources and in the establishment of tuition policies is increasing.

Summary. University autonomy is the product of the struggle between urban middle class intellectuals and the populist State that emerged from the Mexican revolution. The *Universitarios* perceived autonomy as a mechanism to preserve the independence of a liberal humanist space in the face of the emerging authoritarian political system. The State, on the other hand, perceived autonomy in two different ways: as a concession that would provide the State with legitimacy in the face of Vasconcelos' political challenge or as a mechanism that sanctioned the distance between the University and populist education policies.

Factors that affect University autonomy. The limits of University autonomy have varied historically in relation to three structural factors. First, University autonomy increases in situations in which the University has entered a confrontation against the State. Second, autonomy has increased when the University elite and the subordinate groups within the institution have closed ranks or established political alliances. Internal cohesion increases the political strength of the institution improving the relation of forces between the University and the State. On the other hand, autonomy decreases in the presence of internal conflict when the University elites rely on government support to maintain the *status quo*. Third, University autonomy has been limited when important sectors of the University elite and the bureaucracy have established political linkages or alliances with groups inside the State apparatus.

Mechanisms of intervention. In this historical study, I have been able to identify four mechanisms through which the government affects and shapes internal decisions. The first mechanism is direct intervention. There are three instances of direct intervention. These are: the exercise of direct influence on the Governing Board in the designation of University Rector; control over the University budget; and direct political action by tolerating or promoting external political interference in University affairs. The second mechanism is the subordination of University officials. Political allegiance or ideological conformity creates informal chains of command from government to University officials. The third mechanism is the political dependency of University elites and bureaucrats in order to maintain control of the institution in the face of internal conflict. The fourth and most subtle mechanism is the internalization of government designs by University officials, due to expectations about future political careers in UNAM and at the government level.

The relative autonomy of UNAM. The relative autonomy of UNAM should be assessed in the light of the factors and mechanisms that affect University autonomy. The governance organization of UNAM, and the exacerbation of the authoritarian traits of the political system after 1973 have eroded the internal cohesion of the University. Student and union conflicts during the 1970s increased the dependence of University authorities on external government support. The need to expand the operational capacity and broaden the political constituencies of University elites generated a bureaucratization phenomenon that increased political linkages with the government and created ample expectations for political careers. The political cohesion of the Governing Board has increased and the presence of former government officials has remained relatively constant.

Overall, these factors show that the institutional autonomy of the University has weakened in the face of the government. The weakness of structural foundations of University autonomy is an outcome of the internal political organization of UNAM. Given this condition it is possible to establish that:

- University autonomy depends in fact, on the political will of the Executive in the context of historically determined social, political, and economic requirements.

- Consequently, autonomy is lower in those areas that are of fundamental interest to the government.

- The most significant areas of government intervention take place in the political realm. That is, in the appointment of University Rector and in the presence of internal conflict.

- After the economic crisis in 1976 and 1982, government intervention in financial issues like salaries and tuition policies has increased.

- *Libertad de cátedra e investigación* has been increasingly affected by external evaluation, as well as compensatory and research funding programs.

Let us provide a closing summation to this section on the limits of University autonomy. It is important to state that mechanisms of State intervention in University affairs have evolved over time. In the absence of overt political conflict, government intervention in the appointment of authorities, and other University affairs has increasingly relied on subtle mechanisms as opposed to more direct forms of action. I have already argued that the weakening of structural factors affecting University autonomy has enhanced the possibilities of external influences shaping University policies and constraining internal decision–making processes.

Among other things, a political outcome of the conflicts in the 1970s that shaped the relationship between the University and the State during the 1980s was the tightening of bonds between the Federal Government and dominant groups within the University. It is in this context that I make the following argument in opposition to Levy and others. During the 1980s, government intervention in political, academic, and financial affairs of the University may have become more covert; but it has affected as many policy areas and decision–making realms, or more, than in the worse times of open interference.

POLITICS AND CHANGE

Almost all of the interviewees involved in this research have coincided in identifying the most important changes that have occurred at UNAM since the early 1960s. These are the tremendous increase in student enrollment;[62] the expansion and consolidation of a scientific research system;[63] the professionalization of faculty;[64] and the emergence of new social actors—unions and bureaucracy—within the institution.[65] At the same time, many of them agree that the University has not changed its goals and its academic organization.[66]

The University in the 1990s preserves two essential characteristics that were present since its foundation in 1910. First, the University was created as a professionally oriented institution and today it is still organized around the professional schools and geared towards the formation of liberal professionals.[67] Second, the core academic activities of the institution —teaching and research—were split into two separate segments of the organization. Nine decades later, in spite of the expansion of research activities and infrastructure, the organization of UNAM is still segmented into two different subsystems.

The professional University as we know it today was practically in place at the end of the 1950s. The academic organization of UNAM around the professional schools that continues until today was fixated in this period of expansion and splendor of liberal professions. The organization and goals of knowledge production, delivery and distribution, developed after the Second World War, remain almost intact. The basic characteristics of the University were embedded in the governance structures and regulations established since 1945.

Traditional approaches to change in higher education; grounded on theories of social differentiation, resource dependency, and market demands; can only partially explain the transformations and lack of them at the National University. This is why I have addressed the issue of change at UNAM from a political perspective. It is an attempt to explain historical transformations at the National University in relation to the evolution of the Mexican State, the political system, and the political arrangement within the University.

This work has provided a historical account of political conflict at UNAM. Among other things, it reveals that many of the most relevant features of the University have been acquired through changes produced by conflict. Based on this historical analysis of the political evolution of UNAM, it is possible to state that conflict constitutes the most salient explanation for University transformations. In this study, I have identified distinct types of change processes.

The first type involves changes that are the product of confrontations between the University and the State. A few examples are the changes in governance structures and legislation in 1929 and 1933, and the creation of incorporated secondary schools by UNAM to establish a broad alliance against socialist education in 1933–1935.

The second type includes changes that are imposed by external actors. These include financial restrictions through government control of the federal subsidy, societal demands for increased student enrollment, or political demands by the government or other actors.

A third source of changes is intended or unintended outcomes of attempts to control internal conflict and preserve the University political system. This third source of change entails two different possibilities. On the one hand, transformations respond to specific demands by the parties in conflict or to initiatives that seek to divert political attention or provide political legitimacy. On the other hand, there are changes that attempt to contain political unrest or prevent new conflicts.

Finally, I argue that some political changes, the outcome of political confrontations, in turn shape and heavily determine the rationale and dynamics of University change. On the one hand, following Skocpol (1985; 1988 p. 17), I argue that structures and processes that are put in place in order to contain conflict in turn shape future conflicts. On the other hand, structures and political alliances that emerge in response to political challenges introduce new issues and practices that influence the agenda and practices of future transformation attempts.

Throughout this work, I have shown that the nature of political processes at the *Universidad Nacional*, characterized by intense overt politicization and a high degree of conflict, has significant implications for transformation attempts at UNAM. One of the most important consequences of the authoritarian political arrangement, and its inability to channel internal dissent, is the absence of legitimacy of governance forms and the lack of trust between competing sectors of the University. Traditionally, even minor aspects of University policy have become suspect to broad sectors of students and faculty. In many occasions, this situation leads to overt or covert resistance as well as lack of commitment and support towards new policies or transformation initiatives. On the other hand, student and faculty requirements or demands are also visualized as political threats or attempts to challenge the University administration.

This condition feeds into the existing polarization of competing forces within the University. In addition to this, it leads to an extremely complex and costly administrative process that can easily be characterized, in traditional managerial terms, as inefficient, expensive, and superfluous. Traditionally, dominant groups of the University have characterized these problems as deriving from the undesirable politicization of UNAM. In this work I have tried to show that the authoritarian nature of the political arrangement within this institution leads to immobility, administrative complexity, and bureaucratization among other problems that have constrained the possibility of a profound transformation in the nature and structure of the *Universidad Nacional Autónoma de México*.

CLOSING REMARKS

From April of 1999 until February of 2000 the *Universidad Nacional Autónoma de México* was involved in a student strike against tuition increases. This was the third time in the last 13 years that University authorities tried to raise tuition and student fees; the third time that students stopped all activities in this massive institution to defend their constitutional right to free public higher education. Thousands of students marched along the streets of Mexico City. Police forces stormed the University buildings on February 6th, 2000 in order to stop the strike. Hundreds of students were imprisoned and later released along the next ten months. Mexican newspapers were full of articles debating the strike, gratuity of higher education, the Rector's proposal, police intervention, and other related issues. Is this at all surprising?

The latest political confrontation at UNAM combined most of the elements analyzed in this work. Once again, the entrenched mythology of University apoliticization has clouded the understanding of a process that represents the struggle between competing projects for higher education.

Any attempt to go beyond simplistic explanations that depict the student movement as an external conspiracy or a criminal act against the University requires a political understanding of UNAM and its history. This work has shown that a confrontation like this is not uncommon. Moreover, in line with the findings of this research, this confrontation was predictable given financial restrictions imposed on the University, government pressures for tuition increases, and the nature of decision–making processes at UNAM. Events at UNAM highlight the relevance of a study like the one presented here.

This study contributes to the understanding of governance and change at the *Universidad Nacional Autónoma de México* in several ways:

1. The study of the historical evolution in the relationship between the University, as a hegemonic institution, and the State at large explain the development of strong political traditions like autonomy and academic freedom. The struggle between State and University constitutes the external level of conflict. The transition between a period of intense confrontation and the establishment of close ties between these two institutions took place in the context of an authoritarian political system. This explains the high political centrality of UNAM, its intense politicization, and the authoritarian features of its own governance structure since 1945.

2. This work provides ample evidence on the political nature of UNAM in opposition to perspectives that characterize this institution as technical and de–politicized. The study describes the two internal levels of conflict within the University. On the one hand, there is the competition between factions of the dominant group within the restrictive political arrangement centered in executive authorities and the Governing Board. On the other, there are the struggles of students, faculty, and staff versus the governance structure and the dominant groups. The study shows that the political structure has no effective channels for student and faculty representation and participation. This situation has implied that conflict between dominant groups and excluded sectors often takes the form of open confrontation.

3. This study provides an analysis of the origins and content of the hegemonic discourse at UNAM. It shows how this discourse has evolved historically, adapting to the new forms of domination within the University. It shows how dominant groups have used the concepts of autonomy, academic freedom, and de–politicization to articulate internal coalitions in the face of conflict. The concepts of de–politicization and academic merit constitute the legitimating ideology for the political arrangement at UNAM.

4. This study has carefully analyzed the composition and dynamics of political factions within the dominant alliance. It provides a characterization of the basic components of the power ensemble: the University elite and the bureaucracy. This analysis has traced the competition of elite factions over the Rectory and the Governing Board. On this basis, it provides a characterization of the most significant groupings within the elite (populist and elitist scientists, and liberal humanists) and their political evolution. The study on competition among elites reveals the political influence of professional associations and the extent of the domination by medical professionals and its leader Ignacio Chávez.

5. This work provides a study of bureaucratic expansion of UNAM. It shows that in addition to university growth and increased complexity, the University bureaucracy expanded in numbers and positions in response to the elite's need for augmented operational capacity, and a broader political constituency.

6. The assessment on the limits of university autonomy draws heavily on the previous findings. This study provides ample evidence of government intervention in the appointment and removal of Rectors. In addition to this evidence, it develops an argument about the impact of internal political processes, on the subordination of University authorities to government officials and the effective reduction of autonomy. This work analyzes structural internal factors that determine the degree of institutional autonomy and describes the mechanisms of government intervention in political, academic, and financial affairs at the University.

7. Finally, this historical study of the National University shows that political conflict, in general, is the most relevant factor in explaining institutional transformations. In addition to that, this study has identified four distinct sources of change: a) change as the outcome of State–University confrontations; b) changes imposed by external actors; c) change as intended or unintended outcomes of dominant groups in the face of internal conflict; and, d) the effects of structures and processes that have developed in response to internal conflict in shaping the agenda and rationale for change.

Theoretical Implications

There are two types of implications deriving from this study. On the one hand, there are implications for the theory and the study of higher education change. This work provides an alternative conceptual frame emphasizing the political nature of higher education institutions. This case study focuses on an institution that is highly politicized. It may appear as a unique case bearing no relation to "normal" higher education institutions in which political conflict is not evident. I argue that this case study has identified patterns of generalization that can be useful when looking at other higher education institutions. These are the patterns in five distinct areas.

First, the focus on the relationship between university and State as it affects higher education institutions at least in two dimensions: degree of responsiveness or confrontation with the State, and levels of social homogeneity. The case of UNAM shows that the nature of the relationship between university and State has strong effects on its institutional mission and significant influence on the hegemonic discourse of the institution. Social homogeneity reveals the nature of conflict in society, and its effects on higher education institutions. It is possible to assume that a higher degree of social conflict implies an increase on internal divergence and impacts the forms through which this is expressed.

Second, the characteristics of the political system in terms of its levels of political competition and citizen participation have a strong influence on the nature of conflict within higher education. The case of UNAM shows that restricted political competition and citizen participation increases university politicization in two ways. On the one hand, political restrictions placed on other institutions of society force individuals to seek participation channels within the university. On the other, the university is loaded with political issues that correspond to other spheres of society, but cannot be expressed elsewhere. In this sense, the university is loaded with "extraneous" issues and responsibilities.

Third, mainstream theories of change in higher education have made progress in understanding current transformations of higher education. In spite of this, there is a significant debate within the field around explanatory models for change. I do not argue that conflict is the only explanation for change in higher education. It is impossible to deny that transformations in some areas respond to the internal logic of academic disciplines. Gradual institutional adaptation to changes in the environment exists. It is almost common sense to look at how the availability of resources influences University policies and structures. The very existence of a University gives credence to the effects of institutional environments in higher education organizations.

All of these models however, assume some homogeneity of purpose based on a pluralist understanding of society. It is possible to argue that many higher education institutions rarely show high levels of confrontation. The significance of the theoretical model that was proposed in this work is that it addresses both overt and covert conflict and explains the causes of apparent homogeneity. Current trends in higher education suggest the possibility of increased conflict in post–secondary institutions and the importance of addressing change from a political perspective will surely increase.

Fourth, there are competing explanations to account for the notable expansion of managerial sectors or bureaucracies within higher education. Gumport and Pusser (1995) as well as Leslie and Rhoades (1995) have analyzed the weaknesses and strengths of these approaches. In this case study, I have shown an alternative explanation for bureaucratic expansion. Bureaucratic accretion can be analyzed as a consequence of political requirements for operational capacity, campus control, or the expansion of the political constituencies of university leadership.

Fifth, this case study has identified three structural factors that have a strong effect on the degree of university autonomy. These factors may be useful in assessing the level of independence of higher education institutions *vis-à-vis* Executive and Legislative branches of government.

Political Implications

The political implications of this study of UNAM are evident. This study is motivated by my interest and personal involvement in attempts to produce a radical transformation of the National University. In this work, I have tried to expose the political workings of University governance. I have focused on the articulation of political groups and their relations with government factions. University authorities have argued for ages that student and faculty attempts to produce change or resist the administration's initiatives are politically motivated. On the other side, we have tried to argue that both sides are always political and that alternative visions about UNAM compete usually in open confrontation. Reluctance to accept the University's political nature results in a lack of recognition of alternatives posed by those who are adversaries of the administration. The absence of participation channels and negotiation mechanisms transforms every conflict into a vast political confrontation.

Levy's arguments about University autonomy allowed me to focus this critique on a well–structured and informed assessment of the independence of UNAM. Discussing his work is more challenging and productive than addressing ideologized arguments by University authorities and bureaucrats. Nevertheless, engaging Levy's assessment has a practical implication. It has rendered an alternative evaluation that recognizes the limited nature of autonomy at UNAM because of an authoritarian political arrangement.

§

This work has given me the opportunity to bring together a concern for a political understanding of higher education, with a personal commitment to the transformation of the *Universidad Nacional Autónoma de México*. Both paths lead to additional tasks. At the academic level, there is a need to sharpen these analytical tools and explore the possibilities for generalization and theory–building through the analysis of additional cases and the comparison between institutions in different historical contexts. At the political level, there is the need to participate in the collective construction of a social actor that can transform the understanding and political characterization of the *Universidad Nacional* into political action for its transformation.

NOTES

1 Muñoz García, Varela Petito, and Torres Franco (1996).

2 This condition has been sanctioned in a normative frame in the first article of the Organic Law approved by Congress in January 6, 1945:

> Article 1.—The Universidad Nacional Autónoma de México is a public corporation —a decentralized organism of the State —endowed of full legal capacity with the purpose of providing higher education to form professionals, researchers, university professors, technicians that are useful to society; organize and realize research activities, principally about national conditions and problems, and extend the benefits of culture to the largest extent possible (Ávila Camacho 1945 p. 15).

3 Perez Correa (1974 p. 151).

4 Nabor Carrillo was the first coordinator from 1947 to 1953. Fellow populist Alberto Barajas occupied that post during Carrillo's Rectorship from 1953 to 1961.

5 Ignacio González Guzmán was Chávez's Sciences Coordinator from 1961 to 1966. Soberón assumed that post from 1970 to 1973. From this position, he moved to the Rectorship after González Casanova's downfall.

6 In this section heading, I have used the title of Sergio Zermeño's article, *Los olvidados del campus* (1987). In this work, Zermeño described the marginalization of large sectors of faculty and students from access to the decision-making realm at UNAM in the 1980s.

7 For the purpose of this study, I aggregated several disciplines and professional groups into broad disciplinary areas. Then I computed the number of members and days served to assess the relative weight of each group on the Governing Board.

8 The data for each of the disciplines is: Medicine (19.19%), Law (19.16%), and Engineering (8.39%), Chemical Engineering (6.60%), Physics (6.37%), History (6.14%), Architecture (6.03%), Business Administration (5.76%), Economics (4.27%), Philosophy (3.51%), Sociology (2.63%), Biomedical Sciences (2.41%), Mathematics (2.18%), Psychology (1.43%), Veterinary (1.08%), Astronomy (1.06%), Literature (0.83%), and Communication Sciences (0.68%).

9 These calculations are based on 107 individuals that occupied 111 positions in the Governing Board given the fact that four of these individuals were reappointed to this body.

[10] This can be due to the lack of sufficient information on the engineering group.

[11] The Organic Law establishes that two years must have passed after abandoning the board, in order for any former member of this body to be appointed Rector or director.

[12] Four of Chávez's high school friends later became members of the Governing Board. These were Antonio and Manuel Martínez Báez, Salvador Gutiérrez Herrejón, and Gabino Fraga (Romo Medrano 1997 p. 47). Chávez, Zubirán and Baz became friends while they were students in the School of Medicine, a fourth friend from that period, González Ayala, would also become director of that school and a member of the Governing Board (pp. 61, 62). There were some family ties with Trinidad García (Chávez's daughter and Garcías' son were married) (p. 135). Chávez's own son, Ignacio Chávez Rivera, was part of the Governing Board from 1985 to 1997.

[13] Soberón was a disciple and protégé of Ignacio Chávez and Salvador Zubirán. He had been a collaborator of the latter at the *Instituto Nacional de la Nutrición*. He is married to Ignacio Chávez's niece (Romo Medrano 1997).

[14] These were Castro Leal, Gómez Morín, Ocaranza, Baz, De la Cueva, Zubirán, and Garrido. Castro Leal was the Rector during the student movement of 1929. He was responsible for police intervention against the students and had to resign at the students' demand.

[15] Look at the composition of the Constitutive University Congress (González Oropeza 1980) and compare with the list of Governing Board members compiled by Imanol Ordorika.

[16] These include Senators Baz, De Alba, Fournier, Antonio Martínez Báez, Salinas, and Terán Mata; IEPES members Daniel Díaz, Luis Garrido, and Henrique González Casanova. Several of them are registered as official members of the party. The latter group includes Jesús Silva Herzog.

[17] This data has been based on political biographies collected by Roderic Ai Camp (1995a).

[18] Del Valle describes that in most University administrations and in the Governing Board there is always a strong presence by moderate catholic groups (Del Valle 1997). Given the lack of information on the political affiliations and beliefs of Junta members, I was not able to confirm or disprove this statement.

[19] López Cámara however, became a member of the *Confederación Nacional de Organizaciones Populares*, a corporatist branch of the PRI.

[20] In 1975, Rolando Cordera, faculty representative of the School of Economics proposed Dr. Elí de Gortari's candidacy for the Governing Board. The University council voted for the official candidate, Lic. Roberto Alatorre Padilla (Alarcón 1979). In 1981, Dr. Manuel Peimbert, faculty representative of the School of Sciences, proposed Dr. Juan Manuel Lozano. The deans of the School and the Institute of engineering presented Marcos Mazzari (Alarcón 1985). The latter was elected. In 1986, a collective of student and faculty representatives put for-

ward the candidacy of Carlos Tello. The Rector's candidate, Graciela Rodríguez, was elected (Acta de la Sesión del Consejo, 30 de julio de 1986). In 1993, Dr. Sergio Fernández was supported by thousands of student and faculty signatures. The Rector's candidate, Dr. Sergio García Ramírez, was elected by the smallest margin and at a high cost in legitimacy for him and the University administration (Acta de la Sesión del Consejo Universitario, 15 de diciembre de 1993).

[21] Barnés (1998).

[22] The following quotations are part of the author's interview with Luis Villoro (1998).

[23] See Chapter 7.

[24] Villoro (1998).

[25] From UNAM, Cuadros Estadísticos 1929–1979 (1981).

[26] Ibidem.

[27] After the ten-month student strike over tuition (1999–2000) Dr. Manuel Peimbert Sierra became a member of the Governing Board. Manuel Peimbert Sierra is the great grandson of Justo Sierra founder of the modern era of the National University. A world reknown astronomer, Peimbert Sierra was one of the most significant figures of the academic left. He was one of the founders and original leaders of faculty union SPAUNAM. Current rector Juan Ramón de la Fuente proposed his candidacy to the University Council. Economist Rolando Cordera Campos another founder of SPAUNAM in the 1970s was also appointed to the Governing Board after the student strike.

[28] The reputational method identifies the most influential actors as those that are repeatedly named by interviewees. The size of the interviewee pool for this research did not allow for enough repetition.

[29] University Biographies database.

[30] De la Peña (1997); Del Valle (1997); Imaz Gispert (1997); Martínez Della Rocca (1997); Muñoz (1997); Peimbert Sierra (1997); Villoro (1998).

[31] See statement by Mario de la Cueva (in *Excelsior*, July 10, 1969, p. 13–A), also his article *Autocratismo en la Universidad: Negación de los Derechos Humanos* (in *Excélsior*, September 14, 1976, p. 7–A), and statement by Gómez Morín (in *Excélsior*, July 13, 1969 p. 1–A).

[32] García Téllez (1970).

[33] (p. 55).

[34] (Aguirre Cárdenas (1997).

[35] De la Peña (1997); Del Valle (1997); Morales Aragón (1997); Peimbert Sierra (1997); Villoro (1998).

[36] Villoro (1998 and 1999).

[37] Jiménez Espriú (1997).

[38] Board member Henrique González Casanova met with President López Portillo during the morning. Later that same day, the Governing Board met to appoint the Rector. Henrique González Casanova was the current president of the Governing Board during the elective permanent session.

[39] Pérez Arreola (1998).

[40] Jiménez Espriú (1997).

[41] Martuscelli (1997).

[42] Madrazo Cuéllar (1997).

[43] Madrazo Cuéllar (1997). See also Villoro (1998). In this first interview Villoro mentioned Henrique González Casanova, appointed to the Board during the Soberón administration, as one of the most notorious "messengers" of presidential opinions.

[44] Villoro (1998).

[45] Domínguez (1986); Ramírez, Domínguez, and Universidad Nacional Autónoma de México. Centro de Estudios sobre la Universidad (1993).

[46] Martuscelli (1997); Soberón Acevedo (1997).

[47] Imaz Gispert (1997).

[48] Del Valle (1997).

[49] (Castañeda (1987); Imaz Gispert (1997); Moreno (1990).

[50] President Echeverría founded the Consejo Nacional de Ciencia y Tecnología (National Council for Science and Technology) in 1970.

[51] SNI, the National Researchers System was established in 1984. The purpose of this program was to complement faculty earnings in relation to academic productivity.

[52] See Díaz Barriga and Pacheco (1997); Pacheco and Díaz Barriga (1997).

[53] (Muñoz 1997).

[54] See Huacuja Rountree and Woldenberg (1976 pp. 103–104), Mabry (1982) and report by *Proceso* (1977).

[55] See Chapter 5.

[56] See Romo Medrano (1997 pp. 255–437).

[57] Faculty organizers in CCH Vallejo were sanctioned in 1975. This same year, the contracts of faculty union members were terminated in the School of Business and the School of Professional Studies at Cuautitlán (one of the new campuses) (Woldenberg 1988 pp. 284–292 and 414–415). Faculty members were expelled from the schools of engineering and sciences in 1978 (Boletín de la Asamblea General de la Facultad de Ciencias, November 11, 1979).

[58] Villaseñor (1992).

[59] The most significant example is Chávez's refusal to comply with President Díaz Ordaz's demand to continue expanding student enrollments at UNAM. For

example, Rector Rivero Serrano rejected the recommendations of undersecretary for higher education and scientific research Jorge Flores in the meeting of ANUIES (National Association of Universities and Higher Education Institutions) in 1983.

60 All calculations on federal subsidy for UNAM contained in this section are based on a table compiled by the author. See appendix 5.

61 All calculations on student enrollment contained in this section are based on a table compiled by the author. See appendix 2.

62 Aguirre Cárdenas (1997); Imaz Gispert (1997); Martuscelli (1997).

63 De la Peña (1997); Muñoz García (1997); Soberón Acevedo (1997).

64 Guevara Niebla (1997); Imaz Gispert (1997).

65 Martuscelli (1997); Muñoz García (1997).

66 De la Peña (1997); Guevara Niebla (1997); Morales Aragón (1997).

67 Guevara Niebla and Blanco (1990).

Appendices
Appendix 1

DATA SOURCES

University Biographies Database

For the purpose of this study, I compiled a biographical database of 184 University officials. This database provides information on individuals' education histories, academic disciplines, faculty appointments, and administrative positions at the University; government appointments, other employment history, political affiliation, elective positions, military experience, and personal connections, among other data. This database includes: a) 111 members of the Governing Board since its foundation in 1945 until 1997; b) 46 Rectors of UNAM since 1910; c) secretary generals, administrative secretaries, interior secretaries, attorney generals, University treasurers, trustees, scientific research coordinators, humanities and social sciences coordinators, and planning directors from 1973 to 1997.

This biography database was compiled from the following data sources:

- Camp, Roderic Ai. 1995. *Mexican political biographies, 1935–1993.* Austin: University of Texas Press.

- Hurtado, Flor de María, and Mexico. Unidad de la Crónica Presidencial. 1984. *Diccionario biográfico del gobierno mexicano.* México: La Presidencia.

- Hurtado, Flor de María, and Mexico. Unidad de la Crónica Presidencial. 1987. *Diccionario biográfico del gobierno mexicano.* México: La Presidencia.

- Hurtado, Flor de María, and Mexico. Unidad de la Crónica Presidencial. 1989. *Diccionario biográfico del gobierno mexicano.* México: Presidencia de la República Unidad de la Crónica Presidencial-Diana.

- Lajoie, Lucien F. 1972. *Who's notable in Mexico.* Mexico: Who's who in Mexico.

- Pretelín, Rosa, and Leticia Barragán. 1992. *Diccionario biográfico del gobierno mexicano.* México: Presidencia de la República. Unidad de la Crónica Presidencial-Fondo de Cultura Económica.

- Pretelín, Rosa, and Leticia Barragán. 1993. *Diccionario biográfico del gobierno mexicano.* México: Presidencia de la República Unidad de la Crónica Presidencial-Fondo de Cultura Económica.

As well as from personal memoirs and biographies such as:

- Barros Sierra, Javier. 1972. *Javier Barros Sierra, 1968; conversaciones con Gastón García Cantú.* México: Siglo XXI Editores.

- Fernández Mac–Gregor, Genaro. 1969. *El río de mi sangre; memorias.* México: Fondo de Cultura Económica.

- Garrido, Luis. 1974. *El tiempo de mi vida : memorias.* México: Porrúa.

- Méndez, Luis Augusto, and Hermilo de la Cueva. 1977. *Ignacio Chávez.* México: Porrúa.

- Romo Medrano, Lilia Estela. 1997. *Un relato biográfico: Ignacio Chávez, Rector de la UNAM.* México: El Colegio Nacional.

Interviews

In depth interviews were conducted with 24 key informants, a set of relevant political actors who have been politically active and influential during different periods of the history of UNAM. Twenty one of these informants participated in open-ended interviews following a semi–structured questionnaire. Others were asked to respond to specific questions regarding concrete historical events. Some of the informants were interviewed on two occasions. In this list I include two interviews that were not conducted by the author but were used during this investigation. The interviewees were:

1. **Aguirre Cárdenas, Jesús.** Ph. D. in architecture and pedagogy. Former director of the School of Architecture during the confrontation over self–government (*Autogobierno de Arquitectura*). Former member of the Governing Board. Interview by the author, *typed transcription*, México, DF, August 12, 1997.

2. **Barnés, Francisco.** Ph. D. in chemistry. Former president of the student association in the School of Chemistry. Former dean of the School of Chemistry. Former Rector of UNAM (1997–1999). Interview by the author, *typed transcription*, México, DF, February 12, 1998.

3. **Cazés, Daniel.** Ph. D. in anthropology. Director of the Center for Interdisciplinary Studies in Social Sciences and Humanities. Former secretary general of the *Universidad Autónoma de Puebla*. Participant during the initial faculty unionization processes at the UNAM. Interview by author, *interview notes*, México, DF, February 11, 1998.

4. **De la Peña, Luis.** Ph. D. in physics. Emeritus professor in the School of Sciences and the Physics Institute. Founder and leader of the *Consejo Sindical de Profesores de Educación Media y Superior*. Founder of faculty union SPAUNAM. Former faculty representative of the School of Sciences to the University Council. Interview by the author, *typed transcription*, México, DF, July 9, 1997 and March 6, 1999.

5. **Del Valle, Jorge.** MA in social psychology. Founder and leader of faculty union SPAUNAM. Interviews by the author, *typed transcription*, México, DF, July 11 and 24, 1997.

6. **Garrido, Luis Javier.** Ph. D. in sociology. Professor at the Institute for Social Research and the School of Law at UNAM. Op–ed writer for *La Jornada*. Son of former Rector Luis Garrido. Interview by the author, *interview notes*, México, DF, May, 1999.

7. **González Casanova, Henrique.** M.A. in communication sciences. Professor at the School of Social and Political Sciences. Director of the committee on new teaching methods during Pablo González Casanova's Rectorship. Director of the *Colegio de Ciencias y Humanidades*, UNAM. Former member of the Governing Board. Advisor to various Rectors. Interview by the author, *typed transcription*, México, DF, July 18, 1997.

8. **Guevara Niebla, Gilberto.** Biologist. One of the most important student leaders of the *Consejo Nacional de Huelga* during the 1968 student movement. Founder of the faculty union SITUAM at the *Universidad Autónoma Metropolitana*. Education specialist. Interview by the author, *type transcription*, México, DF, July 11, 1997.

9. **Imaz Gispert, Carlos.** Ph. D. education. Student leader of the *Consejo Estudiantil Universitario* from 1986 to 1990. Professor the School of Social and Political Sciences at UNAM. Former president of the *Partido de la Revolución Democrática* in México City. 1997. Interview by the author, *typed transcription*, México, DF, August 5, 1997.

10. **Jiménez Espriú, Javier.** Engineer. Administrative general secretary during the Soberón Administration. Director of the School of Engineering. Candidate to the Rectorship in 1980. Undersecretary for Communications and Transportation for the Federal Government in 1988. Current member of the Governing Board at UNAM. Interview by the author, *typed transcription*, México, DF, July 22, 1997.

11. **Madrazo Cuéllar, Jorge.** Lawyer. Former director of the Legal Research Institute. Former Coordinator for the Humanities and Social Sciences at UNAM during Jorge Carpizo's Rectorship. Attorney general for the Federal Government (1997–2000). Interview by the author, *typed transcrition*, México, DF, July 30, 1997.

12. **Martínez Della Rocca, Salvador.** Ph. D. in sociology. Student leader in 1968. Founder and leader of faculty union SPAUNAM. Education specialist. Former congressman for the *Partido de la Revolución Democrática*. Former member of the Mexico City administration. Interview by the author, *typed transcription*, México, DF, July 10, 1997.

13. **Martuscelli, Jaime.** Ph. D. biomedicine. Former director of the Institute for Biomedical Research during the Soberón administration. Former Coordinator for Scientific Research at UNAM during Rivero Serrano's Rectorship. Undersecretary of Health during the Miguel de la Madrid administration. Currently sub–director of CONACYT. Interview by author, *typed transcription*, México, DF, July 28, 1997.

14. **Morales Aragón, Eliezer.** Economist. Professor of the School of Economics. Founder and secretary general of faculty union SPAUNAM. Leader of unified faculty and staff union STUNAM. Former director of the School of Economics. Interview by author, *typed transcription*, México, DF, July 1, 1997.

15. **Muñoz García, Humberto.** Ph. D. in sociology. Professor at the Institute for Social Research. Director of faculty affairs during the Rivero Serrano administration. Coordinator of the Humanities and the Social Sciences during the Carpizo, Sarukhán, and Barnés administrations. Interview by author, *typed transcription*, México, DF, July 20, 1997.

16. **Muñoz, Inti, 1997.** Sociology student. Student leader at UNAM from 1990 to 1995. Interview by author, *typed transcription*, México, DF, July 27, 1997.

17. **Peimbert Sierra, Manuel.** Ph. D. astronomy. Professor at the School of Sciences and the Astronomy Institute at UNAM. Founder and leader of faculty union SPAUNAM. Former faculty representative of the School of Sciences to the University Council. Member of the *Colegio Nacional*. Interviews by author, *typed transcription*, México, DF, July 17, 1997, and March 6, 1999.

18. **Pérez Arreola, Evaristo.** Lawyer. Founder and leader of staff union STEUNAM and unified faculty and staff union STUNAM until 1989. Former mayor of Ciudad Acuña, México. Interviews by author, *typed transcription*, Cd. Acuña, Mex., February 1and 2, 1998.

19. Pérez Correa, Fernando. Ph. D. sociology. Former director of the *Colegio de Ciencias y Humanidades*. Coordinator of the Humanities and the Social Sciences as well as Secretary General during the Soberón administration. Coordinator of the Humanities and the Social Sciences during the Rivero Serrano administration. Undersecretary of the Interior of the Federal Government from 1984 to 1988. Interview by the author, *interview notes*, México, DF, July 24, 1997.

20. Rojas Bernal, Enrique. Lawyer. Student leader in the 1966 movement that ousted Rector Ignacio Chávez. Interview by Álvaro Delgado, *Proceso*, México, DF, October 2, 1995.

21. Soberón Acevedo, Guillermo. Ph. D. biomedicine. Director of the Institute for Biomedical Research during the Chávez administration. Coordinator of scientific research during the González Casanova administration. Rector of UNAM from 1973 to 1980. Secretary of Health for the Federal Government from 1982 to 1988. Interviews by the author, *typed transcrition*, México, DF, July, 21 1997 and August 14, 1997. Interview by Celia Ramírez, *typed transcription*, México, DF, February 10, 1994.

22. Villoro, Luis. Ph. D. philosophy. Professor at the School of Philosophy and the Institute for Philosophical Research at UNAM. Private secretary to Rector Ignacio Chávez from 1961 to 1965. Former member of the Governing Board. Mexican representative to UNESCO. Interview by the author, *typed transcription*, México, DF, February 12, 1998 and March 30, 1999.

23. Yacamán, Miguel José. Ph. D. in physics. Former director of the Institute of Physics at UNAM. Sub–director of CONACYT. Candidate for the Rectorship at UNAM in 1997. Interview by questionnaire, *typed transcription*, México, DF, July 10, 1997.

24. Zermeño, Sergio. Ph. D. in sociology. Professor at the Institute for Social Research and the School of Social and Political Sciences at UNAM. Interview by the author, *interview notes*, México, DF, April, 1999.

University Laws and Statutes

In this historical study I drew from diverse University laws and statutes. These include the constitutions of the *Real y Pontificia Universidad de México*, the law of 1910 creating the National University, the law of autonomy of 1929, the law of full autonomy of 1933, and the Organic Law of 1945. In addition to this, I reviewed the University Statutes of 1945 and other regulations established at UNAM since that year. The sources for this research were:

• Lanning, John Tate, and Rafael Heliodoro Valle. 1946. *Reales cédulas de la Real y Pontificia Universidad de México de 1551 a 1816*. México: Imprenta Universitaria.

• Universidad Nacional Autónoma de México. 1985. "Ley Constitutiva de la Universidad Nacional de México," in *La Universidad Nacional de México, 1910*. México: Coordinación de Humanidades, Centro de Estudios sobre la Universidad, Universidad Nacional Autónoma de México.

• México, Congreso, and Cámara de Diputados. 1933. *Ley (de 19 de octubre de 1933) Orgánica de la Universidad Autónoma de México*. México, D.F.

• Caso, Alfonso. 1944. *Anteproyecto de Ley Orgánica de la UNAM que el Rector presenta a la consideración del Consejo Constituyente Universitario*. México: Imprenta Universitaria, UNAM.

• Ávila Camacho, Manuel. 1945. "Ley Orgánica de la Universidad Nacional Autónoma de México," in *Legislación Universitaria de la UNAM*, edited by Fernando Serrano Migallón. México: UNAM.

• Universidad Nacional Autónoma de México. Comisión Técnica de Estudios y Proyectos Legislativos. 1977. *Compilación de legislación universitaria de 1910 a 1976*. México: Universidad Nacional Autónoma de México.

University Council Minutes

Access to the University Council minutes has been restricted. For the most part this work has relied on the summaries of these minutes published by the Executive Secretary of the University Council and the Governing Board. Only on one occasion did I request access to the full version of these minutes corresponding to the University Council session of January 22, 1945 when the University Council elected the first members of the Governing Board. Access to these minutes was denied by the Executive Secretary's Office. The summaries of the University Council minutes and the Constituent University council debates were consulted in:

• Alarcón, Alicia Bazán. 1979. *El Consejo Universitario: sesiones de 1924 a 1977*. México: Universidad Nacional Autónoma de México.

• Alarcón, Alicia Bazán. 1985. *El Consejo Universitario: sesiones de 1981 a 1984*. México: Universidad Nacional Autónoma de México.

• González Oropeza, Manuel. 1980. "Actas, síntesis y versiones taquigráficas de las sesiones del Consejo Universitario Constituyente," in *Génesis de la Ley orgánica de la Universidad Nacional Autónoma de México: análisis preliminar de Manuel González Oropeza*. México: Universidad

Nacional Autónoma de México. Centro de Documentación Legislativa Universitaria.

Statistical Sources on UNAM

- Attolini, José. 1951. *Las finanzas de la Universidad a través del tiempo.* México: Escuela Nacional de Economía.
- González Cosío Díaz, Arturo. 1968. *Historia estadística de la Universidad, 1910–1967.* México: Universidad Nacional Autónoma de México Instituto de Investigaciones Sociales.
- UNAM. 1981. *Cuadros Estadísticos 1929–1979.* México, DF: Secretaría General Administrativa, Dirección General de Servicios Auxiliares, Departamento de Estadística.
- UNAM. 1959–1985. *Anuario Estadístico UNAM.* México, DF: UNAM.
- UNAM. 1968–1996. *Presupuesto UNAM.* México, DF: UNAM.
- UNAM. 1981. *Cuadros Estadísticos 1929–1979.* México, DF: Secretaría General Administrativa, Dirección General de Servicios Auxiliares, Departamento de Estadística.
- UNAM. 1986–1998. *Agenda Estadística UNAM.* México, DF: UNAM.
- UNAM. 1996. *Estadísticas del personal académico.* México, DF: UNAM.

Media Sources

EL UNIVERSAL (Mexico, D.F.: *El Universal*)

EXCÉLSIOR (Mexico, D.F. : *Excélsior*)

LA JORNADA (Mexico, D.F. : DEMOS, Desarrollo de Medios)

POLÍTICA (Mexico: Talleres Graficos de Mexico)

PROCESO (Mexico, Cisa).

PUNTO CRITICO (México, Editorial Antares)

UNO MÁS UNO (México, D.F. : Editorial Uno S.A. de C.V)

Union and Student Movement Documents

- Colegio de Profesores de la Facultad de Ciencias. 1973. "Documento de Consejos Departamentales." mimeo.
- Comité Coordinador de Comités de Lucha del IPN y la UNAM, CoCo. 1971. "Boletín."

- Comité Estudiantil de Solidaridad Obrero Campesina, CESOC. 1981. "A 10 Años del 10 de Junio: un breve balance del movimiento estudiantil." México, DF: mimeo.

- Comité Estudiantil de Solidaridad Obrero Campesina. 1982. *25 años de lucha política en la facultad de economía.* México, DF: mimeo.

- Pulido, Alberto. 1981. *Cronología : 50 años de sindicalismo universitario.* [México, D.F.?]: Secretaría de Educación Sindical y Promoción Cultural.

- Pulido, Alberto. 1986. *Las Primeras Luchas del Sindicalismo en la UNAM 1929–1938.* México, DF: STUNAM.

- Ramírez Gómez, Ramón. 1969. *El movimiento estudiantil de México.* México: Era.

- Woldenberg, José. 1988. *Historia documental del SPAUNAM.* México: Universidad Nacional Autónoma de México Facultad de Ciencias Políticas y Sociales y Facultad de Economía : Ediciones de Cultura Popular.

Appendix 2

UNAM: Student Enrollment 1924–1998

YEAR	TOTAL	MALE	%	FEMALE	%
1924	9,622	7,985	82.99%	1,637	17.01%
1925	10,576	7,931	74.99%	2,645	25.01%
1926	10,179	7,388	72.58%	2,791	27.42%
1927	8,431	6,112	72.49%	2,319	27.51%
1928	8,590	5,957	69.35%	2,633	30.65%
1929	6,756	5,110	75.64%	1,646	24.36%
1930	8,031	6,406	79.77%	1,625	20.23%
1931	8,237	6,566	79.71%	1,671	20.29%
1932	9,006	7,114	78.99%	1,892	21.01%
1933	8,215	6,436	78.34%	1,779	21.66%
1934	7,732	6,345	82.06%	1,387	17.94%
1935	8,233	6,755	82.05%	1,478	17.95%
1936	9,804	8,081	82.43%	1,723	17.57%
1937	11,421	9,173	80.32%	2,248	19.68%
1938	12,625	9,775	77.43%	2,850	22.57%
1939	12,969	10,306	79.47%	2,663	20.53%
1940	15,135	12,063	79.70%	3,072	20.30%
1941	16,283	13,021	79.97%	3,262	20.03%
1942	17,508	14,005	79.99%	3,504	20.01%
1943	20,650	16,775	81.23%	3,875	18.77%
1944	20,117	16,494	81.99%	3,623	18.01%
1945	21,394	17,459	81.61%	3,935	18.39%
1946	20,963	17,187	81.99%	3,776	18.01%
1947	20,504	16,667	81.29%	3,837	18.71%
1948	19,135	15,490	80.95%	3,645	19.05%
1949	23,192	19,242	82.97%	3,950	17.03%
1950	24,054	19,981	83.07%	4,703	19.55%
1951	26,827	22,556	84.08%	4,271	15.92%
1952	28,292	23,695	83.75%	4,597	16.25%
1953	29,607	24,913	84.15%	4,694	15.85%
1954	32,652	27,670	84.74%	4,982	15.26%
1955	36,165	30,432	84.15%	5,733	15.85%
1956	36,743	30,835	83.92%	5,908	16.08%
1957	41,304	34,651	83.89%	6,653	16.11%
1958	43,924	36,791	83.76%	7,133	16.24%
1959	49,951	41,536	83.15%	8,415	16.85%
1960	58,519	48,678	83.18%	9,841	16.82%
1961	66,870	55,426	82.89%	11,444	17.11%
1962	70,546	58,003	82.22%	12,543	17.78%
1963	74,063	59,926	80.91%	14,137	19.09%
1964	72,575	58,374	80.43%	14,201	19.57%

1965	73,851	58,579	79.32%	15,272	20.68%
1966	78,094	61,336	78.54%	15,758	20.18%
1967	86,805	67,842	78.15%	18,960	21.84%
1968	95,588	73,948	77.36%	21,604	22.60%
1969	100,754	77,544	76.96%	23,210	23.04%
1970	107,056	83,177	77.69%	23,879	22.31%
1971	121,953	91,887	75.35%	30,066	24.65%
1972	131,442	98,052	74.60%	33,390	25.40%
1973	198,294	143,766	72.50%	54,528	27.50%
1974	217,535	155,481	71.47%	62,054	28.53%
1975	222,982	155,578	69.77%	67,404	30.23%
1976	238,753	162,186	67.93%	76,567	32.07%
1977	271,266	177,580	65.46%	93,686	34.54%
1978	283,466	184,437	65.06%	99,029	34.94%
1979	283,180	183,384	64.76%	99,796	35.24%
1980	294,542	190,053	64.52%	104,489	35.48%
1981	251,971				
1982	270,001				
1983	279,938	171,495	61.26%	108,443	38.74%
1984	255,834	154,319	60.32%	101,515	39.68%
1985	256,693	152,597	59.45%	104,096	40.55%
1986	273,237	153,180	56.06%	108,302	39.64%
1987	266,181	150,501	56.54%	111,473	41.88%
1988	270,710	154,036	56.90%	116,674	43.10%
1989	269,894				
1990	274,409				
1991	271,358				
1992	266,235				
1993	270,249				
1994	263,801				
1995	265,797				
1996	267,486				
1997	268,615				
1998	227,454				

Data from 1958 to 1972 from historical series published in *Anuario Estadístico* 1975, UNAM
Data from 1973 to 1985 from corresponding *Anuarios Estadísticos* UNAM
Data from 1986 to 1988 from corresponding *Anuarios Estadísticos* UNAM

Appendix 3

UNAM Faculty 1931–1996

	Year	Total		Year	Total		Year	Total
(a)	1931	1,145		1953	4,489		1975	14,780
	1932	1,146		1954	5,372		1976	
	1933	1,081		1955	5,314		1977	
	1934	1,023		1956	5,674		1978	18,175
	1935	1,363		1957	6,399		1979	19,190
	1936	1,695		1958	6,405		1980	27,515
	1937	2,343	(b)	1959	4,284		1981	27,933
	1938	2,106		1960			1982	29,660
	1939	2,461		1961	6,214	(c)	1983	
	1940	2,259		1962	6,313		1984	
	1941	2,355		1963	6,370		1985	
	1942	2,786		1964	6,351		1986	28,533
	1943	2,937		1965	6,689	(d)	1987	28346
	1944	3,070		1966	7,290		1988	28903
	1945	3,421		1967	7,764		1989	28787
	1946	3,501		1968	7,721		1990	28852
	1947	3,330		1969	7,902		1991	28333
	1948	3,458		1970	8,885		1992	28158
	1949	3,615		1971	9,707		1993	28732
	1950	3,564		1972	10,286		1994	29207
	1951	3,801		1973	11,040		1995	29366
	1952	3,993		1974.	13,583		1996	30368

(a) From 1931 a 1958, Anuario Estadístico de la UNAM 1959
(b) From 1959 a 1982, Anuario Estadístico de la UNAM
(c) From 1983 a 1986, Anuario Estadístico de la UNAM
(d) From 1987 a 1996, Estadísticas del Personal Académico de la UNAM 1996

Appendix 4

UNAM Staff and Manual Workers

year	total	*confianza*	year	total	*confianza*
1950	3,564		1970	9,126	248
1951	3,801		1971	9,438	
1952	3,993		1972	9,929	
1953	4,489		1973	10,230	513
1954	5,372		1974	11,098	
1955	5,314		1975	13,485	836
1956	5,674		1976		
1957	6,399		1977		
1958	6,405		1978	17,305	
1959	4,284		1979	18,884	
1960			1980	23,716	4808
1961	4,352	128	1981	21,758	
1962	5,014	145	1982	23,647	
1963	5,707	172	1983		
1964	6,144	176	1984		
1965	6,319	172	1985		
1966	6,947	176	1986	25,278	3410
1967	7,182	102	1987	25,454	
1968	7,851	325	1988	25,454	
1969	8,542	309			

Sources:

From 1961 to 1982 Anuario Estadístico UNAM
From 1986 to 1988 Agendas Estadísticas UNAM

Appendix 5

UNAM Total Budget and Federal Subsidy

year	million pesos Budget Current	Subsidy Current	%	Budget Constant (1929=100)	Subsidy Constant 1929=100)
1910					
1911	1.17	1.17	100.00%	1.69	1.69
1912	1.24	1.24	100.00%	1.75	1.75
1913	1.36	1.36	100.00%	1.89	1.89
1914	1.70	1.70	100.00%		
1915					
1916					
1917					
1918	1.56	1.56	100.00%	1.07	1.07
1919	1.45	1.45	100.00%	1.03	1.03
1920	1.80	1.80	100.00%	1.18	1.18
1921	2.47	2.47	100.00%	1.80	1.80
1922					
1923	3.73	3.73	100.00%	3.81	3.81
1924	2.45	2.45	100.00%	2.40	2.40
1925	2.72	2.72	100.00%	2.32	2.32
1926	2.72	2.72	100.00%	2.31	2.31
1927	2.25	2.25	100.00%	2.05	2.05
1928	2.39	2.39	100.00%	2.42	2.42
1929	2.51	2.51	100.00%	2.51	2.51
1930		3.50			3.81
1931		3.42			3.75
1932	3.15	2.82	89.40%	3.77	3.37
1933	3.37	3.00	88.92%	4.47	3.98
1934	1.91	0.05	2.62%	2.12	0.06
1935	2.01	5.05	*	2.51	6.30
1936					
1937		1.00			0.99
1938	5.59	2.00	35.80%	5.05	1.81
1939	5.08	3.21	63.16%	4.32	2.73
1940	5.32	2.50	46.99%	4.86	2.29
1941	5.58	3.00	53.81%	4.31	2.32
1942	5.93	3.50	59.03%	4.09	2.41
1943	6.71	3.50	52.20%	4.22	2.20
1944	7.56	4.00	52.91%	3.93	2.08

	million pesos				
	Budget	Subsidy	%	Budget	Subsidy
year	Current	Current		Constant	Constant
				(1929=100)	1929=100)
1945	10.04	5.20	51.79%	6.43	3.33
1946	10.85	6.20	57.14%	3.42	1.96
1947	12.83	8.00	62.37%	3.32	2.07
1948	14.59	9.50	65.13%	3.67	2.39
1949	15.56	9.50	61.05%	3.42	2.09
1950	17.10	11.00	64.33%	2.59	1.66
1951	19.84	11.00	55.44%	2.42	1.34
1952	21.26	14.00	65.85%	2.50	1.65
1953	23.28	15.85	68.08%	2.79	1.90
1954	40.63	32.89	80.95%	4.46	3.61
1955	48.05	39.89	83.02%	4.64	3.85
1956	56.60	45.89	81.08%	5.22	4.23
1957	67.10	55.89	83.30%	5.93	4.94
1958	93.83	80.32	85.60%	7.94	6.80
1959	115.53	99.78	86.37%	9.67	8.35
1960	146.65	128.29	87.48%	11.70	10.24
1961	166.95	145.29	87.02%	13.19	11.48
1962	194.94	169.28	86.84%	15.13	13.14
1963	235.59	206.33	87.58%	18.19	15.93
1964	258.92	228.62	88.30%	19.17	16.92
1965	311.51	264.78	85.00%	22.65	19.25
1966	359.92	326.57	90.73%	25.83	23.44
1967	401.71	308.71	76.85%	28.03	21.54
1968	506.18	425.21	84.00%	34.65	29.11
1969	608.07	509.97	83.87%	40.59	34.04
1970	631.46	609.47	96.52%	40.15	38.75
1971	792.94	720.12	90.82%	47.79	43.40
1972	1071.26	971.84	90.72%	61.53	55.82
1973	1486.11	1379.18	92.80%	76.15	70.67
1974	1920.91	1795.53	93.47%	79.52	74.33
1975	2735.27	2581.00	94.36%	98.51	92.96
1976	3779.12	3850.10	101.88%	117.51	119.72
1977	5834.50	5616.32	96.26%	140.57	135.31
1978	7850.90	7597.00	96.77%	161.04	155.84
1979	9558.84	9058.70	94.77%	165.90	157.22
1980	11366.00	10350.00	91.06%	156.12	142.17
1981	17395.49	15895.50	91.38%	186.77	170.67
1982	26801.74	24223.45	90.38%	181.08	163.66
1983	41935.99	38605.50	92.06%	140.35	129.20
1984	58386.99	53622.00	91.84%	118.11	108.47
1985	89773.00	84822.53	94.49%	115.12	108.77
1986	138988.06	131150.06	94.36%	95.70	90.30
1987	317844.33	284859.79	89.62%	94.40	84.61
1988	815998.67	784015.41	96.08%	113.17	108.73
1989	997631.00	897680.26	89.98%	115.29	103.74

	million pesos				
year	Budget Current	Subsidy Current	%	Budget Constant (1929=100)	Subsidy Constant 1929=100)
1990	1248521.00	1145521.39	91.75%	113.92	104.52
1991	1639539.35	1510139.35	92.11%	121.96	112.33
1992	2015855.00	1852890.00	91.92%	129.82	119.32
1993	* 2474.71	2284.73	92.32%	145.21	134.06
1994	* 3068.92	2844.42	92.68%	168.35	156.03
1995	* 3932.43	3615.16	91.93%	159.79	146.90
1996	* 5132.72	4720.97	91.98%	155.21	142.76
1997	* 7199.34	6317.71	87.75%	180.48	158.37
1998	* 8039.34	7453.20	92.71%	173.84	161.17

* In nuevos pesos (nuevos pesos=pesos/1000)

Sources:
From 1910 to 1951 Gonzlez , Arturo. 1968. *Ilistoria Estadstica de la Universidad*
From 1968 to 1996 *Presupuesto* UNAM
From 1997 to 1998 *Gaceta* UNAM. Nm. 3 178. April 2, 1998.

Bibliography

Aguayo Quezada, Sergio. 1998. *1968, los archivos de la violencia.* México: Grijalbo.

Aguilar Camín, Héctor and Lorenzo Meyer. 1993. *In the shadow of the Mexican revolution: contemporary Mexican history, 1910–1989.* Austin: University of Texas Press.

Aguirre Cárdenas, Jesús. 1997. Interview by the author. México, DF. *typed transcription.* August 12, 1997.

Alarcón, Alicia Bazán. 1979. *El Consejo Universitario.* México: Universidad Nacional Autónoma de México.

Alarcón, Alicia Bazán. 1985. *El Consejo Universitario.* México: Universidad Nacional Autónoma de México.

Altbach, Philip G. 1974. *University reform: comparative perspectives for the seventies.* Cambridge, Mass.: Schenkman.

Althusser, Louis. 1971. *Lenin and philosophy, and other essays.* London: New Left Books.

Alvarado, María de Lourdes. 1984. "La Escuela Nacional de Altos Estudios. Sus orígenes." In *Memoria del Primer Encuentro de Historia sobre al Universidad.* México: CESU Coordinación de Humanidades UNAM.

Anderson, Bo and James D. Cockroft. 1972. "Control and Cooptation in Mexican Politics." in *Dependence and underdevelopment: Latin America's political development,* edited by James D. Cockroft, Andre Gunder Frank, and Dale L. Johnson. Garden City, NY: Doubleday & Company, Inc.

Appendini, Guadalupe. 1981. *Historia de la Universidad Nacional Autónoma de México.* México: Porrúa.

Apple, Michael W. 1982. *Cultural and economic reproduction in education : essays on class, ideology, and the state.* London; Boston: Routledge & Kegan Paul.

Attolini, José. 1951. *Las finanzas de la Universidad a través del tiempo.* México: Escuela Nacional de Economía.

Ávila Camacho, Manuel. 1945. "Ley Orgánica de la Universidad Nacional Autónoma de México." In *Legislación Universitaria de la UNAM*, edited by Fernando Serrano Migallón. México: UNAM.

Bachrach, Peter and Morton S. Baratz. 1970. *Power and poverty; theory and practice.* New York: Oxford University Press.

Baldridge, J. Victor. 1971. *Power and conflict in the university; research in the sociology of complex organizations.* New York: J. Wiley.

Barnés, Francisco. 1998. Interview by the author. México, DF. *typed transcription.* February 12, 1998.

Barreda, Gabino. 1973. *Estudios (selección y prólogo Jóse Fuentes Mares).* México: Universidad Nacional Autónoma de México.

Barros Sierra, Javier. 1972. *Javier Barros Sierra, 1968; conversaciones con Gastón García Cantú.* México: Siglo XXI Editores.

Barrow, Clyde W. 1993. *Critical theories of the state: Marxist, Neo-Marxsist, Post-Marxist.* Madison, Wis.: University of Wisconsin Press.

Ben-David, Joseph. 1992. *Centers of learning : Britain, France, Germany, United States.* New Brunswick, U.S.A.: Transaction Publishers.

Berdahl, Robert Oliver, Jane Graham, and Don R. Piper. 1971. *Statewide coordination of higher education.* Washington: American Council on Education.

Berger, Peter L. and Thomas Luckmann. 1966. *The social construction of reality; a treatise in the sociology of knowledge.* Garden City, N.Y.: Doubleday.

Bernstein, Basil B. 1971. *Class, codes and control.* London: Routledge and K. Paul.

Blau, P. 1973. *The organization of academic work.* New York: John Wiley.

Bourdieu, Pierre and Jean Claude Passeron. 1977. *Reproduction in education, society and culture.* London ; Beverly Hills: Sage Publications.

Bowles, Samuel and Herbert Gintis. 1976. *Schooling in capitalist America: educational reform and the contradictions of economic life.* New York: Basic Books.

Bremauntz, Alberto. 1969. *Autonomía universitaria y planeación educativa en México.* México: Ediciones Jurídicas Sociales.

Brunner, Jose Joaquín. 1988. *Notas para una teoria del cambio en los sistemas de educacion superior.* Santiago de Chile: FLACSO.

Brunner, José Joaquín. 1989. *Educación superior y cultura en America Latina : función y organización.* Santiago de Chile: FLACSO.

Brunner, José Joaquín. 1990. "Gobierno universitario: elementos históricos, mitos distorsionadores y experiencia internacional." In *Formas de gobierno en la educación superior: nuevas perspectivas,* edited by Cristián Cox D and José Joaquín Brunner. Santiago de Chile: FLACSO.

Burnham, James. 1942. *The managerial revolution: or, what is happening in the world now.* London: Putnam.

Burrell, Gibson and Gareth Morgan. 1979. *Sociological paradigms and organisational analysis: elements of the sociology of corporate life.* London: Heinemann.

Cameron, Kim S. and Mary Tschirhart. 1992. "Postindustrial environments and organizational effectiveness in colleges and universities." *Journal of Higher Education* 63: 87–108.

Camp, Roderic Ai. 1995a. *Mexican political biographies, 1935–1993.* Austin: University of Texas Press.

Camp, Roderic Ai. 1995b. *Political recruitment across two centuries: Mexico, 1884–1991.* Austin: University of Texas Press.

Camp, Roderic Ai. 1996. *Politics in Mexico.* New York: Oxford University Press.

Cárdenas, Enrique. 1996. *La política económica en México, 1950–1994.* México: Colegio de México: Fideicomiso Historia de las Américas: Fondo de Cultura Económica.

Carmona, Fernando. 1970. *El Milagro mexicano.* México: Nuestro Tiempo.

Carnoy, Martin. 1974. *Education as cultural imperialism.* New York: D. McKay.

Carnoy, Martin. 1984. *The state and political theory.* Princeton, N.J.: Princeton University Press.

Carnoy, Martin. 1998. "Globalization and Educational Reestructuring." Interview. Stanford, CA: mimeo.

Carnoy, Martin and Henry M. Levin. 1985. *Schooling and work in the democratic state.* Stanford, Calif.: Stanford University Press.

Carpizo, Jorge. 1978. *El presidencialismo mexicano.* México: Siglo Veintiuno Editores.

Carpizo, Jorge. 1986. "Fortaleza y Debilidad de la Universidad Nacional Autónoma de México." México: Universidad Nacional Autónoma de México.

Carreño, Alberto María. 1961. *La Real y Pontificia Universidad de México, 1536–1865.* México: Universidad Nacional Autónoma de México.

Caso, Alfonso. 1944. *Anteproyecto de Ley Orgánica de la UNAM que el rector presenta a la consideración del Consejo Constituyente Universitario.* Mexico: Imprenta Universitaria, UNAM.

Castañeda, Marina. 1987. *No somos minoría: la movilización estudiantil, 1986–1987.* México: Extemporáneos.

Castells, Manuel. 1996. *The rise of the network society,* Edited by Manuel Castells. Cambridge, Mass.: Blackwell Publishers.

Centeno, Miguel Ángel. 1994. *Democracy within reason: technocratic revolution in Mexico.* University Park, Pa.: Pennsylvania State University Press.

Cerych, Ladislav. 1984. "The Policy Perspective." In *Perspectives on higher education: eight disciplinary and comparative views,* edited by Burton R. Clark. Berkeley: University of California Press.

Clark, Burton R. 1972. "The organizational saga in higher education." *Administrative Science Quarterly* 17:178–184.

Clark, Burton R. 1983. *The higher education system: academic organization in cross-national perspective.* Berkeley: University of California Press.

Cohen, Michael D. and James G. March. 1974. *Leadership and ambiguity: the American college president.* Boston, Mass.: Harvard Business School Press.

Cole, Jonathan R., Elinor G. Barber, and Stephen Richards Graubard. 1994. *The research university in a time of discontent.* Baltimore: Johns Hopkins University Press.

Colegio de Profesores de la Facultad de Ciencias. 1973. "Documento de Consejos Departamentales." Mimeo.

Comité Coordinador de Comités de Lucha del IPN y la UNAM, CoCo. 1971. "Boletín." Suplemento Extraordinario.

Comité Estudiantil de Solidaridad Obrero Campesina. 1982. *25 años de lucha política en la facultad de economía.* México: mimeo.

Comité Estudiantil de Solidaridad Obrero Campesina, CESOC. 1981. "A 10 Años del 10 de Junio: un breve balance del movimiento estudiantil." Interview. México: mimeo.

Consejo Nacional de Poblacion, SPP. 1983. *México: estimaciones y proyecciones de población 1950–2000.* México: CONAPO.

Córdova, Arnaldo. 1973. *La ideología de la Revolución mexicana; la formación del nuevo régimen.* México: Era.

Dahl, Robert Alan. 1966. *Who governs? democracy and power in an American city.* New Haven: Yale University Press.

De la Peña, Luis. 1997. Interview by the author. México, DF. *typed transcription.* July 9, 1997.

Del Valle, Jorge. 1997. Interview by the author. México, DF. *typed transcription.* July 11 and 24, 1997.

Denzin, Norman K. 1989. *The research act: a theoretical introduction to sociological methods.* Englewood Cliffs, N.J.: Prentice Hall.

Díaz Barriga, Ángel and Teresa Pacheco. 1997. *Universitarios, institucionalización académica y evaluación.* México: Universidad Nacional Autónoma de México Coordinación de Humanidades Centro de Estudios sobre la Universidad.

Domhoff, G. William. 1967. *Who rules America?* Englewood Cliffs, N.J.: Prentice-Hall.

Domhoff, G. William. 1970. *The higher circles; the governing class in America.* New York: Random House.

Domhoff, G. William. 1983. *Who rules America now?: a view for the '80s.* Englewood Cliffs, N.J.: Prentice-Hall.

Domínguez, Raúl. 1986. *El proyecto universitario del rector Barros Sierra: estudio histórico.* México: Universidad Autónoma de México.

Ehrenreich, Barbara and John Ehrenreich. 1969. *Long March, short spring; the student uprising at home and abroad.* New York: Monthly Review Press.

Evans, Peter B., Dietrich Rueschemeyer, Theda Skocpol, Social Science Research Council (U.S.). Committee on States and Social Structures, Joint Committee on Latin American Studies, and Joint Committee on Western

Europe. 1985. *Bringing the state back in.* Cambridge Cambridgeshire ; New York: Cambridge University Press.

Fernández MacGregor, Genaro. 1969. *El río de mi sangre; memorias.* México: Fondo de Cultura Económica.

Finn, Chester E., Jr. and Bruno V. Manno. 1996. "American higher education: behind the emerald city's curtain. Hudson Briefing Paper, No. 188."17.

Flores Zavala, Ernesto. 1972. *El estudiante inquieto; los movimientos estudiantiles, 1966–1970.* México: Union Grafica.

Freire, Paulo. 1970. *Pedagogy of the oppressed.* New York: Herder and Herder.

García Téllez, Ignacio. 1970. *La problemática educativa en México.* México: Ediciones Nueva América.

Garciadiego Dantan, Javier. 1996. *Rudos contra científicos: la Universidad Nacional durante la Revolución Mexicana.* México: El Colegio de México. Centro de Estudios Históricos-Universidad Nacional Autónoma de México. Centro de Estudios sobre la Universidad.

Garrido, Luis. 1974. *El tiempo de mi vida: memorias.* México: Editorial Porrúa.

Garrido, Luis Javier. 1982. *El partido de la revolución institucionalizada (medio siglo de poder político en México): la formación del nuevo estado, 1928–1945.* México: Siglo Veintiuno Editores.

Giddens, Anthony. 1984. *The constitution of society: outline of the theory of structuration.* Cambridge, UK: Polity Press.

Gil Mendieta, Jorge, Samuel Schmidt, Jorge Castro, and Alejandro Ruiz. 1997. "A Dynamic Analysis of the Mexican Power Network." *Connections* 20:34–55.

Giroux, Henry A. 1981. *Ideology, culture, and the process of schooling.* Philadelphia, Pa.: Temple University Press.

González Casanova, Henrique. 1997. Interview by the author. México, DF. *typed transcription.* July 18, 1997.

González Casanova, Pablo. 1970. *Democracy in Mexico.* New York: Oxford University Press.

González Casanova, Pablo. 2001. *La universidad necesaria en el siglo XXI.* México: Era.

González Casanova, Pablo and Jorge Pinto Mazal. 1983. *Pablo González Casanova: 6 de mayo de 1970–7 de diciembre de 1972.* México: Universidad Nacional Autónoma de México.

González Cosío Díaz, Arturo. 1968. *Historia estadística de la Universidad, 1910–1967.* México: Universidad Nacional Autónoma de México Instituto de Investigaciones Sociales.

González de Alba, Luis. 1971. *Los días y los años.* México: Era.

González González, Enrique. 1987. "La Legislación Universitaria Colonial (1553–1653)." P. 115 in *Historia de la universidad colonial: (avances de investigación),* edited by Lorenzo Mario Luna Díaz. México: Universidad Nacional Autónoma de México. Coordinación de Humanidades Centro de Estudios sobre la Universidad.

González Oropeza, Manuel. 1980. *Génesis de la Ley orgánica de la Universidad Nacional Autónoma de México: análisis preliminar de Manuel González Oropeza*. México: Universidad Nacional Autónoma de México Centro de Documentación Legislativa Universitaria.

González y González, Luis. 1988. *El oficio de historiar*. Zamora, Mich.: Colegio de Michoacán.

González-Polo y Acosta, Ignacio Francisco. 1983. "La Nueva España y sus motines estudiantiles." In *Las Luchas estudiantiles en México*, edited by Gilberto Guevara Niebla. México: Editorial Línea.

Gortari, Elí de. 1980. *La ciencia en la historia de México*. México: Editorial Grijalbo.

Gramsci, Antonio. 1971. *Selections from the prison notebooks of Antonio Gramsci*, edited by Quintin Hoare and Geoffrey Nowell-Smith. London: Lawrence & Wishart.

Guevara Niebla, Gilberto. 1978. "Antecedentes y desarrollo del movimiento estudiantil de 1968." *Cuadernos Políticos* 17.

Guevara Niebla, Gilberto. 1980. "La educación superior en el ciclo desarrollista de México." *Cuadernos Políticos*.

Guevara Niebla, Gilberto. 1983. *El saber y el poder*. Culiacán, Sinaloa, México: Universidad Autónoma de Sinaloa.

Guevara Niebla, Gilberto. 1985. *La educación socialista en México (1934–1945): antología*. México: El Caballito-Secretaría de Educación Pública. Dirección General de Publicaciones.

Guevara Niebla, Gilberto. 1986. "Las Luchas estudiantiles en México." In *Serie Estado y educación en México*, vol. II, Interview. México: Línea.

Guevara Niebla, Gilberto. 1988. *La democracia en la calle: crónica del movimiento estudiantil mexicano*. México: Siglo Veintiuno Editores; Instituto de Investigaciones Sociales UNAM.

Guevara Niebla, Gilberto. 1997. Interview by the author. México, DF. *type transcription*. July 11, 1997.

Guevara Niebla, Gilberto and Edmundo de Alba Alcaraz. 1981. *La crisis de la educación superior en México*. México: Nueva Imagen.

Guevara Niebla, Gilberto and José Blanco. 1990. *Universidad Nacional y economía*. México: Centro de Investigaciones Interdisciplinarias en Humanidades UNAM-M.A. Porrúa.

Gumport, P. 1993. "The contested terrain of academic program reduction." *The Journal of Higher Education* 64:283–311.

Gumport, P. and B. Pusser. 1995. "A case of bureaucratic accretion: context and consequences." *Journal of Higher Education* 66:493–520.

Hamilton, Nora. 1982. *The limits of state autonomy: post-revolutionary Mexico*. Princeton, N.J.: Princeton University Press.

Hardy, Cynthia. 1990. "Putting power into university governance." Pp. 393–426 in *Higher Education: Handbook of Theory and Research*, vol. VI. New York, NY: Agathon Press.

Huacuja Rountree, Mario and José Woldenberg. 1976. *Estado y lucha política en el México actual*. México: Ediciones El Caballito.

Hughes, Everett Cherrington. 1981. *Men and their work*. Westport, Conn.: Greenwood Press.

Ibarra, David. 1978. *El Perfil de México en 1980*. México: Siglo Veintiuno.

Imaz Gispert, Carlos. 1997. Interview by the author. México, DF. *typed transcription*. August 5, 1997.

Jiménez Espriú, Javier. 1997. Interview by the author. México, DF. *typed transcription*. July 22, 1997.

Jiménez Mier y Terán, Fernando. 1982. *El autoritarismo en el gobierno de la UNAM*. México: Foro Universitario-Ediciones de Cultura Popular.

Jiménez Mier y Terán, Fernando. 1987. *El autoritarismo en el gobierno de la UNAM*. México: Ediciones de Cultura Popular.

Jiménez Rueda, Julio. 1955. *Historia jurídica de la Universidad de México*. México: Facultad de Filosofía y Letras.

Kent Serna, Rollin. 1990. *Modernización conservadora y crisis académica en la UNAM*. México: Nueva Imagen.

Kerr, Clark. 1995. *The uses of the university*. Cambridge, Mass.: Harvard University Press.

Kogan, Maurice. 1984. "The political view." In *Perspectives on higher education: eight disciplinary and comparative views*, edited by Burton R. Clark. Berkeley: University of California Press.

Lanning, John Tate and Rafael Heliodoro Valle. 1946. *Reales cédulas de la Real y Pontificia Universidad de México de 1551 a 1816*. México: Imprenta Universitaria.

Le Goff, Jacques. 1980. *Time, work & culture in the Middle Ages*. Chicago: University of Chicago Press.

Le Goff, Jacques. 1993. *Intellectuals in the Middle Ages*. Cambridge, Mass.: Blackwell.

Lenin, Vladimir Ilich. 1965. *The state and revolution; Marxist teaching on the state and the tasks of the proletariat in the revolution*. Peking: Foreign Languages Press.

Leslie, Larry L. and Gary Rhoades. 1995. "Rising administrative costs: seeking explanations." *Journal of Higher Education* 66: pp. 187–212.

Levy, Daniel C. 1980. *University and government in Mexico: autonomy in an authoritarian system*. New York: Praeger.

Levy, Daniel C. 1986. *Higher education and the state in Latin America: private challenges to public dominance*. Chicago: University of Chicago Press.

Linz, Juan. 1975. "Totalitarian and authoritarian regimes." In *Handbook of Political Science*, vol. III, edited by Fred Greenstein and Nelson Polsby. Reading, Mass.: Addison Wesley.

Lipset, Seymour Martin and Philip G. Altbach. 1969. *Students in revolt*. Boston: Houghton Mifflin.

Lukes, Steven. 1974. *Power: a radical view*. London ; New York: Macmillan.

Luna Díaz, Lorenzo Mario. 1985. "Antecedentes medievales de la Real Universidad de México." In *La universidad en el tiempo*, edited by Universidad Nacional Autónoma de México. Centro de Estudios sobre la Universidad. México: Universidad Nacional Autónoma de México Coordinación de Humanidades Centro de Estudios sobre la Universidad.

Luna Díaz, Lorenzo Mario. 1987a. "El desarrollo de la conciencia corporativa universitaria y la política eclesiástica en Nueva España." In *Historia de la universidad colonial: (avances de investigación) La Real Universidad de México, estudios y textos*; edited by Lorenzo Mario Luna Díaz. México: Universidad Nacional Autónoma de México Coordinación de Humanidades. Centro de Estudios sobre la Universidad.

Luna Díaz, Lorenzo Mario. 1987b. "El surgimiento de la organización corporativa en la universidad medieval." In *Historia de la universidad colonial: (avances de investigación) La Real Universidad de México, estudios y textos*; edited by Lorenzo Mario Luna Díaz. México: Universidad Nacional Autónoma de México Coordinación de Humanidades. Centro de Estudios sobre la Universidad.

Luna Díaz, Lorenzo Mario. 1987c. "La Real Universidad de México. Historia de la universidad colonial." In *Historia de la universidad colonial: (avances de investigación) La Real Universidad de México, estudios y textos*, vol. 1, Interview by Lorenzo Mario Luna Díaz. México: Universidad Nacional Autónoma de México Coordinación de Humanidades. Centro de Estudios sobre la Universidad.

Mabry, Donald J. 1982. *The Mexican university and the state: student conflicts, 1910–1971*. College Station: Texas A&M University Press.

Madrazo Cuellar, Jorge. 1997. Interview by the author. México, DF. *typed transcrition*. July 30, 1997.

Marsiske, Renate. 1985. "La Universidad Nacional de México y la autonomía." In *La Universidad en el tiempo*, edited by Universidad Nacional Autónoma de México. Centro de Estudios sobre la Universidad. México: Universidad Nacional Autónoma de México; Coordinación de Humanidades. Centro de Estudios sobre la Universidad.

Martínez Assad, Carlos R. 1979. *El laboratorio de la Revolución: el Tabasco garridista*. México: Siglo Veintiuno Editores.

Martínez Della Rocca, Salvador. 1983. *Estado, educación y hegemonía en México, 1920–1956*. México: Editorial Línea.

Martínez Della Rocca, Salvador. 1986. *Estado y universidad en México, 1920–1968: historia de los movimientos estudiantiles en la UNAM*. México: J. Boldó i Climent.

Martínez Della Rocca, Salvador. 1997. Interview by the author. México, DF. *typed transcription*. July 10, 1997.

Martínez Della Rocca, Salvador and Imanol Ordorika Sacristán. 1993. *UNAM, espejo del mejor México posible: la universidad en el contexto educativo nacional*. México: Era.

Martuscelli, Jaime. 1997. Interview by the author. México, DF. *typed transcription.* July 28, 1997.

Marx, Karl. 1972. "A Contribution to the Critique of Political Economy." In *The Marx-Engels reader*, edited by Robert C. Tucker. New York: Norton.

Marx, Karl and Friedrich Engels. 1967. *Capital; a critique of political economy.* New York: International Publishers.

Massy, William F. 1992. *Measuring performance: how colleges and universities can set meaningful goals and be accountable.* Stanford, Calif.: SIHER.

Massy, William F. 1996. *Resource allocation in higher education.* Ann Arbor: University of Michigan Press.

Massy, William F. and Robert Zemsky. 1996. "Information technology and academic productivity." *Educom Review* 31:12–14.

Mayo, Sebastián. 1964. *La educación socialista en México; el asalto a la Universidad Nacional.* Rosario, Argentina: Bear.

Mendieta y Núñez, Lucio. 1956. *Historia de la Facultad de Derecho.* México: Universidad Nacional Autónoma de México. Dirección General de Publicaciones.

Menegus Bornemann, Margarita. 1987. "La Economía y las Finanzas de la Universidad en el Siglo XVI." In *Historia de la universidad colonial: (avances de investigación)*, edited by Lorenzo Mario Luna Díaz. México: Universidad Nacional Autónoma de México. Coordinación de Humanidades Centro de Estudios sobre la Universidad.

Mets, Lisa A. and Marvin W. Peterson. 1987. *Key resources on higher education governance, management, and leadership: a guide to the literature.* San Francisco: Jossey-Bass Publishers.

México, Congreso, and Cámara de Diputados. 1933. *Ley (de 19 de octubre de 1933) Orgánica de la Universidad Autónoma de México.* México, D.F.

Meyer, John W. and Brian Rowan. 1978. "The structure of educational organizations." in *Environments and organizations*, edited by M.W. Meyer. San Francisco: Jossey-Bass.

Meyer, Lorenzo. 1981a. "El primer tramo del camino." In *Historia general de México*, vol. 2, edited by Bernardo García. México: El Colegio de México.

Meyer, Lorenzo. 1981b. "La encrucijada." In *Historia general de México*, vol. 2, edited by Bernardo García. México: Colegio de México.

Michels, Robert. 1958. *Political parties: a sociological study of the oligarchical tendencies of modern democracy.* Glencoe, Ill.: Free Press.

Milam, John H., Jr. 1991. "The presence of paradigms in the core higher education journal literature." *Research in Higher Education* 32:651–668.

Miliband, Ralph. 1969. *The state in capitalist society.* London: Weidenfeld & Nicolson.

Miliband, Ralph. 1977. *Marxism and politics.* Oxford: Oxford University Press.

Mills, C. Wright. 1956. *The power elite.* New York: Oxford University Press.

Molina Piñeiro, Luis and Arturo Sánchez Vázquez. 1980. *Descripción de un conflicto.* Mexico: Universidad Nacional Autónoma de México.

Mora, José María Luis. 1963. *Obras sueltas de José María Luis Mora, ciudadano mexicano.* México: Porrúa.

Morales Aragón, Eliezer. 1997. Interview by the author. México, DF. *typed transcription.* July 1, 1997.

Moreno, Rafael. 1990. *La reforma universitaria de Jorge Carpizo de y su proyección actual.* México: Universidad Nacional Autónoma de México.

Mosca, Gaetano and Arthur Livingston. 1939. *The ruling class: (Elementi di scienze politica).* New York: McGraw-Hill.

Mouffe, Chantal. 1979. *Gramsci and Marxist theory.* London ; Boston: Routledge & Kegan Paul.

Muñoz García, Humberto. 1989. "Politica y Universidad." Mexico: mimeo.

Muñoz García, Humberto. 1997. Interview by the author. México, DF. *typed transcription.* July 20, 1997.

Muñoz García, Humberto, Gonzalo Varela Petito, and José Luis Torres Franco. 1996. *Los valores educativos y el empleo en México.* México: Instituto de Investigaciones Sociales UNAM; Centro Regional de Investigaciones Multidisciplinarias UNAM; M.A. Porrúa.

Muñoz, Inti. 1997. Interview by the author. México, DF. *typed transcription.* July 27, 1997.

Ocaranza, Fernando. 1943. *La tragedia de un rector.* México: Talleres linotipográficos Numancia s. de r. l.

Offe, Claus. 1975. "The theory of the capitalist state and the problem of policy formation." In *Stress and contradiction in modern capitalism: public policy and the theory of the State,* edited by Leon N. Lindberg. Lexington, Mass.: Lexington Books.

O'Gorman, Edmundo. 1960. *Seis estudios históricos de tema mexicano,* edited by Universidad Veracruzana and Facultad de Filosofía Letras y Ciencias. Xalapa: Unversidad Veracruzana.

Ordorika, Imanol 1988. "¿Cuál de todos mano?" *Nexos,* September 1, 1988.

Ordorika, Imanol. 1996. "Reform at Mexico's National Autonomous University: Hegemony or Bureaucracy." *Higher Education* 31:403–427.

Ordorika, Imanol. 1999a. "Poder, política y cambio en la educación superior." In *Universidad contemporánea: Política y gobierno,* vol. II, edited by Hugo Casanova Cardiel and Roberto Rodríguez Gómez. México: Centro de Estudios sobre la Universidad, UNAM y Grupo Editorial Miguel Ángel Porrua.

Ordorika, Imanol. 1999b. "Power, polítics, and change in higher education: the case of the National Autonomous University of Mexico." Ph. D. Thesis, School of Education, Stanford University, Stanford, Ca.

Ornelas, Carlos. 1995. *El sistemas educativo mexicano: la transición de fin de siglo.* México: Centro de Investigación y Docencia Económicas, Nacional Financiera; Fondo de Cultura Económica.

Ornelas, Carlos and David Post. 1992. "Recent University Reform in Mexico." *Comparative Education Review* 36:278–297.

Pacheco, Teresa and Ángel Díaz Barriga. 1997. *La profesión: su condición social e institucional.* México: Miguel Ángel Porrúa.

Pareto, Vilfredo. 1935. *The mind and society, a treatise on general sociology.* New York: Dover.

Parry, Geraint. 1969. *Political elites.* New York: Praeger.

Peimbert Sierra, Manuel. 1997. Interview by the author. México, DF. *typed transcription.* July 17, 1997.

Peimbert Sierra, Manuel. 1999. Interview by the author. México, DF. *interview notes.* March 6, 1999.

Pérez Arreola, Evaristo. 1998. Interview by the author. Cd. Acuña, Mex. *typed transcription.* February 1and 2, 1998.

Pérez Correa, Fernando. 1974. "La Universidad: Contradicciones y Perspectivas." *Foro Internacional* XIV:127–155.

Pérez Correa, Fernando. 1997. Interview by the author. México, DF. *interview notes.* July 24, 1997.

Perez Rocha, Manuel. 1974. "Profesores en la UNAM. Federación o club privado?" in *Excélsior*, México, DF.

Perkin, Harold. 1984. "The historical perspective." In *Perspectives on higher education: eight disciplinary and comparative views*, edited by Burton R. Clark. Berkeley: University of California Press.

Perkin, Harold. 1997. "History of Universities." In *ASHE reader on the history of higher education*, ASHE Reader Series, edited by Lester F. Goodchild and Harold S. Wechsler. Needham Heights, MA: Simon & Schuster Custom Publishing.

Peterson, Marvin W. 1985. "Emerging developments in post-secondary organization theory and research: fragmentation and integration." Ißn *Organization and governance in higher education*, ASHE Reader Series, edited by Marvin W. Peterson. MA: Ginn Press.

Pfeffer, Jeffrey and Gerald R. Salancik. 1978. *The external control of organizations: a resource dependence perspective.* New York: Harper & Row.

Pinto Mazal, Jorge. 1974. *La autonomía universitaria: antología.* México: Universidad Nacional Autónoma de México, Comisión Técnica de Legislación Universitaria.

Poniatowska, Elena. 1971. *La noche de Tlatelolco; testimonios de historia oral.* México: Era.

Portantiero, Juan Carlos. 1978. *Estudiantes y política en América Latina: el proceso de la reforma universitaria (1918–1938).* México: Siglo Veintiuno.

Portantiero, Juan Carlos. 1981. *Los usos de Gramsci.* S.l.: Folios Ediciones.

Poulantzas, Nicos Ar. 1973. *Political power and social classes.* London: NLB; Sheed and Ward.

Poulantzas, Nicos Ar. 1978. *State, power, socialism.* London: NLB.

Proceso. 1977. "Autoridades que utilizan porros." *Proceso*, May 16, 1977, pp. 12–17.

Pulido, Alberto. 1981. *Cronología: 50 años de sindicalismo universitario.* [México, D.F.]: Secretaría de Educación Sindical y Promoción Cultural, STUNAM.

Pulido, Alberto. 1986. *Las primeras luchas del sindicalismo en la UNAM 1929–1938.* México: STUNAM.

Pusser, Brian. 1999. "The Contest Over Affirmative Action at the University of California: Theory and Politics of Contemporary Higher Education Policy." Doctoral Dissertation Thesis, School of Education, Stanford University, Stanford, CA.

Pusser, Brian and Imanol Ordorika. 2001. "Bringing political theory to university governance: the University of California and the Universidad Nacional Autónoma de México." Pp. 147–194 in *Higher education: handbook of theory and research*, vol. XVI, edited by John C. Smart. New York: Agathon.

Raby, David L. 1974. *Educación y revolución social en México, 1921–1940.* México: Secretaría de Educación Pública.

Ramírez, Celia and Raúl Domínguez. 1993. *El rector Ignacio Chávez: la universidad nacional entre la utopía y la realidad.* México: Universidad Nacional Autónoma de México. Coordinación de Humanidades. Centro de Estudios Sobre la Universidad.

Ramírez Gómez, Ramón. 1969. *El movimiento estudiantil de México.* México: Era.

Rashdall, Hastings. 1936. *Universities of Europe in the Middle Ages*, edited by F. M. Powicke and Alfred Brotherston Emden. Oxford: New York: Clarendon Press; Oxford University Press.

Readings, Bill. 1996. *The university in ruins.* Cambridge, Mass.: Harvard University Press.

Rhoades, Gary. 1998. *Managed professionals: unionized faculty and restructuring academic labor.* Albany: State University of New York Press.

Rhoades, Gary L. 1993. *Beyond "the state": interorganizational relations and state apparatus in post-secondary education*, vol. VIII, edited by John C. Smart. New York: Agathon.

Rhoades, Gary and Robert Rhoads. 2000. "Graduate student unionization in the United States: social movement towards what ends?" in *Association for the Study of Higher Education*, Interview. Sacramento, Ca.

Rojas Bernal, Enrique. 1995. Interview by Álvaro Delgado. México, DF. *Proceso.* October 2, 1995.

Romo Medrano, Lilia Estela. 1997. *Un relato biográfico: Ignacio Chávez, rector de la UNAM.* México: El Colegio Nacional.

Rosas, María. 2001. *Plebeyas batallas: la huelga en la Universidad.* México: Era.

Salmerón, Fernando. 1966. "Philosophers of the twentieth century." In *Major trends in Mexican philosophy*, edited by Mario de la Cueva. Notre Dame, Ind.: University of Notre Dame Press.

Sánchez, George Isidore. 1944. *The development of higher education in Mexico.* New York: King's crown press.

Silva Guerrero, Lucila. 1979. "Cronología del Sindicalismo en la Universidad Nacional Autónoma de México (1929–1979)." *Cuadernos del Centro de Documentación Legislativa* 1:125–165.

Silva Herzog, Jesús. 1974. *Una historia de la Universidad de México y sus problemas.* México: Siglo Veintiuno Editores.

Slaughter, Sheila. 1988. "Academic Freedom and the State: Reflections on the Uses of Knowledge." *Journal of Higher Education,* 59(3): 241–262.

Slaughter, Sheila. 1990. *The higher learning and high technology: dynamics of higher education policy formation.* Albany: State University of New York Press.

Slaughter, Sheila. 1991. "The "official" ideology of higher education: ironies and inconsistencies." in *Culture and ideology in higher education: advancing a critical agenda,* edited by William G. Tierney. New York: Praeger.

Slaughter, Sheila and Larry L. Leslie. 1997. *Academic capitalism: politics, policies, and the entrepreneurial university.* Baltimore: Johns Hopkins University Press.

Smith, Peter H. 1979. *Labyrinths of power: political recruitment in twentieth-century Mexico.* Princeton, N.J.: Princeton University Press.

Soberón Acevedo, Guillermo. 1994. Interview by Celia Ramirez. México, DF. *typed transcription.* February 10, 1994.

Soberón Acevedo, Guillermo. 1997. Interview by the author. México, DF. *typed transcrition.* July, 21 1997.

Soberón Acevedo, Guillermo, J. Cuauhtémoc Valdés Olmedo, and María de los Angeles Knochenhauer. 1983. *La universidad ahora: anotaciones, experiencias y reflexiones.* México: Colegio Nacional.

Sotelo Inclán, Jesús. 1982. "La educación socialista." In *Historia de la educación pública en México,* edited by Fernando Solana, Raúl Cardiel Reyes, and Raúl Bolaños Martínez. México: Fondo de Cultura Económica.

Talavera, Abraham. 1973. *Liberalismo y educación.* México: Secretaría de Educación Pública. Dirección General de Educación Audiovisual y Divulgación.

Torres Bodet, Jaime. 1969. *Memorias.* México: Porrúa.

UNAM. 1981. *Cuadros Estadísticos 1929–1979.* México: Secretaría General Administrativa, Dirección General de Servicios Auxiliares, Departamento de Estadística.

Universidad Nacional Autónoma de México. 1977. *Informe del Rector.* México: UNAM.

Universidad Nacional Autónoma de México. 1980. *Informe del Rector.* México: UNAM.

Universidad Nacional Autónoma de México. 1985a. *La Universidad Nacional de México, 1910.* México: Coordinación de Humanidades, Centro de

Estudios sobre la Universidad, Universidad Nacional Autónoma de México.

Universidad Nacional Autónoma de México. 1985b. *Siete discursos de toma de posesión.* México: Universidad Nacional Autónoma de México. Coordinación de Humanidades. Centro de Estudios sobre la Universidad.

Universidad Nacional Autónoma de México. 1995. "Legislación universitaria de la UNAM." UNAM.

Universidad Nacional Autónoma de México. Comisión Técnica de Estudios y Proyectos Legislativos. 1977. *Compilación de legislación universitaria de 1910 a 1976.* México: Universidad Nacional Autónoma de México.

Valadés, Diego. 1974. *La Universidad Nacional Autónoma de México: formación, estructura y funciones.* México: Universidad Nacional Autónoma de Mexico Comisión. Técnica de Legislación Universitaria.

Vázquez, Josefina Zoraida. 1992. "La República restaurada y la educación: un intento de victoria definitiva." In *La Educación en la historia de México, Lecturas de historia mexicana,* edited by Josefina Zoraida Vázquez. México: El Colegio de México. Centro de Estudios Históricos.

Vázquez, Mariano. 1961. "Porqué renuncié a la Junta de Gobierno." In *Excélsior,* Interview. México, DF.

Villaseñor, Guillermo. 1992. "Educación superior: planeación y realidad 1980–1990." In *Educación Superior y Desarrollo Nacional,* edited by Salvador Martínez Della Rocca. México: Instituto de Investigaciones Económicas, UNAM.

Villegas Moreno, Gloria. 1984. "La Universidad de Justo Sierra y la Revolución." In *Memoria del Primer Encuentro de Historia sobre al Universidad.* México: CESU Coordinación de Humanidades UNAM.

Villoro, Luis. 1998. Interview by the author. México, DF. *typed transcription.* February 12, 1998.

Villoro, Luis. 1999. Interview by the author. México, DF. *notes on telephone interview.* March 30, 1999.

Weber, Max, C. Wright Mills, and Hans Heinrich Gerth. 1946. *From Max Weber: essays in sociology.* New York: Oxford University Press.

Weick, Karl E. 1976. "Educational organizations as loosely coupled systems." *Administrative Science Quarterly* 21:1–19.

Weiler, Hans N. 1983. "Legalization, Expertise, and Participation: Strategies of Compensatory Legitimation in Educational Policy." *Comparative Education Review* 27:259–277.

Weir, Margaret, Ann Shola Orloff and Theda Skocpol. 1988. *The Politics of social policy in the United States.* Princeton, N.J.: Princeton University Press.

Wences Reza, Rosalío. 1984. *La Universidad en la historia de México.* México: Línea; Universidad Autónoma de Guerrero; Universidad Autónoma de Zacatecas.

Wilkie, James Wallace, Edna Monzón de Wilkie, and Ramón Beteta. 1969. *México visto en el siglo XX, por James W. Wilkie y Edna Monzon de Wilkie.* Mexico: Instituto Mexicano de Investigaciones Economicas.

Williams, Raymond. 1977. *Marxism and literature.* Oxford: Oxford University Press.

Wirt, Frederick M. and Michael W. Kirst. 1972. *The political web of American schools.* Boston: Little Brown.

Woldenberg, José. 1988. *Historia documental del SPAUNAM.* México: Universidad Nacional Autónoma de México. Facultad de Ciencias Políticas y Sociales. Facultad de Economía-Ediciones de Cultura Popular.

Wolin, Sheldon S. 1991. "The new public philosophy." *Democracy*, No. 1, Oct. 1981: 23–36.

Zea, Leopoldo. 1966. "Positivism." Pp. 328 in *Major trends in Mexican philosophy*, edited by Mario de la Cueva. Notre Dame, Ind.: University of Notre Dame Press.

Zea, Leopoldo. 1974. *Positivism in Mexico.* Austin: University of Texas Press.

Zemsky, Robert and William F. Massy. 1990. "Cost Containment: Committing to a New Economic Reality." *Change* 22:16–22.

Zermeño, Sergio. 1978. *México, una democracia utópica: el movimiento estudiantil del 68.* México: Siglo Veintiuno Editores.

Zermeño, Sergio 1987. "Los olvidados del Campus." *Nexos*, August 1, 1987.

Index

academic freedom (libertad de cátedra), 8, 51, 53, 60, 62–63, 68,
80, 101, 115–116, 125, 140,
158, 164, 170, 174, 177,
180–181, 196, 198, 200, 207,
208, 213–214, 219, 223
academic work, 25, 94, 99, 126, 184,
188n
accountability, 8, 44, 208, 217, 218
Aceves Parra, Salvador, 71n, 73n, 93,
123
Administración. *See* Facultad de
Comercio y Administración
agenda, 9, 13–14, 161, 224
control, 29, 32, 34, 221
political, 27, 31, 113
Alemán, Miguel, 82–86, 89, 91, 93,
106n, 108n
Alba Andrade, Fernando, 111n, 159
analytical perspectives, 17–20
functional, 10, 17, 18
interpretive, 17, 18
organizational, 6, 10, 17–19
societal, 10, 17–19
Arquitectura. *See* Facultad de
Arquitectura
Athenaeum of Youth (Ateneo de la
Juventud), 47, 48, 53, 70n
authoritarianism, 7, 8, 10, 12, 23, 26,
27, 37, 40, , 101, 129
authoritarian State, 7, 8, 12, 27,
35n, 38–42, 43, 44, 191–226

emergence, 12, 37–76
consolidation, 12, 40, 77–96
crisis or decline, 12, 40, 97–112,
113–190
authority, 7, 20, 51, 59, 67, 101, 118,
130, 146n, 152n, 207
of professionals, 25, 101, 207
University (UNAM) authorities, 7,
8, 9, 50, 60, 64, 67, 73, 77,
104, 105, 114, 119, 129, 130,
183
autonomy, 3, 7, 8, 9, 10, 16n, 21, 60,
80
autonomy and accountability,
217–218
campus and academic, 8, 62, 68,
101, 131–134, 213–215
financial, 8, 209, 215–217
political, 8, 209–213
principle of, 63
Ávila Camacho, Manuel, 38, 54–56,
59, 60, 72n, 73n, 74n, 79,
81–83, 91, 93, 100, 106n,
107n, 108n, 195
Ayala González, Abraham, 79, 91, 92,
93, 105n, 108n
Azuela, Salvador, 58, 72n, 88

Bachrach, Peter, 29
Barajas, Alberto, 91
Baratz, Morton S., 29
Barnés, Francisco, 204